"Housing supply and house prices are worsening problems worldwide – and often planning is seen to be the cause. *Politics, Planning and Housing Supply in Australia, England and Hong Kong* provides an important contribution to understanding these issues, putting land use planning into the political context in three distinct institutional and market environments."

Christine Whitehead, Emeritus Professor for Housing Economics London School of Economics

Politics, Planning and Housing Supply in Australia, England and Hong Kong

In recent years, many nations have asked why not enough housing is being built or, when it is built, why it isn't of the highest quality or in the best, most sustainable, locations. *Politics, Planning and Housing Supply in Australia, England and Hong Kong* examines the politics and planning of new homes in three very different settings, but with shared political traditions: in Australia, in England and in Hong Kong. It investigates the power-relationships and politics that underpin the allocation of land for large-scale residential schemes and the processes and politics that lead to particular development outcomes.

Using a comparative framework, it asks:

- how different systems of urban governance and planning mediate the supply of land for housing;
- whether and how these system differences influence the location, quantity and price of residential land and the implications for housing outcomes;
- what can be learned from these different systems for allocating land, building consensus between different stakeholders, and delivering a steady supply of high quality and well located homes accessible to, and appropriate for, diverse housing needs.

This book frames each case study in a comprehensive examination of national and territorial frameworks before dissecting key local cases. These local cases—urban renewal and greenfield growth centres in Australia, new towns and strategic sites in England, and major development schemes in Hong Kong—explore how broader urban planning and housing policy goals play out at the local level. While the book highlights a number of potential strategies for improving planning and housing delivery processes, the real challenge is to give voice to a broader array of interests, reconstituting the political process surrounding planning and housing development to prioritise homes in well-planned places for the many, rather than simply facilitating investment opportunities for the few.

Nicole Gurran is Professor of Urban and Regional Planning at the University of Sydney, Australia.

Nick Gallent is Head of the Bartlett School of Planning and Professor of Housing and Planning at University College London, UK.

Rebecca L. H. Chiu is Head and Professor at the Department of Urban Planning and Design, and the Director of the Centre of Urban Studies and Urban Planning of the University of Hong Kong, China.

Routledge Research in Planning and Urban Design
Series editor: Peter Ache
Radboud University, Nijmegen, Netherlands

Routledge Research in Planning and Urban Design is a series of academic monographs for scholars working in these disciplines and the overlaps between them. Building on Routledge's history of academic rigor and cutting-edge research, the series contributes to the rapidly expanding literature in all areas of planning and urban design.

A full list of titles in this series is available at: www.routledge.com/series/RRPUD. Recently published titles:

Actor Networks of Planning
Exploring the Influence of ANT
Yvonne Rydin and Laura Tate

Neoliberal Spatial Governance
Philip Allmendinger

Placemaking
An Urban Design Methodology
Derek Thomas

Ideology, Political Transitions, and the City
The Case of Mostar, Bosnia and Herzegovina
Aleksandra Djurasovic

Place and Placelessness Revisited
Robert Freestone and Edgar Liu

Sustainable Regeneration of Former Military Sites
Samer Bagaeen and Celia Clark

Politics, Planning and Housing Supply in Australia, England and Hong Kong
Nicole Gurran, Nick Gallent, and Rebecca L. H. Chiu

Politics, Planning and Housing Supply in Australia, England and Hong Kong

Nicole Gurran, Nick Gallent, and Rebecca L. H. Chiu

NEW YORK AND LONDON

First published 2016
by Routledge
711 Third Avenue, New York, NY 10017

and by Routledge
2 Park Square, Milton Park, Abingdon, Oxon OX14 4RN

First issued in paperback 2018

Routledge is an imprint of the Taylor & Francis Group, an informa business

© 2016 Taylor & Francis

The right of Nicole Gurran, Nick Gallent, and Rebecca L. H. Chiu to be identified as authors of this work has been asserted by them in accordance with sections 77 and 78 of the Copyright, Designs and Patents Act 1988.

All rights reserved. No part of this book may be reprinted or reproduced or utilized in any form or by any electronic, mechanical, or other means, now known or hereafter invented, including photocopying and recording, or in any information storage or retrieval system, without permission in writing from the publishers.

Trademark notice: Product or corporate names may be trademarks or registered trademarks, and are used only for identification and explanation without intent to infringe.

Library of Congress Cataloging in Publication Data
Names: Gurran, Nicole, author. | Gallent, Nick, author. | Chiu, Rebecca Lai-Har, author.
Title: Politics, planning and housing supply in Australia, England and Hong Kong / by Nicole Gurran, Nick Gallent and Rebecca Chiu.
Description: New York, NY: Routledge, 2016. |
Series: Routledge research in planning and urban design |
Includes bibliographical references.
Identifiers: LCCN 2015050401|
ISBN 9781138937147 (hardcover) | ISBN 9781315676432 (ebook)
Subjects: LCSH: Housing—Australia—Planning. | Housing—England—Planning. | Housing—China—Hong Kong—Planning. | Land use, Urban—Australia—Planning. | Land use, Urban—England—Planning. | Land use, Urban—China—Hong Kong—Planning. | Housing policy—Australia. | Housing policy—England. | Housing policy—China—Hong Kong. | Urban policy—Australia. | Urban policy—England. | Urban policy—China—Hong Kong.
Classification: LCC HD7287 .G87 2016 | DDC 333.33/8--dc23
LC record available at http://lccn.loc.gov/2015050401

ISBN 13: 978-1-138-59506-4 (pbk)
ISBN 13: 978-1-138-93714-7 (hbk)

Typeset in Sabon
by Florence Production Ltd, Stoodleigh, Devon, UK

Contents

List of Figures   xi
List of Tables   xiii
Notes on Authors   xiv
Preface   xv
Acknowledgments   xviii

1 Introduction: Politics, Planning, and Housing Supply   1

Perspectives from Comparative Planning and Housing Studies   2
   Approach and Methods   4
Comparative Markers for Analysis   5
   Urban Settlement and Housing Demand   8
   Government Support for Housing Production and Consumption   9
   Land Use Planning, Development Control, and Housing Supply   13
   System of Housing Production   15
   Housing Product Diversity   16
   Power and Control in the Planning System   20
Structure of the Book   23
References   25

2 Urban Planning, Politics, Land, and Housing Supply in Australia   29

Introduction   29
Urban Planning and Housing Provision in Australia   30
   Public Housing and Government Involvement in Land Supply   33
   Rise of Environmental Planning, Urban Containment, and the Infrastructure Backlog   34
Housing Problems in the New Millennium   35
Government Responses to the Housing Affordability Problem   38
   Scope of Urban Planning, and Roles of the Public and Private Sectors   40
   The Planning Process   40

Planning for Affordable Housing   47
*The Political Arguments about Planning, Housing, and
  Land Supply*   50
*Conclusions: Implications for Addressing Housing Affordability
  in the New Millennium*   53
References   54

3 Planning and Property Politics in Sydney's Urban Renewal and Growth Centres   59

Introduction   59
Australia's Changing Housing System, and the Role of Planning   60
  The Housing "Shortage" in NSW   62
The Case Studies   66
  Green Square   66
  Rouse Hill   73
Comparison of Housing Outcomes in Case Study Areas   78
*Conclusion: Property Politics, Planning, and Constraints
  to Affordable Housing Supply*   83
References   84

4 Power and Democracy in the English Planning System   87

Introduction   87
Power and the Scope of Planning   88
Decision Making and the Governance of Urban Planning   92
Urban Planning and Land Supply   101
Conclusions: Power and Influence in Planning and Development   108
References   111

5 Delivering New Homes on Major Development Sites in England   115

Introduction   115
The Housing Crisis and Major Sites   118
Strategic Planning and Major Sites   120
Case Study Sites   122
  Stevenage, Hertfordshire   124
  Ashford, Kent   129
  Ebbsfleet, Kent   138
A Future for Major Sites in England?   148
  1. Value Capture, Infrastructure, and Planning Gain   148
  2. Top–Down Planning and Local Opposition/Democracy   149
  3. Overloading of Existing Infrastructure—Public Concern   150
  4. Policy Shift and "Regulatory Risk"   151

　　　　5. Market Cycles and Viability   151
　　　　6. Flexible Planning?   152
　　　　7. Major Sites and Cross-Border Working   153
　　Closing Remarks   154
　　References   155

6　Power and Decision Making in Hong Kong's Planning System　　　　159

　　Introduction   159
　　Scope of and Power within Urban Planning   162
　　　　Landownership and Disposal System   162
　　　　The Planning System and its Scope   166
　　　　Territorial Development Plans   169
　　　　District Plans   170
　　　　Development-Related Tools   171
　　　　Plan-Making and Enforcement Processes: Power Relations
　　　　　　and Politics   172
　　　　The Making of Territorial and Subregional Plans: Incremental
　　　　　　Public Participation since 1990   173
　　　　The Making of District Plans: from Elitist to Mass Participation
　　　　　　Since 2005   177
　　Conclusion: Planning, Governance, and Housing Supply   180
　　References   182

7　Land Supply and New Housing Provision in Hong Kong　　　　185

　　Introduction   185
　　The Market Situation and the Land Search Efforts   186
　　Planning Governance and Housing Supply since 1998   194
　　　　South East Kowloon Development Scheme: Transforming
　　　　　　Governance   194
　　Land Search in a Buoyant Market: Quantity Versus Quality   198
　　　　Small-Scale Development Projects   202
　　　　Large-Scale New Development Projects   202
　　　　Tung Chung New Town Extension   204
　　Conclusion   208
　　Notes   209
　　References   209

8　Conclusion: Planning, Democracy, and Control in the Delivery of New Homes　　　　213

　　Landownership and Development Rights   213
　　　　Allocation of Development Rights   214
　　　　Landownership and Proactive Planning   218

Representative Democracy and Power in the Planning Process 219
  Representative Democracy and Reform 220
  Politics 220
Lessons 224
  Are There Optimal Approaches to Planning for Housing Supply? 226
References 226

Index 229

Figures

1.1	Housing Provision, Australia, England, and Hong Kong (based on annual averages, 2001–2014)	16
2.1	Dwelling Completions and House Prices, Australia, 1986–2014	30
2.2	Australia's Urban Settlement Structure	37
2.3	Composition of Dwelling Commencements by Sector, Australia, 1984–2015	39
3.1	Green Square and Rouse Hill Metropolitan Context	67
3.2	Green Square Development Area and Precincts	69
3.3	Population Growth, Green Square and South Sydney Villages, 2001–2011	71
3.4	Mixed Residential and Commercial Development under Construction Surrounding the Green Square Train Station	72
3.5	Rouse Hill	75
3.6	Apartments and Open Space, Victoria Park/Green Square	79
3.7	Comparison of Dwelling Stock, 2001–2011, Green Square Renewal and Rouse Hill Development Areas	80
3.8	House under Construction, Rouse Hill	80
3.9	Apartments Surrounding the Library and Central Square, Rouse Hill Town Centre	81
3.10	Mortgage and Rent Payments, Green Square, Rouse Hill, and Sydney (2011)	81
3.11	Median Sales Prices, All Dwellings, 2001–2015	82
5.1	House Prices and Houses Built in England	119
5.2	Housing Affordability in England	121
5.3	Three Study Sites, England	123
5.4	Proposed Stevenage West Development	127
5.5	Ashford and its Major Urban Extensions	131
5.6	New Housing in the Ashford Growth Area, 2010	132
5.7	Thames Gateway Development Corridor	139
5.8	Ebbsfleet Valley Development Sites	141
5.9	Castle Hill (Eastern Quarry), Looking toward Swanscombe	144
5.10	Ebbsfleet Urban Development Corporation	146

xii *Figures*

6.1	Spatial Development of Hong Kong	168
6.2	Hierarchy of Plans in Hong Kong	168
6.3	Spatial Plan Under the 2030 Planning Vision and Strategy, 2007	171
6.4	Plan-Making Process, Hong Kong	178
6.5	Planning Application Process, Hong Kong	179
7.1	Hong Kong House Price Trends, 1986–2014	187
7.2	Hong Kong Price-to-Income Ratio, 1997–2014	188
7.3	Housing Commencements in Hong Kong (Private Housing)	191
7.4	Planned Developments in Proposed Reclamation Areas of South East Kowloon Development, 2004	197
7.5	Major and Controversial Land Development Projects, 2011–2014, Hong Kong	198
7.6	Tung Chung Extension	206
7.7	Village Housing in Tung Chung West	206
7.8	Public Rental Housing in Tung Chung West	207

Tables

1.1	Key Characteristics, Australia, England, and Hong Kong, 2014	9
1.2	Financing Housing Production and Consumption, Australia, England, and Hong Kong	10
1.3	Characterization of Land Use Planning, Development Control, and Housing Supply Systems in Australia, England, and Hong Kong	14
1.4	System of Housing Production, Australia, England, and Hong Kong	15
1.5	Housing Product Diversity Australia, England, and Hong Kong	17
1.6	Power and Control within the Planning System	21
2.1	Legal Scope of Urban Land Use Planning Systems in Australia	41
2.2	Key Stages in the Land Use Planning Process, Australia	45
2.3	The Role of Different Actors in the Urban Land and Housing Development Process, Australia	48
3.1	Completed and Projected New Dwellings, Green Square and "South Sydney Villages", 2015	73
7.1	Sources of Residential Land, 2014–2015	193
7.2	Planning Revisions of South East Kowloon Development Scheme, 1992–2012	195
7.3	Major Land Development Projects, 2008–2014	199

Notes on Authors

Nicole Gurran is Professor of Urban and Regional Planning at the University of Sydney, where she leads the university's Urban Housing Lab research incubator and the Australian Housing and Urban Research Institute node. She has authored numerous publications on land use planning, housing, and the environment in Australia, including *Australian Urban Land Use Planning: Policy, Principles and Practice* (Sydney University Press, 2011, in its second edition). Nicole is also a professionally qualified planner and Fellow of the Planning Institute of Australia. Nicole is Practice Editor of the journal *Urban Policy and Research,* published by Taylor & Francis.

Nick Gallent is Head of the Bartlett School of Planning and Professor of Housing and Planning at University College London. He has twenty years' experience in UK universities and a track record in housing-related research and publication. Nick is the co-author or editor of twelve previous books—including *Delivering New Homes* (Routledge, 2003, with Matthew Carmona and Sarah Carmona), *Decent Homes for All* (Routledge, 2007, with Mark Tewdwr-Jones), and *The Rural Housing Question* (Policy Press, 2010, with Madhu Satsangi and Mark Bevan)—and numerous peer-reviewed articles. He is a Chartered Town Planner, a fellow of the Royal Institution of Chartered Surveyors and a Fellow of the Academy of Social Sciences. He is also editor of the journal *Progress in Planning*, published by Elsevier.

Rebecca L. H. Chiu is Head and Professor at the Department of Urban Planning and Design, and the Director of the Centre of Urban Studies and Urban Planning of the University of Hong Kong. Her current research interests center on housing and urban sustainability issues in high-density Asian cities, especially in China, comparative housing policies in Asia, and housing policy transfer. She is the Founder Chairman of the Asia Pacific Network for Housing Research and the Director of the Affordable Housing Research Network at the University of Hong Kong. She has been appointed to government boards and appeal panels related to housing, planning, urban renewal, and natural and heritage conservation in Hong Kong.

Preface

What does a studio flat in central London, a mansion in outer Sydney, and a one-bedroom apartment in downtown Hong Kong have in common? In 2015, all were worth approximately a half million pounds Sterling, or around twelve to fourteen years of median annual earnings. For the global investor, all might offer attractive prospects for future growth, but for most aspiring first-time buyers the housing market seems increasingly out of reach.

So how has it come about that house prices and rents have become unaffordable to average wage-earning households in these three very different cities? If lack of space for housing development might explain real estate pressures in land-limited Hong Kong, the same could hardly be said about the sprawling suburbs of Sydney. But concerns about sluggish rates of residential production have dominated policy debates linked to housing affordability in Australia since at least the new millennium. So too in England, where rates of new house building have recently hit an all-time low, despite buoyant population growth and astronomical house prices in the global metropolis of London.

Much of the blame has focused on the planning system, or government control of land supply, as an explanation for inadequate housing output and consequent affordability pressures. Thus, many commentators—within governments and beyond—have called for reforms to the decision-making processes governing land release and development control. Indeed, over the past decade or so, numerous changes to urban planning and land-release procedures have been advanced in many countries. These range from adjustments to local and regional frameworks for growth management through to system-level interventions that alter the balance of power between local residents, property owners, private-sector developers, and the state.

But could land supply and planning-system constraints plausibly explain why high house prices and buoyant population growth have failed to trigger increased house building across the very different settings of England, Hong Kong, and Australia? How could the very different land-supply and planning systems in three distinct cities and nations work in the same way to constrain housing output and elevate housing prices? Have urban reforms helped increase housing output and effectively tackled price pressures?

Critical analysis of urban reform agendas points to the political and economic logics of neoliberalism as a driving force of changes to land use planning systems (Davoudi, 2011; Haughton & Allmendinger, 2012; Gurran & Phibbs, 2013; Gurran et al., 2014). Similar analyses accompany accounts of housing policy reforms across much of the world (Lee & Zhu, 2006; Beer et al., 2007; Jacobs & Manzi, 2013; Rolnik, 2013). But underlying these critiques is a series of very real, yet unresolved, questions—why have levels of new housing production slowed in many nations; what are the key constraints on new development; and how might these constraints be best addressed?

Despite a plethora of important academic studies (predominantly by housing scholars) that have pointed to undersupply in housing markets, as well as a mountain of government reports in countries including the United Kingdom and Australia, we are no closer to understanding the dynamics of housing development "on the ground." Of course, concern about levels of housing production chimes with particular political interests, such as those of producer groups and financiers, who will always advocate more favorable—usually less prescriptive and more flexible—approaches to regulation. Debates about new housing development will also intersect with local-level politics and the concerns of local residents—home owners in particular—who fear the impacts of change on local amenities or the social milieu.

What is missing from these discussions is analysis of the actual ways in which housing development takes place in the twenty-first century and the extent to which perceived constraints—regulatory or community in origin—actually operate in practice to mediate the supply of new homes in quantitative and qualitative terms. In this book we seek to bridge this gap.

The genesis of the book began in 2013 with seed-funding from the University of Sydney and the university's Henry Halloran Trust, which sponsored a meeting and public seminar at the University of Hong Kong in July 2014. The themes of the day were housing supply and urban planning reform—at the time hot topics in all three of our case study locations. The rhetoric seemed strikingly similar: governments and housing developers drawing attention to low levels of housing production and high house prices, and pushing for reforms to systems of land release and development control. While the concerns of local communities and their local representatives (over the pace and scale of new development, and its impact on environmental quality, neighborhood amenities, and property values) intersected with land supply and planning reform agendas, other interests—such as the affordability pressures affecting lower-income renters and aspiring home owners—seemed overshadowed.

Prior to the meeting in Hong Kong, the three authors worked on individual country "cases," using a broad framework for comparative analysis. Addressing what we saw as a gap in the policy and research literature on land use planning system barriers to housing production, our focus was squarely on operational questions surrounding the scope of land use planning, development control, and infrastructure provision, and the ways in which these arrangements reflected and reinforced political interests and historically evolved structures of power.

The Hong Kong event was attended by more than two hundred people, despite it being a hot and humid Saturday afternoon. Nick and Nicole were astonished by the turnout, but it seemed that the question of housing supply and the planning system had struck a chord with policy makers and planning practitioners in Hong Kong, as it had in Australia and England. What we observed at this event, and through the meetings and discussions that followed, was an appetite for understanding the mechanics of planning and housing development as it occurs in other places, as a starting point for better-informed domestic policy reflection and improved practice, and as a basis for challenging the uneven politics of property and housing provision, which must be confronted and understood before real change can be progressed.

Nicole Gurran
Nick Gallent
Rebecca L. H. Chiu

December 2015

Acknowledgments

This book was made possible with the generous funding provided by the University of Sydney's Henry Halloran Trust and International Development Program.

We are grateful to Nicole Solana and Judith Newlin at Routledge's New York office, who have been a source of encouragement and who have helped keep the project on track. The excellent maps and diagrams were drawn and redrawn by Sandra Mather at Liverpool University. At the University of Sydney, colleagues within the Urban Housing Lab research incubator, including Dr. Jennifer Kent, Catherine Gilbert, Dr. Somwrita Sarkar, and Professor Peter Phibbs, were a great sounding board as the book developed, and Dr. John Lea provided very helpful feedback on the draft manuscript. Sandra Nichols, through the University of Sydney, assisted with the final draft. Most of the photos are our own but Land Securities in the UK kindly supplied the shots of the Ebbsfleet Valley and Sam Phibbs captured the photos in Chapters 2 and 3. Rebecca would like to thank Mr. Jimmy Leung and Miss Ophelia Yuen Sheung Wong for their useful comment on the drafts of Chapters 6 and 7, Mr. Kang Sum Lee for the photographic support, and Dr. Jie Li for her assistance in preparing the illustrations of these two chapters. Research drawn on in these chapters was funded by a grant from the Research Grants Council of the Hong Kong Special Administrative Region, China (Project no. HKU 742811H). Thanks are also due, as ever, to our families for their support and tolerance. Nicole thanks her husband, Raju, and children Ravi, Neeva, Saru, and Anoushka. Nick's support team include his wife, Manuela, and daughters Marta and Elena.

1 Introduction
Politics, Planning, and Housing Supply

Planning is a key and highly politicized element of public policy. Planning decisions have a propensity to radically change urban and rural environments, to create winners and losers in an economic sense, and also to alter people's lives and the wellbeing of communities. Those decisions, therefore, are often contested and subject to national and local scrutiny. The politics of planning, and of housing development, is a core public policy concern around the world. Periodically, many nations stop and ask why not enough housing is being built or, when it is built, why it is not of the highest quality or in the best, most sustainable, locations. Housing outcomes are determined by a complex national politics, by power play, and by the forces of democracy; they therefore reflect the will of vested interests and of a well-housed majority, which would often prefer to see its amenity protected than opportunity extended to the poorly housed.

This book examines these issues, exploring the politics and planning of new homes in three settings which are very different, but which have shared political traditions: Australia, England, and the Hong Kong Special Administrative Region (SAR). We cast a spotlight on the power relationships and politics that underpin the allocation of land for large-scale residential schemes and thereafter the processes and politics that lead to particular development outcomes. As well as drawing out key conceptual and practical lessons, the book frames each of its case studies in a comprehensive examination of national/territorial frameworks (themselves analyzed in comparative perspective) before dissecting key local cases as a means of answering the book's central question: Are there optimum approaches to planning for housing development, in terms of setting an appropriate framework for allocating land and regulating development proposals, building consensus across local communities and between different stakeholders, and delivering a steady supply of high-quality and well-located homes accessible to, and appropriate for, diverse housing needs? In order to answer this question, it is necessary to situate the planning process within its wider economic and political context.

In this introductory chapter we provide a basis for this wider contextual framework, outlining how different systems of governance and urban planning can mediate the supply of land for housing, and the roles playedby government, planning authorities, developers, property owners, and the public in this process. We ask whether and how differences in land use planning systems—across the processes of land use planning and development control, structures of power, property rights, and development entitlement—might influence the location, quantity, and price of residential land and the implications for housing outcomes, particularly for the fate of large-scale strategic housing development. This sets the scene for understanding large strategic housing sites as locations of intense political and democratic scrutiny and as potential epicenters of conflict centered on the exercise of power and conflicting rights and needs, and as litmus tests of the efficacy of planning/political systems to deliver against the needs of growing populations.

Perspectives from Comparative Planning and Housing Studies

Patterns of housing provision and occupation are shaped by distinct, historically evolved relationships between the state, the market, and private property. While the state intervenes through urban planning to manage the impacts of development, the scope and impacts of this intervention are mediated by systems of landownership and associated rights and obligations (Simpson & Chapman, 1999; Buitelaar & Segeren, 2011). Comparative planning and housing studies can shed light on these processes and their outcomes (Kemeny & Lowe, 1998; Chiu, 2008; Stephens, 2011; Stephens & Norris, 2011). Such work helps explain the origin of new policy information and approaches, while calling into question the validity of assumptions and evidence borrowed from elsewhere (Healey, 2013).

A major attraction of comparative research is the opportunity to undertake "thought" experiments, to speculate on how a shift in the balance between one element of a particular system might affect another. For instance, in the context of growing concern over levels of new housing production relative to rates of population growth, household formation, and rising housing prices, many governments worldwide worry that urban land use planning systems impose oppressive constraints on new development. Arguably, such concerns are rarely grounded in an analysis of actual development processes. Further, the risks of dismantling development controls are significant—potentially degrading urban and environmental quality—while the benefits (assumed increases in rates of housing production) are not necessarily straightforward. Thus, comparative research offers a "low-risk" opportunity for testing assumptions about the potential risks or benefits of system change. Nevertheless, for such comparisons to be valid and useful, it is important to recognize the contextual differences arising from historically evolved systems of housing provision and urban governance. Furthermore, Chiu (2010, 2013) points out that questions of policy transfer must be grounded in a thorough understanding of the policy environment of the originating country (e.g. financial and land resources, regulatory and institutional control, and governance structure) and its national, social, and historical roots. Only by recognizing the embeddedness of policy might it be possible to identify interventions that are genuinely transferrable.

Previous comparative studies have sought to identify which balance of government intervention and market freedom in urban and housing development produces economically or socially optimal outcomes (Barlow & Duncan, 1992). Forms of government intervention span the financial settings for housing and infrastructure production (grants, subsidies, taxes, or finance) to the rules and procedures for deciding the location and design of homes, the obligations of developers, and the extent of community involvement in these decisions. Types of urban regulation (for instance, the extent to which a planning system is discretionary or more rigid in character) may also have important implications for the quantity, quality, and volume of housing and other development (Booth, 1996).

Here, the scale of intervention—i.e. centralized control versus locally devolved decision making—may determine the responsiveness of new development to local circumstances (Barlow & Duncan, 1992), and the extent to which decisions reflect "party politics," producer interests, or those of resident/home owner groups. Such questions are at the heart of any analysis of the role of politics in housing provision. The distance afforded by comparison can illuminate the structural conditions that enable particular interests to prevail.

All of these considerations are relevant to our three-country comparison of urban governance and housing outcomes in Australia, England, and Hong Kong. However, our particular focus in this book is the ways in which the politics of planning and housing provision—the interests of governments and of different producer and consumer groups—are mediated through particular urban governance arrangements, and the implications for new housing supply. Housing supply is our focus, since land and dwelling production is the housing output most directly attributable to the planning system. Other outcomes—such as the cost and distribution of homes across different social groups—are directly and indirectly influenced by planning system decisions (particularly decisions affecting the quantity, quality, and location of new homes), but causality is more difficult to attribute. Further, many other domestic, and progressively international, factors affect demand in the increasingly "financialized" housing market (Rolnik, 2013). These include demographic change, economic growth, the cost and availability of housing credit, the relative value of other investments, and so on (Barker, 2014).

To explore questions concerning the role of planning in mediating housing supply across our three different case studies, we focus on two scales of analysis—1) the bird's eye overarching view, tracing the evolution of the three systems of urban governance in the planning arena; and 2) the level of the strategic development site—where arrangements are played out in practice. Our chief focus is the ways in which politics has shaped planning policy in Australia, England, and Hong Kong, and how, at local levels, political and economic power has been mediated—or unleashed—through the planning system in the production of new homes.

Approach and Methods

One of the limitations of comparative urban and housing research is that it is almost impossible to reduce highly complex phenomena—whole nations and their systems of urban governance and housing provision—into neat units of analysis for comparison. We have not attempted such a task in this book. Rather, our approach has been to develop both a "macro view" and a "micro view" of urban governance, planning, and housing outcomes in each of our three countries, addressing as part of this task basic markers for comparison. These included an attempt to explain the "scope" of urban planning in each case, the key techniques of development control (plan making, zoning, and the permitting process), and questions of landownership and political power in the decision process. We are interested in the balance of influence across the state, civil society, and the private sector (property owners and developers) in each case, as well as the balance of power between central and local governments, or local government and communities, at the plan-making and development control/implementation stages. Ultimately, we are concerned with the ways in which specific aspects of the urban planning system intersect with the wider framework for housing provision.

Thus, the three cases are each examined in two chapters: The first of each pair of chapters provides a national and territorial overview of urban governance, planning, and the housing system, before the second chapters explore how broader frameworks and contexts deliver particular local challenges and outcomes on major strategic sites. Our focus on strategic sites for housing delivery is deliberate. While planning and infrastructure decisions impact on the trajectory of urban change within a city or region in gradual and incremental ways, newly constructed homes amount to a very small proportion of the entire dwelling stock (about 0.5 percent annually in England, and around 2 percent in Australia). This means that the impacts of urban planning on the wider housing market are somewhat limited. However, at regional and subregional scales, strategic sites where housing is delivered at volume will have an important price-setting impact. Notwithstanding the growing importance of "infill" development, it is on large-scale strategic sites—in "greenfield" (undeveloped) and "renewal" (previously developed) contexts—that the planning system intersects with new housing supply at a significant scale. Yet there is surprisingly little analysis of this important context for housing production. Across the "gray" urban policy literature (such as that produced by government and quasi-government agencies, industry sources, and consultants), the focus has tended to be placed on general barriers to new development: perceived problems with the pace of new land release, restrictive development standards, complicated, slow, and uncertain decision processes, and obstructive home owners. But this catalog of complaints—probably familiar to planners nearly everywhere—is rarely substantiated with a deep analysis of where production barriers exist and how precisely they have impacted on housing provision.

Similarly, there is an extensive empirical literature on relationships between the planning system and housing market outcomes, largely rooted in econometric analytical techniques (see Bramley, 2013, and Hincks et al., 2013, for reviews; White & Allmendinger, 2003). However, by necessity this work reduces the planning system to a generalizable series of proxy measures (such as rates of development approval/refusal, or the character and weight of statutory development controls). To draw valid comparisons from this work would require Herculean efforts to develop equivalent measures of planning constraint between, say, Sydney, with its system of piecemeal zoning and codified development standards, and London, with its discretionary, negotiated model. But, more importantly, it would probably miss the point. When it comes to significantly increasing the supply of houses in all of our three case studies—and, indeed, we suspect in many other locations around the world—the policy settings and conventions applying to exceptional sites slated for large-scale new development are probably more important than the generalizable framework governing incremental urban change. Thus, studies of the politics of new land supply—such as the factors affecting local planning authorities in their decisions regarding residential land release (Matthews et al., 2015)—and the ways in which local developers' experiences with particular planning authorities mediate their decisions (Monk & Whitehead, 1999)—highlight the importance of more grounded analyses of planning and housing provision.

Therefore, while a loose framework for comparison was imposed initially as we developed each of the three case study accounts, we also allowed each country to "tell its own story," ensuring that our predetermined framework did not presuppose a particular interpretive outcome. We then reconsidered each of the case studies in the context of wider markers for comparison, informed by the literature on comparative urban research as outlined below but also guided by the emergent themes that seemed to resonate particularly in one or more of our countries.

Comparative Markers for Analysis

As noted, there is a rich, if patchy, literature on comparative urban and housing analysis. Overall, much of the field is dominated by urban geographers, who compare cities and urban regions and their regimes of governance (Stoker & Mossberger, 1994; DiGaetano & Strom, 2003). This work intersects with the growing volume of research on how global ideas circulate (McFarlane, 2011) through processes of "policy transfer"

(Hambleton & Taylor, 1994; Dolowitz & Marsh, 2000; Harris & Moore, 2013). There is also an important and growing stream of comparative housing studies (Kemeny & Lowe, 1998; Stephens, 2011).

However, systematic, comparative studies of urban planning systems (understood in the widest possible sense to encompass strategic spatial decision making, infrastructure provision, and development regulation)—are remarkably rare. One of the exceptions to prove the rule is Philip Booth's 1996 volume on certainty and discretion in development control systems across Europe, the USA, and Hong Kong. Attempts to consider housing and urban planning systems together—that is, to compare the ways in which particular systems of urban governance and planning mediate housing outcomes—are few and far between. An important exception is the series of studies undertaken by James Barlow and his colleagues during the 1990s (Barlow, 1990; Barlow & Duncan, 1992; Barlow & King, 1992; Barlow, 1993; Barlow, 1995). What we find instructive about these contributions is the detailed attention both to systems of housing provision (situated in the wider context of government economic and welfare settings) and to urban planning. This wide canvas allows consideration of the multiple (and distinct) factors affecting housing production and consumption, and the ways in which different systems of urban regulation come to mediate different outcomes. Comparing owner-occupied housing supply and planning in Britain, France, and Sweden, Barlow asks simply

> ... whether similar problems of house and land price inflation, land supply constraints, planning disputes and so on emerge, despite the very different housing provision and land use planning systems that are present
>
> (Barlow 1990, p. 4)

More recently, a special issue of the journal *Housing Studies*, edited by Paris (2007), investigated the relationship between planning and affordable housing across four systems in different geographical locations—England (Whitehead, 2007), Ireland (Norris & Shiels, 2007), Australia (Beer et al., 2007), and Hong Kong (Chiu, 2007)—and concluded that planning's influence over the supply of *affordable housing*, in particular, is limited. But the contributions did not examine the influence of planning and governance on the broader housing supply. Likewise, Whitehead et al. (2009) examined the benefits and costs of land use regulations in different parts of the UK, post-socialist countries in Eastern Europe, and Hong Kong, but did not delve into the impacts of the increasingly participatory planning systems.

Across the comparative literature, debates persist over whether nations are "converging" toward a similar trajectory (often shorthand for marketization), despite very different starting positions, or whether groups of similar nation states are in fact diverging both in approaches to key policy problems and in system/market outcomes (Holzinger & Knill, 2005). However, a preoccupation with questions of "convergence" and "divergence" implies a type of "path dependence" that is immune to disruption. An alternative—perhaps more grounded—purpose of comparative research is to test whether particular interventions (perhaps borrowed from "overseas") might in fact disrupt a current trajectory (e.g. Barlow, 1993; Barlow et al., 2003; Oxley et al., 2014). This form of research can be a precursor to "policy transfer" but needs careful qualification through systematic analyses of contextual differences.

Comparative research can also provide a basis for exposing domestic policy assumptions; in effect, seeing whether proposed remedies to existing problems have been successful in other places (e.g. White & Allmendinger, 2003; Moore & McKee, 2012; Austin et al., 2014). This technique is underpinned by research methods that involve careful assemblage and scrutiny of different policy claims and outcomes. Our interest in this book is more sympathetic to these two applied rationales for comparative research than more theoretical questions of system convergence or divergence. Nevertheless, in the final summation certain similarities in housing outcomes—despite profound system differences—do emerge across Australia, England, and Hong Kong.

Drawing on the lessons from comparative housing and urban studies literature, the key "markers" for comparative analysis of our cases focus on the scope of urban planning within the wider, historically evolved framework for urban and housing development. This implies that in addition to our close analysis, as set out in the case study chapters (on the "scope" of urban planning in each system, techniques of development control, landownership, and political power across the state, civil society, and the private sector), we must establish a basis for conceptual "equivalence," which is critical to comparative research (Kemeny & Lowe, 1998; DiGaetano & Strom, 2003). Although this study does not set out to compare the housing provision systems across the three case studies, it is necessary to draw out the principal similarities and differences defining the distinct systems of housing provision (e.g. arrangements for housing production: private enterprise and non-profit and finance, and the variety of housing options delivered for different social groups) in each case in this introductory chapter in order to reveal the housing contexts within which the planning systems are operating.

Turning to these planning systems, attention is now drawn to important features of the urban governance arrangements defining each country/city. These include: relationships between central and local government where applicable; approaches to the release of land; the articulation of controls governing the type and density of development; decision processes for determining and contesting particular proposals; and the balance of power between central and local authorities and communities. In particular, opportunities for public participation in decision processes, the balance between political and professional autonomy in determining development applications, and the extent to which developers and/or third parties can contest or legally appeal decisions, are significant dimensions. Other important systemic factors to unpack include arrangements, responsibilities, and funding mechanisms for providing infrastructure, as well as mechanisms for value capture following land rezoning, the issuing of planning permission, or major public investment to support transport or urban renewal.

Urban Settlement and Housing Demand

The geography and settlement structures of our three case studies have important bearings on the nature of housing and the parameters and constraints affecting new production. Equally, demographic drivers—such as population growth and household formation rates—are traditionally the major considerations in relation to understanding patterns of housing need and demand.

As shown in Table 1.1, England has the largest population and a much higher population density than Australia (at 413 persons per square kilometer), but less than 30 percent of people live in England's major cities. This stands in contrast to Australia, where nearly two-thirds of the population live in a few, large cities despite an overall population density of only three persons per hectare. Hong Kong has the highest urban density: 6,690 persons per kilometer, eclipsing that of England's largest city, London, and more than seventeen times the density of Sydney, Australia (Table 1.1). Of course, these differences in density must in part reflect constraints on urban expansion, whether inherent (defined by geography in the case of Hong Kong), historically evolved (as in the case of Australia's pattern of concentrated settlement), or imposed (as has been claimed is the case in England). Such constraints have a major bearing on the capacity to satisfy housing demand by the release of new land for housing development. Another important difference between our three cases is that Australia's population growth rate is higher than either England or Hong Kong (comprised of both high international immigration and a buoyant birth rate), although its larger overall land mass implies a greater capacity to accommodate this growth.

Despite these differences, all three case study areas are struggling with housing affordability pressures. In England and Australia these pressures have been concentrated particularly in the high growth and employment regions (the east and southeast coast in Australia and the southeast of England), but in all three cases house price inflation has far exceeded wage growth over the past decade.

While numerical data are limited, one consideration when understanding housing demand is the growing internationalization of housing markets. In recent years a small but growing proportion of housing demand has derived from international investors (Rolnik, 2013). This international demand introduces a new dimension to understanding future market pressures, since planning forecasts focus on localized demographic trends (and sometimes

Table 1.1 Key Characteristics, Australia, England, and Hong Kong, 2014

	Australia	England	Hong Kong
Population (million)	23.9	54.3	7.2
Population growth	1.8%	0.8%	0.8%
Percentage of population in major cities (larger than one million people)	60%	29%	100%
Population density (persons per square kilometer)	3	413	6 690
Population density of largest city (persons per square kilometer)	380 (Sydney)	5285 (London)	6 690
Ratio of median house prices to median household earnings	6–8:1	8–10:1	14–16:1

Sources: Fox & Finlay, 2012; Census and Statistics Department, 2015; Department for Communities and Local Government, 2015b; ONS, 2015; World Bank, 2015; Worldometers, 2015

economic factors to allow for increased demand for larger primary properties or second homes). The focus for foreign investment in real estate has been on global cities—such as Hong Kong, London, and Sydney—while impacts on the overall domestic housing market are as yet unclear (Rogers et al., forthcoming), they are thought by some to be significant (Valentine, 2015) or potentially significant (Gallent, 2015). It may also be the case that housing *development* is also increasingly international, with new evidence that Chinese firms, for instance, are following Chinese real estate investors to other markets such as Australia (Lui & Gurran, 2015).

Government Support for Housing Production and Consumption

This leads to the question of how governments intervene to support housing production or consumption. Support might relate to the provision of housing (housing construction and management, by the private sector, public or not-for-profit organizations, or individuals) and/or to the ways in which housing is "consumed" (purchased or rented by its occupants). There is also considerable potential for differences in the ways in which such support is provided, which might range from direct grants for housing production, through to implicit taxation benefits for housing consumption. Importantly, when there is limited control over how in-kind (such as free state-owned land) or in-cash subsidies or financial incentives for consumers are used, it is likely that house prices and/or rents will increase more than the rate of new supply.

The different forms of support for housing provision and consumption in Australia, England, and Hong Kong are summarized in Table 1.2.

Table 1.2 Financing Housing Production and Consumption, Australia, England, and Hong Kong

Support	Australia	England	Hong Kong
Producer support			
Grants for private housing producers	Periodic Commonwealth/state grants available to address local infrastructure blockages	Builders Finance Fund for private schemes that have slowed down or stalled from 2015; grants to support delivery of Starter Homes availability at 20 percent below market value, also from 2015	N/A
Grants for social/not-for-profit housing providers	Very limited Commonwealth/state funds for social housing development (financing around 1,500–2,500 dwellings per annum)	Limited Affordable Housing Capital Funding (2015–2018)	N/A (Proceeds from the subsidized sale schemes and the rental income from retail properties in public housing development finance the social housing sector, after a one-off government injection of permanent capital in 1987)
Reduced interest rates on loans for housing producers/state finance	N/A	Some preferential private lending practice given the low risk associated with sector	N/A
Tax relief for housing producers	N/A	Partial recovery of input VAT possible on "Affordable Rent" housing	N/A

Access to government land for housing development	Limited, and commercial return to government usually required	Local authority land used in this way; requirement for significant affordable housing inclusion when public land developed	Government supplies free land for all public rental housing projects and cost-priced land for owner-occupier housing projects provided by the Hong Kong Housing Authority, a public organization which is the main subsidized housing provider
Planning system mechanisms to provide land, funding, or completed dwellings for affordable sector	Limited, and in some jurisdictions only	Extensive and established mechanisms under "planning gain" (Section 106 of 1990 Town and Country Planning Act) requirements	N/A
Producer support tied to affordable outcome	Social housing and planning system mechanisms only	Not always: market rescue schemes in 1990s and today (including Builders Finance Fund); also post-2015 Starter Home initiative delivers a market discount rather than "affordability" linked to local wages	N/A

Consumer/investor support

Mortgage interest tax relief (family home)	No	No—Mortgage Interest Relief at Source (MIRAS) ceased in 1988	A small income tax concession for all mortgagors
Mortgage interest tax relief (landlords)	"Negative gearing" for investment properties (landlords can offset finance and other costs against whole income tax liability)	Yes, landlords have been able to use interest paid on mortgage to offset tax bill. This will stop in 2017, to be replaced by a less generous tax credit system	N/A

continued . . .

Table 1.2 Continued

Support	Australia	England	Hong Kong
Consumer/investor support . . . Continued			
Other favorable tax treatment for family home	No capital gains tax on sale of family home, preferential treatment in pension asset test	No capital gains tax on sale of family home	No capital gains tax on sale of family homes generally if occupancy is longer than two years
Other favorable tax treatment for property investment	Discount on capital gains tax if property held for more than twelve months	Local Council Tax not in proportion to property values; higher valued property is undertaxed	Generally, profit tax for sale of home of less than two years
Grants to assist with home purchase	Cash grants for first home buyers (sometimes limited to new homes only)	Help to Buy equity loans on properties valued at up to £600,000; Social Homebuy and Right to Acquire support in social sector	Terminated in 2003. Between 1987 and 2003, provided interest-free loans for down-payment.
Rental subsidies	Limited means-tested rental subsidy	Means-tested Housing Benefit	Means-tested public rental housing to about 30 percent of households. Rents about 25 percent of market rent
Financial support limited to new homes only	No, but some small targeting of first home buyer's grant	Yes, Help to Buy is restricted to new-build homes	Direct provision of subsidized owner-occupier housing 1976–2002, then reactivated from 2011. Covering about 14 percent of households.

Source: The authors

As shown, support for housing production differs significantly across the three countries, with Australia characterized by minimal production-side support in comparison to England, where capital subsidies for social housing production persist (albeit having been highly reduced), and to Hong Kong, where the broad-based public housing system is self-financing due to the institutional structure of subsidized housing provision. In both England and Hong Kong there are established arrangements to provide land for affordable housing development (government land in Hong Kong and contributions made through the planning system in England). In Australia and England, at least, support for housing "consumption"—in the form of tax concessions in particular—appears to outweigh support for new dwelling production.

Land Use Planning, Development Control, and Housing Supply

Beyond the financing of housing production, it is clearly important to consider the land use planning and development control systems that regulate how new housing is produced and how the existing housing stock is renewed or adjusted. Barlow (1990) identifies three types of development control, which he casts as "positive" (trying to direct housing producers to a desired outcome, generally only possible with the use of government resources and contractual agreements between housing providers and the state), "negative" (because the government simply sanctions or denies housing development), or "intermediate" (where strategic plans are legally binding) (Table 1.3). Booth (1996) distinguishes between "negative" forms of development control (simply permitting or refusing a development) and more strategic regulation through "a continuum from strategic policies to the eventual decision on a particular development proposal for a given plot" (Booth, 1996, p. 6). Under ideal conditions, there is a clear trajectory from the strategic policy framework to the legally enforceable development rights and constraints that are clearly understood by all parties and consistently applied. However, implementation gaps mean that it may also be the case that the development rules (often expressed through land use zones and quantifiable development standards (or "design codes") such as street setbacks and maximum heights) might appear detached from or even inconsistent with the strategic framework. Similarly, depending on the level of discretion available to decision makers responsible for determining proposals, there may also be intense political pressures to approve or refuse a proposal despite compliance/inconsistency with prevailing controls.

Booth suggests that, in general terms, "rule-bound" systems (with limited discretion available to interpret the rules in relation to the merits of an individual case) are often characterized by administrative decision-making processes (professional planners applying regulatory criteria under delegated authority). By contrast, discretionary systems that interpret criteria with reference to the "merit" of a particular case are often characterized by political determination processes that are likely to be less predictable. It has also been suggested that political decision processes are more likely to be bound by local home owner interests (Hawkins, 2011; Matthews et al., 2015). The balance between certainty and flexibility and local versus wider-level interests has been a key theme in planning reform agendas across the United Kingdom and in Australia (Gurran et al., 2014), and emerges as a critical issue in the case studies that follow.

Table 1.3 summarizes these different approaches to land use planning and development control across Australia, England, and Hong Kong on a continuum from "negative" control through development-permitting only through to "intermediate" (more strategic forms of regulation) and "positive" planning whereby government has capacity to drive housing production (or other development outcomes) more directly. In nations characterized by primarily regulatory planning systems, new housing supply depends almost solely on the private sector to bring forward development proposals and enact approved schemes. In such systems, patterns of housing development typically follow market cycles, although the existence of a strong not-for-profit sector able to operate counter-cyclically during down-

Table 1.3 Characterization of Land Use Planning, Development Control, and Housing Supply Systems in Australia, England, and Hong Kong

Planning, development control, and housing supply	Australia	England	Hong Kong
"Negative" Control over the nature and location of development, solely by the use of development permits		✓	
"Intermediate" Control over the nature and location of development by the establishment of detailed and legally binding land use plans, where developer rights and obligations are known and fixed	✓		✓ Modification by planning application may be allowed
"Positive" State ownership of development land, coupled with a system of production based on contractual agreements between developers/providers and the state		Partial—Section 106 requirements securing land for affordable housing, government grants for development	✓

Source: The authors, drawing on Barlow (1990)

turns in the market can improve stability. As shown in Table 1.3, only Hong Kong retains the capacity to proactively stimulate and guide the development process through state ownership of land.

System of Housing Production

Another important dimension of the housing system is the way in which housing is actually initiated and produced. Barlow (1990) distinguishes between systems defined by speculative development for profit, systems where profit making or not-for-profit institutions are balanced or where profit dominates, and "self-development" by individual householders. Thus, residential development might come about through the efforts of private (for-profit) land development and/or housing construction firms, public (or quasi-public) institutions, or individual households who acquire land and commission a builder to construct their home to an agreed design.

There are marked differences in the systems of housing production across our three case studies (Table 1.4). While in Australia the majority of new homes are produced as a result of individual household contracts between builders (of either single homes, and increasingly of multi-unit developments), in England housing production is largely speculative (Figure 1.1).

Table 1.4 System of Housing Production, Australia, England, and Hong Kong

Housing production classification	Australia	England	Hong Kong
"Non-speculative" production dominated by not-for-profit (or limited-profit) developers and/or state authorities	2–3 percent of housing production only	15 percent of housing production	44 percent of housing production
"Speculative" production organized by private development companies (including corporatized state entities)	Around 10 percent of land and housing production	Around 75 percent of housing production	56 percent of housing production
"Non-speculative" production organized by individual households (i.e. initiated and contracted via financial contract pre-construction)	Around 90 percent of dwellings (single-family homes and apartments) contracted before construction	Around 10 percent of housing production	Minimal

Source: The authors, drawing on Barlow's 1990 classification of housing production modes and various national level studies, namely National Housing Supply Council 2009; Hong Kong Housing Authority 2015

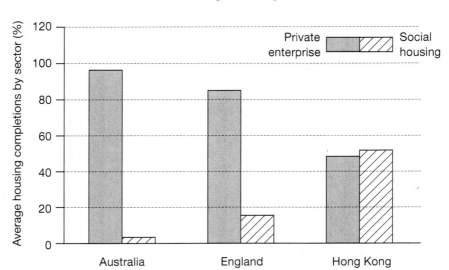

Figure 1.1 Housing Provision, Australia, England, and Hong Kong (based on annual averages, 2001–2014)

Sources: (ABS, 2015; Department for Communities and Local Government, 2015a; Hong Kong Housing Authority, 2015)

In Hong Kong, housing production has appeared relatively balanced between private enterprise and social provision over the past decade, although there have been significant year-on-year shifts linked to fluctuation in the level of public subsidy (Hong Kong Housing Authority, 2015). The relative implications of these different systems of housing provision are discussed at greater length in the case study chapters.

While data are currently inadequate, it may be the case that involvement by international or external (from within China but outside of Hong Kong is considered external but not international) housing developers (in turn, marketing to the international real estate market) may also affect the character of new housing production in distinct but as yet uncharted ways (Lui & Gurran, 2015).

Housing Product Diversity

What do these arrangements amount to, in terms of housing options for different cross-sections of the community? Table 1.5 provides a starting point for comparing the range of tenure options and their distribution across the three case studies.

As shown, tenure arrangements differ significantly across the three cases, with Australia and England dominated by home ownership, although rates of owner-occupation have been gradually falling in the wake of the 2007/08

Table 1.5 Housing Product Diversity Australia, England, and Hong Kong

Tenure types, costs, and benefits	Social renting			Private rental			Assisted/shared home ownership			Home ownership		
	Australia	England	Hong Kong	Australia	England	Hong Kong	Australia	England	Hong Kong	Australia	England	Hong Kong
Proportion (households) (%)	4	17.7	30.4	28	18.1	13.9	Small, numbers n/a	0.8	15.9	68	63.4	52.1 (including assisted HOS)
Entry costs	Low	Low	Low	Deposit (one month's rent)	Deposit (four to six weeks' rent)	Deposit (two months' rent)	Low	Low	Low	High —20 percent deposit/ equity)	High —20 percent deposit	Very high (private housing)— 30 percent down payment
Recurrent expenditure	Low (25–30 percent of income)	Low	Low (14 percent of income)	Variable/ High	Variable: high in some markets	High	Moderate (25–30 percent of income)	Moderate	Moderate	Variable —high for recent purchasers	Variable: high in some markets	Moderate (currently very low interest rate)
Ease of access	Ten-year waiting list, means-tested	Means-tested, depends on need category	Means-tested, currently 3.7 years' waiting time	Variable	Variable	Variable	Limited availability	Limited availability	Currently very limited availability	Variable —5 percent of stock nationwide affordable to low-income households	Low: declining uptake prompting government support	Good availability but currently unaffordable (P/I ratio: 16:1)

continued …

Table 1.5 Continued

Tenure types, costs, and benefits	Social renting			Private rental			Assisted/shared home ownership			Home ownership		
	Australia	England	Hong Kong	Australia	England	Hong Kong	Australia	England	Hong Kong	Australia	England	Hong Kong
Security of tenure	Means-tested	High	High	Low—six-month lease	Low—six to twelve-month Assured Shorthold Tenancy (AST)	Usually one year fixed and one year floating. Renewability varies	High	High	High	High	High, unless mortgagee defaults on loan	High
Choice of location and dwelling type	Low	Low—"right to buy" has reduced availability in popular locations and also availability	Low—a max. of three choices of location is offered. Dwelling size depends on family size	Medium	Medium	Restricted by affordability	Medium	Medium—concentration of products in particular locations	Medium	High, but restricted by affordability	High, but huge variations in affordability	High, but restricted by affordability

Dwelling control (i.e. upkeep, management)	None	None of single-family homes	Can request elderly-friendly retrofitting, Active resident participation	None	None	High	High	High	High	High	High
Property ownership	None	None	None	None	None	Shared	Shared	Full	Highest	Highest	Highest
Capital gains/risks	None	None	None	None	None	Shared	Shared	Have to return subsidy at prevalent price upon resale	Highest	Highest	Highest

Source: The authors, adapted from Barlow & Duncan (1992) and national housing statistic sources; Census and Statistics Department, Hong Kong Special Administrative Region (2012), 2011 Census Data, generated through the Interactive Data Dissemination Service on 24/1/2013 (percentage does not add to 100 because there is a small sector of rent-free/accommodation provided by employer)

20 *Introduction: Politics, Planning, Housing*

Global Financial Crisis (GFC). While England has a significant social housing sector (17 percent), offering secure tenure and affordable rents, nearly half of households in Hong Kong reside in subsidized accommodation.

Around 16 percent of households in Hong Kong occupy "shared" home ownership—a scheme by which equity is shared between the household and government or a not-for-profit entity at resale, reducing up-front and recurrent costs to provide affordable but secure accommodation, with provision for modest capital gain. However, government support for this scheme in Hong Kong was suspended between 2002–2011. Ironically, both Australia and England have begun programs to increase shared ownership opportunities in recent years.

Power and Control in the Planning System

Within the overarching framework of the planning system, rules governing housing development influence the capacity of different interest groups—corporations or individuals—to extract profit from the development process and housing market. In turn these potential benefits and the relative resources of each group will have implications for their level of political organization and potential influence over the planning framework overall—including participation rights and the obligations of developers—and, in particular, the spatial policy framework for assigning land uses, infrastructure investment, and decisions on particular proposals.

Drawing on Booth's (1996) framework for understanding planning systems by reference to degrees of regulation or discretion, we can add an explicitly political dimension. Thus, Table 1.6 attempts to conceptualize the planning system with reference to relative forms of power (political, state/bureaucratic, developer/producer), landowners, local residents (i.e. including non-home-owning tenants), and interest groups (representing producers, environmental issues, low-income tenants, business groups, and resident home owners). With reference to these groups it summarizes the ways in which power is exercised through the planning system at different points in the process of land allocation and development control across the three case studies.

As shown, there are significant differences in the allocation of power and control across the three planning systems. While the Australian states exercise strong control of local plan making and decisions, in England the balance appears tipped toward local communities. While Australia's regulatory system implies some codification of development rights (and obligations), discretionary provisions enable higher levels of government to exercise flexibility in awarding development approval as well. Australian developers are able to challenge refusals or onerous development conditions in court, but community groups and their advocates have little recourse to legal review in the event of a decision they oppose. By contrast, in Hong Kong the shift has been very much toward increased community consultation and engagement in major planning decisions, while in England local

Table 1.6 Power and Control within the Planning System

	Australia	England	Hong Kong
Strategic spatial planning (non-statutory)—land allocation for housing, nature, industry, etc. Infrastructure funding decisions	State government-led Public exhibition Written submissions received State government	Local government-led, land and site allocation (indicative) National/local	Government-led (only one-tier), wide public consultation in previous two strategic plans Government as proposer Legislative Council as approver
Land use zoning and definition of development controls	Local/state government Public exhibition, written submissions received Landowner/developer can initiate process	Not currently applicable but discussions around "permission in principle" zoning for some brownfield sites linked to 2015 Housing and Planning Bill	Recommended by Town Planning Board (TPB), approved by Chief Executive-in-Council. TPB chaired by a government official, but mainly comprised of professional and community leaders. Public representations (objection or support) permitted. Objections must be heard; and if not withdrawn, will be submitted to Chief-Executive together with the proposed plan
Development proposals and control	Developer initiates, state/local authority determines Public exhibition and written submissions received	Developer (for-profit/not-for-profit) proposes Local government determines	Anyone can initiate, including non-property owner, Town Planning Board (TPB) determines. Proposals exhibited for public views. If objections not upheld, can seek for review by TPB, and eventually judicial review, or submission to Appeal Court

continued ....

Table 1.6 Continued

	Australia	England	Hong Kong
Regulatory/discretionary in character	Mixed system—statutory plans and controls imply development rights; discretionary assessment confers them	Discretionary with some recent adjustments to permitted development rights, giving communities control over some minor development and allowing, for example, office-to-residential conversions	Development rights follow statutory plans and controls. Uses always permitted or may be permitted upon application are listed in the zoning plans. TPB considers applications cautiously to avoid legal challenges
Value-capture mechanisms	No real mechanisms, but development contribution charges (fixed or negotiated) for infrastructure in most state jurisdictions. Very limited affordable housing inclusion schemes in some states	Past attempts to tax "betterment" abandoned; contributions negotiated through Section 106 agreements or fixed through charging schedule based on Community Infrastructure Levy (CIL). Compulsory Purchase possible, but at intended use value	N/A
Appeal rights and mechanisms	Developer can appeal a refusal or against the conditions of development approval, limited third-party appeal rights	Developer can appeal; national government can intervene	Developer/owner can ask for a review hearing and subsequently lodge an appeal of a refusal or against conditions of development approval. May seek judicial review or submission to the Appeal Court

Source: The authors

autonomy over development has been reinforced by recent system reforms under post-2010 "localism" (Jacobs & Manzi, 2013).

Structure of the Book

The next six chapters of this book explore how these profound differences in approach to urban regulation and housing development play out on the ground. Our first port of call is Australia. In Chapter 2 we dissect the sociocultural origins of Australia's current planning approaches, settlement structure, and housing challenges. The chapter illustrates how, over the past twenty years, a mounting housing affordability crisis in Australia has generated much scrutiny of the ways in which the planning system might affect the housing market. In canvassing these debates, the chapter explains how Australian planning, which combines elements of both the English (discretionary assessment) and American (zoning) traditions has become the focus of an increasingly contested politics of land and housing supply.

Chapter 3 carries forward the national analysis of Australia into metropolitan, and then local, case studies, focusing on the state of New South Wales and particular discourses, development patterns and outcomes in the Greater Sydney area. Detailed case studies on the delivery of new homes through major development sites in outer urban "greenfield" and inner-city "brownfield" settings highlight the distance between the rhetoric of planning system constraint and the reality of market-driven production, which is facilitated by public coordination and investment but largely unbounded by public obligations. The chapter ends by asking whether the politics of property in Australia has blinded the policy imagination to fairer approaches for housing provision across high-demand urban regions.

Chapter 4 reflects on the scope and evolution of planning in England, unpacking a seventy-year narrative in which there have been key shifts in the locus of power and an extension of local democracy. At the beginning of this period, planning was operating in a "delivery mode"; it was leading urban change through post-war urban renewal and the delivery of New Towns. But, midway through, it switched to a "regulatory mode" as the volume of direct public investment was eclipsed by private development. In this regulatory mode, the key power of planning has been to lever public goods from the development process, a power derived from its control over development rights, but which diminishes during low points in the economic cycle. Regulatory-mode planning in England is strongest in rising markets. Given this reality, this chapter considers the changing relationships (and the shifting contours of power) that determine planning outcomes. It looks, in particular, at the changing role of the local state, the power of market actors, and the growing influence (it seems) of community groups. Of particular concern in Chapter 4 is the recent undersupply of housing in England and the regularity at which major housing sites have become "stuck" and bogged down in local political struggles.

In the fifth chapter, three highly significant case studies are examined using the frameworks developed generally in Chapter 1 and localized in Chapter 4. These three sites are Stevenage West, a pair of urban extensions in the Ashford Growth Area, and the Ebbsfleet Valley site in the London Thames Gateway. These are all critical sites of the type that needed (and need) to be built if the government is to substantially increase housing supply in England in line with projections of demographic need. The Stevenage West site figured in the New Town plans for Stevenage in the 1960s. The Ashford extensions are part of a regional planning aspiration that became a national flagship policy with the publication of the Labour government's Communities Plan in 2003. And the Ebbsfleet Valley site has been through several plan iterations, the most recent of which sees it as the first of a new generation of garden cities in England. These are all highly political sites. Stevenage West is a cross-jurisdictional site that has seen no development since its plan allocation in 1998. Ashford has seen substantial growth and there are plans to put 15,000 homes in a former clay pit at Ebbsfleet. These cases are presented and analyzed in light of the changing scope, scale, and nature of planning in England.

Hong Kong provides a contrast to Australia and England in many respects, but also shares some political and democratic traditions. But urban planning in Hong Kong continues to operate in the "delivery mode" that was gradually lost in England (and in Australia) in the decades after the Second World War. This is because land is state-owned. State ownership enables the delivery of a large public housing program and the generation of significant public revenue from land sale. This makes urban planning an expedient government instrument for the fast achievement of an array of socioeconomic objectives. However, as the planning process has become increasingly participatory and politicized since 1997, coupled with the long economic depression and market slump after the Asian financial crisis, the system has manifested trends similar to those observed in Australia and England: housing land supply has stagnated and there are now great difficulties in securing sufficient land to meet buoyant demand, causing rapid rises in housing costs and deepening affordability problems. Again building on the comparative framework and markers developed in Chapter 1, the first of the Hong Kong chapters analyzes how enhanced democracy and participation is now impacting on Hong Kong's housing outcomes in both quantitative and qualitative terms, highlighting the trade-offs and the underlying market forces shaping the planning approach to the provision of residential land.

The issues brought to light in Chapter 6 are exemplified in Chapter 7 by two key sites—the South East Kowloon Development Scheme at the old airport site and the Tung Chung New Town Extension—and by reference to other major planning projects. Chapter 7 examines the history of these new development areas and tracks the political debate and community involvement in their allocation as major new housing locations and in the master-planning of the proposed schemes. Of particular concern is the way in which the planning process has interfaced with community actors and the degree to which the strategic priorities of government and community ambition can be satisfactorily reconciled. This analysis is set against a backdrop of rising house prices (and declining affordability), critical challenges in land supply (in part due to the suspension of new land development from 1999 to 2007), and two opposing democratic trends: the rise in participatory planning and the centralization of control over land development, typified by public landownership.

What can be learnt from the three experiences of delivering new homes on major development sites? What are the key drivers of political discourse and has there been any detectable shift in the balance of power between different actors in the development process given the greater social complexity (i.e. a mix of needs, aspirations, actors, etc.) with which planning now has to grapple? These are some of the major questions that are addressed in this book's concluding chapter. The national or territorial experiences and local illustrations are drawn together to synthesize a broader view of the politics (and questions of democracy) that are central to the way planning takes place and delivers particular outcomes. The conclusion rounds in on two core issues: the ownership of land and development rights and the influence of representative democracy on housing outcomes. It considers the extent to which, despite community involvement in housing development (ostensibly aiming to achieve locally tailored solutions), overall outcomes are the product of wider democratic processes that privilege a well-housed property-owning majority at the expense of a poorly-housed minority.

References

ABS (Australian Bureau of Statistics). (2015). *Building Activity, Australia (Cat 8752.0)*. Canberra: Australian Bureau of Statistics (ABS).

Austin, P., Gurran, N., & Whitehead, C. E. (2014). Planning and affordable housing in Australia, New Zealand and England: common culture; different mechanisms. *Journal of Housing and the Built Environment*, 29(3), 455–472.

Barker, K. (2014). *Housing: Where's the Plan?* London: London Publishing Partnership.

Barlow, J. (1990). Owner-occupier housing supply and the planning framework in "boom regions": Examples from Britain, France, and Sweden. *Planning Practice and Research*, 5(2), 4–11.

Barlow, J. (1993). Controlling The Housing Land Market—Some Examples From Europe. *Urban Studies*, 30(7), 1129–1149.

Barlow, J. (1995). The politics of urban-growth—Boosterism and nimbyism in European boom regions. *International Journal of Urban and Regional Research*, 19(1), 129–144.

Barlow, J., Childerhouse, P., Gann, D., Hong-Minh, S., Naim, M., & Ozaki, R. (2003). Choice and delivery in housebuilding: Lessons from Japan for UK housebuilders. *Building Research and Information*, 31(2), 134–145.

Barlow, J. & Duncan, S. (1992). Markets, states and housing provision: Four European growth regions compared. *Progress in Planning, 38,* Part 2, 93–177.

Barlow, J. & King, A. (1992). The state, the market, and competitive strategy: The housebuilding industry in the United Kingdom, France, and Sweden. *Environment and Planning A, 24*(3), 381–400.

Beer, A., Kearins, B., & Pieters, H. (2007). Housing affordability and planning in Australia: The challenge of policy under neo-liberalism. *Housing Studies, 22*(1), 11–24.

Booth, P. (1996). *Controlling Development: Certainty and Discretion in Europe, the USA and Hong Kong.* London, Bristol, PA: UCL Press.

Bramley, G. (2013). Housing market models and planning. *Town Planning Review, 84*(1), 9–34.

Buitelaar, E. & Segeren, A. (2011). Urban structures and land. The morphological effects of dealing with property rights. *Housing Studies, 26*(5), 661–679.

Census and Statistics Department. (2015). *Hong Kong: The Facts.* Hong Kong: Information Services Department.

Chiu, R. L. (2008). Government intervention in housing: Convergence and divergence of the Asian Dragons. *Urban Policy and Research, 26*(3), 249–269.

Chiu, R. L. (2013). The Transferability of Public Housing Policy Within Asia: Reflections from the Hong Kong-Mainland China Case Study. In J. H. Chen, M. Stephens, & Y. Man (Eds.) *The Future of Public Housing.* Berlin: Springer, pp. 3–12.

Davoudi, S. (2011). Localism and the reform of the planning system in England. *Disp, 47*(4), 92–94.

Department for Communities and Local Government. (2015a). *Live Tables on Housebuilding (Table 241).* London: Department for Communities and Local Government.

Department for Communities and Local Government. (2015b). *Live Tables on the Housing Market and House Prices.* London: Department for Communities and Local Government.

DiGaetano, A. & Strom, E. (2003). Comparative urban governance—An integrated approach. *Urban Affairs Review, 38*(3), 356–395.

Dolowitz, D. P. & Marsh, D. (2000). Learning from abroad: The role of policy transfer in contemporary policy-making. *Governance—an International Journal of Policy and Administration, 13*(1), 5–24.

Fox, R. & Finlay, R. (2012). *Dwelling Prices and Household Income.* Canberra: Reserve Bank of Australia.

Gallent, N. (2015). Investment, global capital and other drivers of England's housing crisis. *Journal of Urban Regeneration & Renewal, 9*(2), 122–138.

Gurran, N., Austin, P., & Whitehead, C. (2014). That sounds familiar! A decade of planning reform in Australia, England, and New Zealand. *Australian Planner, 51*(2), 186–198.

Gurran, N. & Phibbs, P. (2013). Housing supply and urban planning reform: The recent Australian experience, 2003–2012. *International Journal of Housing Policy,* 1–27.

Hambleton, R. & Taylor, M. (1994). Transatlantic urban policy transfer. *Policy Studies, 15*(2), 4–18.

Harris, A. & Moore, S. (2013). Planning histories and practices of circulating urban knowledge. *International Journal of Urban and Regional Research, 37*(5), 1499–1509.

Haughton, G. & Allmendinger, P. (2012). Spatial planning and the new localism. *Planning Practice & Research*, 28(1), 1–5.

Hawkins, C. (2011). Electoral support for community growth management policy. *Social Science Quarterly*, 92(1), 268–284.

Healey, P. (2013). Circuits of knowledge and techniques: The transnational flow of planning ideas and practices. *International Journal of Urban and Regional Research*, 37(5), 1510–1526.

Hincks, S., Leishman, C., & Watkins, C. (2013). Planning and housing: Concepts, policy instruments and market analysis. *Town Planning Review*, 84(1), 1–7.

Holzinger, K. & Knill, C. (2005). Causes and conditions of cross-national policy convergence. *Journal of European Public Policy*, 12(5), 775–796.

Hong Kong Housing Authority. (2015). *Housing in Figures*. Hong Kong: Hong Kong Housing Authority.

Jacobs, K. & Manzi, T. (2013). New localism, old retrenchment: The "big society", housing policy and the politics of welfare reform. *Housing Theory & Society*, 30(1), 29–45.

Kemeny, J. & Lowe, S. (1998). Schools of comparative housing research: From convergence to divergence. *Housing Studies*, 13(2), 161–176.

Lee, J. & Zhu, Y. P. (2006). Urban governance, neoliberalism and housing reform in China. *Pacific Review*, 19(1), 39–61.

Lui, S. & Gurran, N. (2015). Foreign investment in Australian housing: Effects of China's domestic housing policy changes on international investment demand. *Paper presented to the 2015 Australasian Housing Conference February 2015*. Hobart, Tasmania: AHNR.

Matthews, P., Bramley, G., & Hastings, A. (2015). Homo economicus in a big society: Understanding middle-class activism and NIMBYism towards new housing developments. *Housing, Theory and Society*, 32(1), 54–72.

McFarlane, C. (2011). Travelling Policies, Ideological Assemblages. In C. McFarlane, *Learning the City*. Hoboken, NJ: Wiley-Blackwell, pp. 115–152.

Monk, S. & Whitehead, C. M. E. (1999). Evaluating the economic impact of planning controls in the United Kingdom: Some implications for housing. *Land Economics*, 75(1), 74–93.

Moore, T. & McKee, K. (2012). Empowering local communities? An international review of community land trusts. *Housing Studies*, 27(2), 280–290.

Norris, M. & Shiels, P. (2007). Housing affordability in the Republic of Ireland: Is planning part part of the problem or part of the solution? *Housing Studies*, 22(1), 45–62.

ONS. (2015). *Annual Mid-year Population Estimates, 2014*. London: Office for National Statistics (ONS).

Oxley, M., Brown, T., Richardson, J., & Lishman, R. (2014). *Boosting the supply of affordable rented housing: Learning from other countries*. Leicester, UK: De Montfort University and Places for People.

Paris, C. (2007). International perspectives on planning and affordable housing. *Housing Studies*, 22(1), 1–9.

Rogers, D., Lee, C., & Yan, D. (2015). The politics of foreign investment in Australian housing: Chinese investors, translocal sales agents and local resistance. *Housing Studies*, 30(5), 730–748.

Rolnik, R. (2013). Late neoliberalism: The financialization of homeownership and housing rights. *International Journal of Urban and Regional Research*, 37(3), 1058–1066.

Simpson, F. & Chapman, M. (1999). Comparison of urban governance and planning policy—East looking West. *Cities, 16*(5), 353–364.

Stephens, M. (2011). Comparative Housing Research: A "system-embedded" approach. *International Journal of Housing Policy, 11*(4), 337–355.

Stephens, M., & Norris, M. (2011). Introduction to special issue: Comparative housing research. *International Journal of Housing Policy, 11*(4), 333–336.

Stoker, G. & Mossberger, K. (1994). Urban regime theory in comparative perspective. *Environment and Planning C-Government and Policy, 12*(2), 195–212.

Valentine, G. (2015). Theorizing Multiculturalism and Diversity: The Implications of Intersectionality. In T. Matejskova & M. Antonsich (Eds.) *Governing through Diversity*. Berlin: Springer, pp. 145–160.

White, M. & Allmendinger, P. (2003). Land-use planning and the housing market: A comparative review of the UK and the USA. *Urban Studies, 40*(5–6), 953–972.

Whitehead, C., Chiu, R. L., Tsenkova, S., & Turner, B. (2009). *Land Use Regulation: Transferring Lessons From Developed Economies*. Berlin: Springer.

World Bank. (2015). *World Development Indicators*. Washington, DC: World Bank.

Worldometers. (2015). Worldometers—real time world statistics [website]. Retrieved from www.worldometers.info. Accessed on December 15, 2015.

2 Urban Planning, Politics, Land, and Housing Supply in Australia

Introduction

One of the most puzzling attributes of housing markets is the seemingly unpredictable relationship between demand—expressed through real estate prices—and supply responses expressed in the production of new homes. Australia, with one of the world's most expensive housing markets, is an interesting context in which to examine these dynamics. Despite abundant land and buoyant population growth, residential development faltered in the new millennium, raising widespread concerns about housing supply and affordability. By 2014, the national housing shortage was estimated to be around 284,000 dwellings, or 3 percent of Australia's housing stock (NHSC, 2014). This shortfall emerged not as a consequence of an absolute land shortage, or even economic downturn. Rather, it followed an unprecedented housing boom (1996–2004), during which time the national median house price doubled but rates of new house building barely changed (Figure 2.1).

In this context, there has been intense political debate over the causes of Australia's housing problems, the impacts of urban planning on land supply for housing development, and the accessibility of home ownership. These debates echo concerns about government intervention in land supply and housing development being played out in England and Hong Kong, as outlined in the chapters to follow, yet Australia's case is colored by a deep-seated ambivalence over the role of the state and the market in regulating private development and in delivering housing outcomes across the income spectrum. To understand how Australia's distinct system of urban planning has evolved and the implications for contemporary housing supply, this chapter draws on primary and secondary historical sources, more-recent urban policy and planning documents, legislation, media articles, and material produced by community and industry groups, as well as data on patterns of land and new housing supply. A key theme throughout the chapter is how underlying perspectives on the notions of home, private property, and the role of government vis-à-vis the market, are reflected in the narratives surrounding Australian housing and planning policy.

30 *Australia: Urban Planning and Housing*

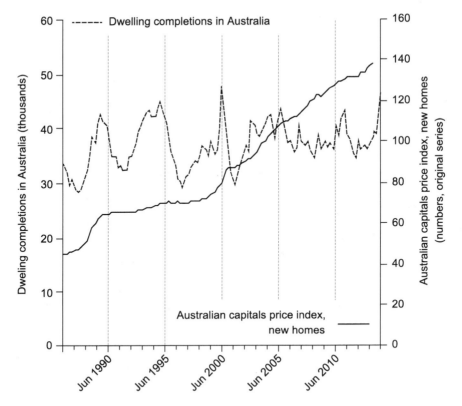

Figure 2.1 Dwelling Completions and House Prices, Australia, 1986–2014
Source: Australian Bureau of Statistics, 2015a; Australian Bureau of Statistics, 2015b

The chapter first sketches the evolution of urban settlement and planning trends and characteristics in Australia. Second, it outlines the contemporary scope of Australian urban planning, the various roles of the public and private sector in the mediation of property and development rights, key elements and players in the planning decision-making process, and the ways in which urban planning intervenes in processes of land supply, particularly land supply for housing. The final section of the chapter reflects on the implications of Australia's particular systems of planning and housing provision for addressing housing affordability problems in the new millennium.

Urban Planning and Housing Provision in Australia

From the early days of white settlement as a British penal colony in the late eighteenth and early nineteenth centuries, urban Australia was shaped by the housing aspirations of her new arrivals:

> The decision to seek a new life in Australia was often the last step in a journey that had already led the emigrant, by stages, from a village or provincial home to London, Liverpool or Glasgow. The homes these emigrants created in the new land were based on those essentially British ideals which the cities of the homeland had nurtured, but which they denied to the majority of their inhabitants
>
> (Davison, 2000, p. 7)

British laws and ideals were applied to the new settlement from the outset. The first governor of Sydney, Arthur Phillip, had bold visions for the city. Imagining a grander future beyond the British government's ideas for a lowly convict depot, Phillip introduced building and subdivision regulations to avoid the housing problems plaguing England under industrialization (Marsden, 2000). However, almost from the outset these plans were constrained by a shift to granting land in freehold title that tipped power toward the landholder. Subsequent governors "... did not care to hinder private builders nor to improve public building standards" (Marsden, 2000, p. 27).

Regulations that were established (for fire and sanitation) drew heavily on earlier British laws, often well out of date and barely adapted for local circumstances. Even these were generally ignored or resisted. Indeed, the early suburbanization of Australia's major cities was in part driven by an attempt to evade regulation:

> Australian colonists were motivated to escape regulation, to buy their own plot and to use it as they wished, building homes without restriction. One factor in the early suburbanisation of Australian cities was an expression of this desire to escape restrictions introduced by city councils, such as the *Melbourne Building Act*, passed in New South Wales (NSW) in 1849. Enforcement of the expensive specifications affected settlement because people who wished to use cheaper designs and materials were encouraged to move beyond central Melbourne, the area of jurisdiction and the city council's boundaries.
>
> (Marsden, 2000, p. 28)

For many emigrants—displaced from the overcrowded cities of England, Scotland, and Ireland—home ownership symbolized escape from "tyrannical landlords" (Davison, 2000, p. 19). A single-family home was important to most, although perspectives on private space varied, with English emigrants placing the highest value on the detached house and garden, and most likely to settle in the newly expanding suburbs. Thus, Australia's distinct urban housing typology reflected deep-seated notions about privacy and freedom:

> Freedom from the neighbours, freedom from the landlord, freedom from the boss: these, as much as the moral, sanitary, and social ideals for the

ideal English middle class, were the homeland dreams on which the Australian home were founded.

(Davison, 2000, p. 20)

Within the inner cities, overcrowding and disease soon became rampant, prompting a wave of public health regulations from the late 1870s, all of which also tended to promote outward urban settlement.

By the mid-nineteenth century, builders and building firms had become an important part of the housing market, with the consequence of speculative land subdivision and building becoming a major driver for state intervention. Tensions between speculative builders and state and municipal regulations emerged during housing booms of the 1870s–1880s and again in the early 1920s. By this time, the building industry had organized representation in the form of the Master Builders Association, which called attention to the constraining effects of Sydney's building regulations:

> Building, health and other regulations make it impossible to erect a home at a figure that had any possible relation to the average workers' income
> (Master Builders' Association, 1925, quoted in Marsden, 2000, p. 31)

Australia achieved formal independence from Britain in 1901 and established a three-tier federated system of commonwealth (national-level), state/territorial, and local government. From this time, governments intervened more strongly in the regulation of subdivision and in enforcing minimum building standards, predominantly set by state/territorial governments. However, for the most part, urban land was already in the private sector and held in freehold title. This meant that the private-sector landowners and developers drove much of the process of urbanization, aside from periods of specific government intervention in the post-war years and during the 1970s, discussed below. An exception was the foundation of the new capital city of Canberra, which was designed as the seat of federal government to exemplify modern planning and housing standards and to escape the problems associated with land speculation that had beset the colonial cities (Sandercock, 1975). Retaining control of land was thought central to this objective, so a system of ninety-nine-year leases was introduced and remains to this day.

Although town planning laws were introduced by the states from the late 1920s onward (predominantly empowering local government to control private land use), these laws mainly affected the design of new sub-urban housing areas, which resulted in a mandatory "bylaw" form of suburban sprawl across most of Australia:

> By insisting upon minimum block sizes and detached houses, they have enforced by law the Australian "suburban ideal."
> (Marsden, 2000, p. 39)

At the same time, there was a strong reluctance to interfere with the rights (and economic value) of property ownership, beyond modern planning powers such as land use zoning used in the "richer suburbs" to quarantine residential areas from industry and "unacceptable residential uses such as blocks of flats" (Marsden, 2000, p. 38). Thus, the early evolution of urban planning in Australia was shaped by a strong, culturally embedded resistance to regulation, combined with an equally strong belief in the significance of home ownership and private property rights.

Public Housing and Government Involvement in Land Supply

During the early twentieth century, the states experimented with social rental housing schemes, and undertook slum clearance initiatives during the 1920s and 1930s (Troy, 2009). However, by the early 1940s, national-level concern about a growing housing shortage led to the establishment in 1943 of a Commonwealth Housing Commission to examine future housing requirements. The scope of the Commission's agenda was broad, in keeping with its mission to ensure that all Australians were able to rent or purchase a home without being "exploited by excessive profit" (Troy, 2009, p. 10). The Commission made a number of recommendations for wider urban planning, including the nationalization of land (or development rights); and the introduction of betterment taxes to address speculation and secure broader public welfare benefits through the urban development process.

Although the majority of these recommendations were never implemented, one of the major outcomes was the enactment of the first Commonwealth State Housing Agreement (CSHA) in 1945. This agreement provided funding support to the states for public housing. In return, the states were obliged to introduce appropriate town planning laws, and establish State Housing Authorities to undertake public housing construction and administer assistance programs for home purchasers and renters. This first of eight CSHAs established the differing roles of the Commonwealth and state governments in relation to housing, and set the basis for a wide range of programs for public housing construction in the 1950s.

In the 1970s, state land development organizations (an initiative of the short lived Whitlam Labor government) played a significant role in moderating the market for greenfield land release on the edges of the major cities (Troy, 2012). However, by the new millennium, those states that had retained land development functions had reorganized around a corporatized model required to deliver significant commercial returns to government (McGuirk & Dowling, 2009).

Similarly, up until the late 1980s, the State Housing Authorities were major housing producers, although the operation of policies to support home ownership, including tenant "right to buy" schemes, meant that the stock was not necessarily retained in the sector. Thus, although around 12 percent of total housing output in the mid-1980s was funded under the CSHA, only around 6 percent of households resided in public housing. By this time there was a shift away from the broad commitment to social welfare through affordable housing provision and universal access to public housing, toward home ownership and a residualized social housing sector:

> The gradual transformations of the 1945 CSHA which shifted the focus over the subsequent eight Agreements from the provision of public housing through welfare housing to residual social housing not only recognised the primacy of owner occupation, they served also to create and entrench the problems of alienation and concentrations of social disadvantage the CHC had sought to change and to weaken urban planning in the states.
>
> (Troy, 2009, p. 22)

Although the original CSHA was framed around the close synergies between housing and urban planning, and the idea of a comprehensive national housing policy, this was never fully realized. Over time, responsibility for CSHA negotiation and administration became concentrated within social welfare portfolios at commonwealth levels, and the special purpose State Housing Authorities, which caused a narrowing of housing policy and a bifurcation between public- and private-sector provision. The urban planning policies and systems of the states and territories remained focused on responding to private-sector development proposals rather than the more proactive public planning undertaken during the brief period of the early 1970s.

Rise of Environmental Planning, Urban Containment, and the Infrastructure Backlog

By the end of the 1970s, the planning policy interests of the states had begun to shift toward environmental and heritage concerns. Greater provision was made for public participation during the plan-making and development assessment processes. The responsibility for policy direction remained with the states, who increasingly sought to influence the spatial evolution of major cities and towns through metropolitan-wide and regional-level strategic processes, with varying degrees of success. The states also retained executive power for land allocation (generally via legally enforceable land use zoning), although detailed spatial planning and density/design controls were the domain of local government. Depending on the political orientation and financial capacity of local governments, various approaches to local planning and development control thus emerged.

A fiscal crisis in the 1980s led to significant changes across the Australian public sector, many of which affected local government as the least powerful tier. Local governments were increasingly expected to undertake higher-level services with reduced access to central funding. Economic shifts—

particularly the decline of employment in manufacturing industries, and subsequently agriculture, had profound implications for the settlement structure of Australia. Until the 1970s, populations in inner city areas had been declining, with growth occurring primarily in the urban fringe and major regional towns (Gurran & Blakely, 2007).

This began to reverse in the 1980s, particularly in Sydney, where the "compact city" model (also called "urban consolidation") became an increasingly popular planning policy in the context of worsening traffic congestion (Searle, 2007; Freestone, 2010). Urban consolidation represented an opportunity to reduce expenditure on new infrastructure and unlock the value of former industrial sites, particularly those near the inner city. The policy was also thought an important tool for realigning the urban housing stock—predominantly detached, large homes—with the changing demographic profile of smaller, aging, households.

By the late 1990s, urban consolidation was the major paradigm for Australian metropolitan planning, implemented in states such as New South Wales (NSW) via state policies that could override local planning controls by directly rezoning land for higher-density housing development if local councils failed to prepare satisfactory schemes of their own (Gurran, 2008). The principles of urban consolidation underpinned the metropolitan plans for each of the Australian capital cities, although for residents of existing communities the prospect of higher density apartments surrounding established suburbs remained extremely contentious (Ruming et al., 2012). Developers and industry lobby groups too claimed that urban consolidation policies created a shortage of greenfield land for housing development, while restrictive local planning controls were preventing the construction of higher-density homes in established areas.

Housing Problems in the New Millennium

Despite such tensions, in world terms, Australia's housing system delivered enviable outcomes, particularly over the post-war period, with widespread home ownership and a flexible private rental sector offset by viable and modern public housing (Paris, 1993). This was achieved under a policy environment that, relative to other OECD countries, was "market-supportive" rather than "welfare state" in orientation. Key elements of this "market-supportive" system included generous taxation benefits supporting property ownership, central government funding of key urban infrastructure and facilities, and an emphasis on private-sector housing provision. High physical standards of Australian housing—much of which was produced in the post-war period—became institutionalized by a land development industry working in concert with volume "project" home builders. By the 1960s, the dominant form of new housing development occurred on land released in residential estates, served by basic roads, with provision made for public open space. Infrastructure funding arrangements differed across the states and territories, although modest developer contributions (or dedications of land) were progressively introduced from the 1970s onward. Carrying forward earlier practices, it was common for residential estates to be governed by private-developer covenants prescribing housing design, siting, building materials, and even landscaping requirements (Freestone, 2010). While local planning instruments governed land uses and housing density (including heights, building set-backs, and minimum lot sizes), these private developer covenants acted to propagate the distinctive brick-and-tile project home that has typified late-twentieth-century-Australian suburbia.

The benefits of the volume house building system in greenfield estates included economies of scale, competition between builders, and the relatively low overheads associated with detached single- or two-story dwellings. The building industry was able to operate with great flexibility, utilizing a subcontracting system that enabled many small firms to adjust to changing demand, year-round, under Australia's benevolent climate. Yet the system was not entirely market-driven (McGuirk & Dowling, 2009). As outlined in the previous section, government land developers ("land commissions"), a legacy of the short-lived Whitlam (Labor) government, played an important role in acquiring rural land and releasing it for residential development, as a means of moderating the market. The land commissions operated in all states except Queensland, although they were progressively corporatized from the late 1980s onward.

However, a number of structural changes were combining to disrupt Australia's housing system over this period, including labor-market adjustments (increased female participation but also in increasingly polarized labor-market opportunities), financial deregulation in the 1980s (resulting in more accessible mortgage finance), demographic changes (such as declining household sizes), and reduced funding for public housing construction. Nevertheless, with overall rates of home ownership remaining stable (at around 70 percent), the effects of these underlying structural changes (initially delaying home purchase among younger cohorts)—were masked (Yates, 2011a).

By the middle of the 1990s, this began to change. Financial deregulation in the late 1980s was followed by a period of falling interest rates, and wages growth, fueling demand for housing. Cash grants for first home buyers were introduced in 2000, initially to cushion the impacts of a new Goods and Services Tax (GST), and later used to stimulate demand for new housing following the GFC, exacerbating inflationary pressures (Yates, 2011b). Overall population in the major cities also ballooned, driven primarily by international migration, while the trend toward smaller households meant that household formation rates exceeded population growth. All these factors combined with ongoing support for home ownership in the form of highly advantageous taxation arrangements for housing investment. By the mid-1990s, house prices in the capital cities began to rise faster than incomes and continued to rise until mid-2004.

On the supply side, there were inherent constraints. In addition to the nation's concentrated urban settlement pattern, with economic activity and employment opportunities clustered in the major cities (Figure 2.2), Australians have an enduring preference for homes within established suburbs (Productivity Commission, 2004), limiting the extent to which new stock in greenfield locations could moderate price inflation. Indeed, over the period, the price differential between inner and peripheral urban areas intensified (Ellis, 2014). By around 2008, the estimated shortfall between new housing production and forecast requirements (projected household formation) had reached around 30,000 dwellings per year, and the shortage of affordable rental accommodation was estimated to be over half a million dwellings—or around 5 percent of the nation's entire housing stock (Australian Institute of Health and Welfare, 2013; NHSC, 2012).

By this point, Australia's housing system had undergone a structural transformation, with the median house price moving beyond the reach of moderate income earners for the first time since the post-war period (Yates, 2011). Rates of home ownership among younger cohorts dropped throughout

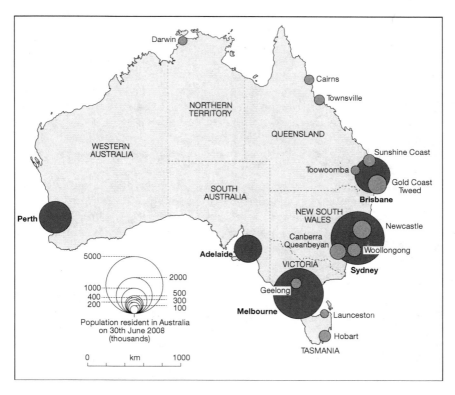

Figure 2.2 Australia's Urban Settlement Structure
Source: Adapted from Major Cities Unit (2010, p. 39)

the decade, and the proportion of households in owner-occupation slipped from its twenty-year rate of 70 percent to 68 percent in 2013. Although the majority of Australians in home ownership had enjoyed the increase in benefits associated with the growth in housing equity over this period, there was growing concern about accessibility for aspiring purchasers, as well as the labor market and wider effects stemming from affordability constraints.

Government Responses to the Housing Affordability Problem

At the national level, government responses to housing affordability problems have been muted. There has been a series of inquiries and special working groups, commencing with a Productivity Commission report on barriers to home ownership (2004), Parliamentary inquiries on housing affordability (Parliament of Australia, 2008; Parliament of Australia, 2015), and investigations of the performance of the land use planning system (Local Government and Planning Ministers' Council, 2011; Productivity Commission, 2011) and the need for reform (COAG Reform Council, 2012). In addition, between 2008 and 2013 a quasi-independent National Housing Supply Council advised on aspects of the land and housing supply pipeline and overall affordability trends (NHSC, 2014). The establishment of this body was no doubt influenced by the UK's National Planning and Housing Advice Unit, and there was much cross-fertilization of policy ideas and techniques at this time (Gurran et al., 2014). However, unlike its English counterpart, the Australian supply council rarely stepped beyond its mandate to monitor and advise on housing supply, implying that increased housing production would resolve affordability pressures affecting lower-income groups.

In the context of industry concern over sluggish rates of new housing production, and widespread criticism of planning systems and processes including via the range of policy processes outlined above, the states and territories have implemented rolling programs of regulatory reform since the new millennium. To some extent, these efforts have sought to enhance the implementation of the compact city agenda, by introducing new mechanisms and quasi-government authorities (including corporatized government land development agencies) to facilitate more coordinated and contained processes of land release, infrastructure funding, and provision. But there has also been a major focus on procedural reforms, designed to standardize local planning instruments, speed up decision making, and "fast-track" significant developments. These reforms have been enacted through various legislative changes that have typically reduced the scope for local discretionary decision making by elected representatives in favor of codified development entitlements, flexible approval paths, and "expert" panel determination (Ruming & Gurran, 2014).

However, specific initiatives to directly increase the supply of Australia's affordable housing have been limited (Gurran & Ruming, 2015). The states and territories have largely withdrawn from public or affordable housing development. As noted above, since the 1980s the trend has been toward a residualized public housing sector, with the primary focus being a form of housing assistance for low-income renters, provided as income support under a Commonwealth-funded rental subsidy. One consequence of this shift has been a marked withdrawal of government involvement in house building, falling from around 12 percent of output in the mid-1980s to around 2 percent in 2013, aside from a brief boost as economic stimulus in the context of the Global Financial Crisis. A tax incentive for affordable rental housing construction (the National Rental Affordability Scheme) operated from 2009 and supported around 35,000 dwellings but was dumped by the Liberal government soon after it came to power in 2013 (Groenhart & Gurran, 2015).

Although many other nations (including England and Hong Kong, as outlined in this book) have used the planning process to support affordable dwellings as an intrinsic component of overall housing development, Australia's state planning laws permit few such opportunities. Consequently, over the past three decades the nature of housing provision in Australia has shifted sharply from a system involving some public supply to one that is almost entirely dependent on the private sector (Figure 2.3). Thus, although output over time has remained relatively steady, the proportion of new housing development that is dedicated to be affordable to low and moderate income groups has declined markedly.

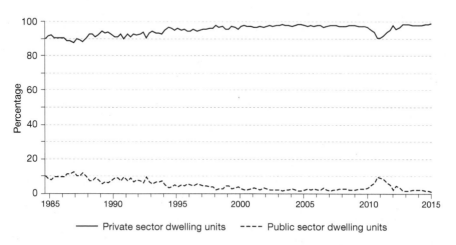

Figure 2.3 Composition of Dwelling Commencements by Sector, Australia, 1984–2015

Source: 8752.0 Building Activity, Australia, (Table 37. Number of Dwelling Unit Completions by Sector, Australia (Original Series))

In this context, the land use planning process has become even more significant in delimiting housing opportunities in Australian cities and regions. The following sections provide an overview of this process, including the different roles of the public and private sector, arrangements for infrastructure funding and provision, and opportunities to secure affordable housing for low and moderate income groups.

Scope of Urban Planning, and Roles of the Public and Private Sectors

As noted, responsibility for urban planning in Australia rests with the six states and the two self-governing territories. Neither land nor housing concerned the drafters of the Australian Constitution in 1900, so both portfolios became state powers by default. Table 2.1 summarizes the overarching legislation governing Australian land use planning across the states and territories.

The legislation establishes the scope of urban planning and the extent to which plans and decisions can consider social and public good outcomes beyond the physical dimensions of development. Under each system there are limited powers of compulsory acquisition to enable infrastructure or nature conservation (and all properties acquired are entitled to market compensation). Although betterment taxing (whereby the value created by a planning decision or public investment is taxed) is not formally practiced, each jurisdiction has varying arrangements for requiring developers to make contributions toward infrastructure and services. In the major development areas there is increasingly a trend to require contributions toward regional infrastructure (particularly for transport) as well.

As shown, the objectives of Australian planning laws emphasize physical and environmental aspects of the development process, and only the states of South Australia and NSW refer to affordable housing as falling within the remit of the planning system.

The Planning Process

Table 2.2 summarizes the key stages in Australia's land use planning process, from the allocation of land for particular uses through to the application for permission to develop, and appeal if the application is denied. Land allocation is the first stage in the planning process, beginning with the preparation of a comprehensive instrument to apply to an entire local government area (there are around five hundred local government entities in Australia). The usual standard involves twenty to twenty-five years' land supply for various residential and non-residential purposes, calculated with respect to projected population and household change (using state-supplied data), forecast employment trends, and an assessment of land capacity, often involving detailed environmental studies. This strategic planning stage may

Table 2.1 Legal Scope of Urban Land Use Planning Systems in Australia

State/territory	Legislation	Key objectives
ACT	Planning and Development Act 2007	"To provide a planning and land system that contributes to the orderly and sustainable development of the ACT ... consistent with the social, environmental and economic aspirations of the people of the ACT ... in accordance with sound financial principles" (s6)
NSW	Environmental Planning and Assessment Act 1979	"The proper management, development and conservation of natural and artificial resources [,] the promotion and coordination of the orderly and economic use and development of land [,] the provision and coordination of community services and facilities [,] ecologically sustainable development [,] the provision and maintenance of affordable housing [,] and the promotion of public participation" (s5).
NT	Planning Act 1999	"To plan for, and provide a framework of controls for, the orderly use and development of land", with subsidiary goals relating to the sustainable use and protection of the natural environment and resources; protection of amenity; and community consultation (s2A(2))
QLD	Sustainable Planning Act (SPA) 2009	"To seek to achieve ecological sustainability [by] ensuring the process is accountable, effective and efficient and delivers sustainable outcomes [,] managing the effects of development on the environment"; and coordinating and integrating planning at local, regional and state levels(s3). Further detail is provided under section 5, which states that decision-making processes should be "accountable, coordinated, effective and efficient," and "take account of short and long-term environmental effects of development at local, regional, State and wider levels"
SA	Development Act 1993	"To provide for proper, orderly and efficient planning and development [,] sustainable development and the protection of the environment [,] to encourage the management of the natural and constructed environment in an ecologically sustainable manner [,] to advance the social and economic interests and goals of the community [, to] provide for appropriate public participation in the planning process and the assessment of development proposals"; to provide for "cost

continued ...

Table 2.1 Continued

State/territory	Legislation	Key objectives
		effective" technical standards for buildings including the adoption of national standards, and increased housing choice and access to affordable housing (s3)
TAS	Land Use Planning and Approvals (LUPA) Act 1993	Objectives for the planning process include ensuring that "the effects on the environment are considered" in plan making and assessment, and providing for "consideration of social and economic effects when decisions are made" (Schedule One, Part Two)
VIC	Planning and Environment Act 1987	"The fair, orderly, economic and sustainable use, and development of land"; the "protection of natural and man-made resources and the maintenance of ecological processes and genetic diversity." Objectives for the "planning framework" include ensuring that "the effects on the environment are considered and provide for explicit consideration of social and economic effects when decisions are made about the use and development of land" and "the achievement of planning objectives through positive actions by responsible authorities and planning authorities"; and providing an "accessible process for just and timely review of decisions without unnecessary formality." (Extracts from s4)
WA	Planning and Development Act (PDA) 2005	The purposes of the Act include providing "for an efficient and effective land use planning system in the state"; and promoting "the sustainable use and development of land in the state" (s3)

Source: Adapted from Gurran, 2011, p. 141

involve negotiations with the private sector and will almost certainly involve some "sounding out" of potential landowners and developers to determine the likelihood of development opportunities being taken up. Developers may also request that their site be rezoned and, indeed, do so frequently in higher-value markets.

Once completed, the draft plan indicating proposed development patterns and change is publicly exhibited, and may be subject to adjustments before being legally made. Although the use of land use zones as a form of land categorization fell out of favor among some planning authorities around the turn of the millennium, there has been a trend back to formal zoning. Advocacy by bodies such as the influential "Development Assessment Forum" (a coalition of industry lobby groups, as well as state planning agencies and the Commonwealth) has influenced the increasing use of standardized zoning in Australian local plans since the early 2000s, as standardized development controls are seen to improve development certainty (Development Assessment Forum, 2012). However, local planners often fear this standardization as undermining place-based planning, and communities tend to experience codified entitlements as an erosion of certainty, since their capacity to influence decisions regarding the scale and appearance of specific development proposals is much reduced.

Thus, the designation of land use zones sends an important signal regarding potential development entitlement. However, in practice most forms of development (aside from straightforward uses such as simple dwellings) still require a process of merit assessment against zone objectives and development criteria. Even so, most applications (around 95 percent in NSW) are approved (Gurran & Phibbs, 2014), implying a very predictable system.

Planning approval confers time-limited development entitlement, subject to conditions. The entitlement is usually activated once the project commences (for instance, some services are installed in the case of a subdivision or demolition of a structure in the case of a redevelopment area). Of course, this is not necessarily the end of the process, as the developer ultimately retains the option to develop, even once approval is granted, and may indeed choose instead to sell the site, which is now more valuable with planning permission, or to hold until more favorable market conditions arise. Thus, during times of market downturn—or if a landholder prefers to hold out for maximum prices—significant sites can and do remain in suspension.

If permission to develop is refused, the developer can appeal to a special purpose court, even if the refusal is because the proposal is inconsistent with the prevailing planning rules. Third-party appeals by those not directly involved in the development (i.e. the landowner/developer and the consent authority) are strictly limited in most jurisdictions to matters of administrative process rather than the merits of a proposal (with the exception of the state of Victoria, where residents are able to appeal against certain types of development, including residential projects).

The provision of infrastructure depends on the location and type of development. Within existing areas, local authorities can recoup expenditure on infrastructure and community facilities through development contributions, which are payable by developers as a condition of planning approval. These are usually calculated via a formula designed to recognize the marginal impact of each new household or employee on the demand for existing infrastructure and services. A similar approach applies to new-release greenfield areas; however, the amount charged is usually higher because of the costs of supplying basic infrastructure and connecting to existing networks. Local government or the developer will roll out these services depending on the scale of the development and what is negotiated between both parties. Water, sewerage, and electricity services are, however, managed by corporatized suppliers who operate independently of the planning process, so their costings and scheduling decisions can represent a significant constraint to new development in greenfield locations and, to some extent, can constrain major development in existing locations where utility upgrades are required.

Decisions about rezoning, particularly from rural to urban land on the fringes, have important implications for the costs and efficiency of local and regional infrastructure programs, so sequential and contiguous development is preferred. However, across the various jurisdictions, arrangements now exist to enable developers to "accelerate" release of their own precinct, often by providing all of the major infrastructure up front and then recouping their own expenditure from subsequent developers and house builders. As discussed in the next chapter, such provisions can be problematic because they can result in piecemeal development that provides limited opportunities for the provision of wider regional retail, community, and transport facilities.

The entire process from the identification of land through to the installation of infrastructure and the construction of a dwelling typically takes around ten years (Productivity Commission, 2011). In part, this timeframe may reflect unique characteristics of Australia's contemporary land development and housing industry.

Land development is dominated by specialized land development firms who undertake site acquisition, rezoning where needed, and subdivision, often also installing basic facilities (roads, footpaths, playgrounds, etc.). There is a high concentration of large firms within Australia's land development industry, with more than 70 percent of plots in Sydney being developed by one of ten major developers (NHSC, 2011), making the industry a powerful market and political force. New dwellings are typically delivered through an individual contract between households and builders, with very little speculative building activity. Australia's building firms therefore have relatively low overheads, and are able to sub-contract specialized tasks and maintain a small workforce, often involving casual laborers. This process is changing somewhat with the increasing provision of medium-density housing (now around 35 percent of all dwelling production), but remains the norm. Furthermore, finance requirements demand that around 70 percent of the development is contracted as "presales" before medium- and high-density development can proceed.

Overall, the separation between land developers and builders means that landowners have economic incentives to sell land or development sites at optimum market value. Unlike builders who depend on ongoing volume for profit, land developers make profit by purchasing when the market is low (and waiting until it picks up) or by identifying discount sites and then increasing value by securing a change in planning rules—either a rezoning or change of development controls—to allow a higher value use. While this model—whereby land remains dormant until individual households contract a builder—prevents the surplus of speculative homes seen in some markets,

Table 2.2 Key Stages in the Land Use Planning Process, Australia

Stage	Public sector	Private sector	Development entitlement?
Land allocation for particular uses; establishment of density/design criteria or standards	Demographic/environmental study (often regional scale) Preparation of draft plan to reclassify ("rezone") the land—could be initiated by local government, state government, or special quasi-government development corporation Land uses will be subject to design criteria or standards associated with particular development type and/or locations Exhibition for public comment Adjustment if required (and re-exhibition) Approval—by state/territorial government, or delegate	May request that land be "rezoned" (land owned or subject to "option" to purchase)—known as a "spot rezoning" Sometimes application for particular development submitted at the same time as rezoning request	Implied entitlement to carry out land uses permitted in zone, but most categories of development still require discretionary assessment against development standards
Development application (including subdivision of land)	Received by local/territorial government authority, or if more significant or controversial development,	Initiates development application. Prepares supporting studies etc. as required	Time limited development entitlement granted, with conditions

continued ....

Table 2.2 Continued

Stage	Public sector	Private sector	Development entitlement?
	will be referred to a panel or to state government		
	Public exhibition, submissions considered (more significant developments)		
	Referral to other agencies (more significant applications)		
	Assessment by local or state government		
Appeal	Different arrangements for review of decisions within local government and by special purpose appeals tribunals/courts	May appeal decision to approve/refuse, conditions of consent, or delayed decision through specialist courts.	May be granted on appeal
	Very limited third-party appeal rights (most jurisdictions)	No appeal for rezoning applications, aside from administrative review	
Arrangements for infrastructure provision	Local infrastructure funded through contributions by developers and through local taxes, arrangements differ by state/territory	Responsible for infrastructure contribution or provision as per condition of planning approval	Contingent on payment or provision of infrastructure mandated in plan
	Regional/state/national infrastructure funded by state/commonwealth (states now seeking development contributions for regional items)		

it can also contribute to the fragmented patterns of housing development that prevail in Australia's outer metropolitan regions. Of course the near total dependence on the private sector to finance and deliver new homes in Australia also means that there are very few levers available for government to directly generate increased housing production.

The description provided above underscores the important role played by private developers, compared with other players, in Australia's contemporary urban land and housing development process. Recalling the discussion on planning systems in Chapter 1, Table 2.3 summarizes these roles as "proactive" versus "reactive" stances at each stage in the process.

As shown, private developers are generally far more proactive in the planning process than the public sector or the community. Consequently, property owners and other local residents are therefore also forced into a reactive stance as developer-initiated rezonings or projects are proposed. In some cases, quasi-government development organizations operate in relation to sites regarded significant for their strategic location or due to their potential contributions to housing growth, particularly when public land is involved. Over the past decade there has been a resurgent interest in the potential role of government land organizations, although the scale of their activities remains modest (van den Nouwelant et al., 2014). In 2009/10, government land organizations delivered fewer than 2,000 dwellings or lots in all jurisdictions, aside from the Australian Capital Territory (ACT), where the government land development authority governs land supply through the leasehold system (Productivity Commission, 2011). The major role of these government land organizations has been in catalyzing major development and renewal areas.

Planning for Affordable Housing

Within the heavily reactive planning system described above, there are very limited legal mechanisms to secure affordable housing outcomes for lower-income groups. Indeed, there has been much government ambivalence and industry hostility toward enabling local authorities to require affordable housing inclusion as part of new development, with some notable exceptions (Gurran et al., 2008).

In the states of NSW and South Australia, planning legislation was amended (in the years 2000 and 2005), to enable the planning system to address affordable housing through requirements that certain developments contribute to the supply of affordable homes. Affordable housing is usually measured in Australia by reference to income criteria (up to 120 percent of median household income) and housing costs (up to 30 percent of gross income), but eligibility for specific forms of subsidized affordable housing differs according to program. In NSW, modest inclusionary zoning schemes have generated a cash contribution toward local housing projects within selected, high-value inner-city locations, but the state has never extended

Table 2.3 The Role of Different Actors in the Urban Land and Housing Development Process, Australia

Stage/role	State government	Local government	Developer	Property owners/local residents
Zoning of new land for development	*Proactive* Oversight and final approval, sets policy direction (criteria for site selection), takes direct responsibility for special sites	*Reactive* Usually applies state policy criteria to local context, proposes sites, and manages study and draft plan application process	*Proactive/reactive* Often lobbies/applies directly for particular sites, also involved in public consultation processes. Lobbying techniques include political donations, agreements for extra infrastructure provision, meetings with planning authorities, written submissions. Some developers will react by acquiring land once zoning complete	*Reactive* Will be formally consulted through zoning process. Techniques of opposition include written submissions and direct protest
Rezoning of land for different land use ("spot rezoning")	*Reactive* Usually oversight and final approval	*Reactive* Will assess application for spot rezoning	*Proactive* Applies and lobbies for rezoning	*Reactive* Responds to proposed rezoning via written submission/protest at council meeting, direct protest

Development/application for permission to develop	*Reactive* If major proposal, state will be the approval authority. Very little public development	*Reactive* Usually the approval authority	*Proactive* Makes the application, then, if approved, decides if and when to sell, develop, or hold. Able to appeal decision if not favorable	*Reactive* Responds to proposal via written submission/protest at council meeting, direct protest. Rarely has right of appeal
Infrastructure provision, including transport and community facilities	*(Moderately) proactive* Supplies major roads, schools, hospitals, recreational areas, etc. Sometimes intervenes to activate development through infrastructure spending. Increasingly imposes own charges for regional infrastructure. Some jurisdictions allow developers to "leapfrog" existing urban areas if they provide their own services	*Reactive* Infrastructure provision occurs along with development, funding contributions sought from developers according to different formulae. Local taxes also used to fund infrastructure provision and augmentation	*Moderately proactive* Drives infrastructure supply through development process, though actual provision may be by local authority or by developer	*Reactive* Generally not involved in infrastructure decisions but funds provision through property taxes, including new requirements

the approach more widely because of industry opposition. In 2009, the *NSW State Environmental Planning Policy: Affordable Rental Housing* sought to incentivize affordable rental housing in existing residential areas, but was subsequently severely curtailed in the face of local resident opposition (Davison et al., 2012; Ruming, 2014).

In South Australia, the approach involves incorporating an affordable housing requirement when land is rezoned to enable housing, or up-zoned to enable increased housing density. The requirement is that 15 percent of the development includes homes affordable to low- or moderate-income groups, for rent or purchase, with the developer able to recoup the costs of this provision through sale to eligible householders or to an affordable housing provider. This approach has yielded over 4,000 dwellings since its introduction in 2005/06 (Austin et al., 2014). However, the lack of capital funding for affordable housing construction means that the model is largely limited to the sale of homes to those on lower and moderate incomes.

In the state of Western Australia, the government has introduced affordable housing targets in new development areas, but these are typically where the government has contributed land or other capital. In the Australian Capital Territory, the leasehold system of land (whereby the government maintains land title but grants ninety-nine-year leases to occupants) has supported more ambitious targets of 15–20 percent affordable housing on new and in urban infill contexts. Design solutions (implemented by adjustments to planning controls) have driven cost savings (smaller allotments overall in developments). These have been applied to homes available for purchase by eligible households on home-purchase, equity-share (with the government retaining a proportion of the equity), or land-rent bases (where the household purchases the dwelling but rents the land) (ACT Planning and Land Authority, 2010).

However, a major weakness of these planning-based mechanisms for affordable housing is that, in the absence of a significant capital funding stream for social provision, the development of Australia's affordable housing supply largely depends on private-sector activity. In turn, this depends on the market. At the same time, the imposition of planning requirements for affordable housing inclusion has been seen to add to the regulatory burden facing private-sector developers, and thus counterproductive to the overarching objective of promoting new housing supply as a means of moderating prices across the market.

The Political Arguments about Planning, Housing, and Land Supply

In the context of Australia's rising property prices and falling rates of home ownership, the major policy question was why the market did not adequately respond to the ongoing demand for homes. In the context of a sustained housing boom from the mid-1990s, this question became intensely political. At the commonwealth level it was argued that fundamental constraints within state and local land use planning systems was preventing an adequate supply response. This position was exemplified by former Prime Minister John Howard, as articulated in a televised interview with the Australian Broadcasting Commission (ABC). Brushing aside the proposition that historically low interest rates might explain house price inflation, John Howard blamed "State and Territory governments for pushing up the price of new houses, by choking off supply" (Greg Jennett, 2006, transcribed in Lateline, 2006):

> The fundamental cause of the high cost of the first home is the cost of land, and until State governments understand and accept that and they stop bowing to green pressure and they release more land, and this applies particularly in Sydney, we're going to have a problem.
> (Lateline 2006)

Howard's own political views on land supply enabled his government to claim credit for the wealth effects of house price growth that benefited the majority of the home-owning electorate, while berating the state and local governments for containing land supply. Many of these underlying ideas about the impacts of planning on the housing market were in global circulation at the time, promulgated by international property consultant firm Demographia (Phibbs & Gurran, 2008; Gurran & Phibbs, 2015). Similar ideas have also been embraced in New Zealand, where there was a strong political backlash against urban containment and growth management (Murphy, 2014).

Ideological think tanks, such as Australia's Institute for Public Affairs, ran a dedicated campaign to highlight the purported impacts of planning on the "Great Australian Dream" of home ownership (Moran, 2006). Works such as this were intended to demonize government intervention through planning as an instrument for alienating private property rights and denying younger generations the choice to purchase a home where they choose:

> Two vital tenets of modern economies involve first, the respect for individual property rights, and second, that governments should not restrict people's choices. . . . Yet contemporary urban planning is very much about both restricting choice and socialising individual property rights. These come about, most obviously, by rationing access to land. Planning systems are in place across all major Australian urban areas. Invariably, they reduce the quantity of land that is available for conversion into housing. Australia's ration-induced high prices for new developments on the periphery lift prices throughout the city. The way forward involves ensuring far greater rights for landowners to use their property in ways they prefer it to be used.
> (Moran, 2006, pp. 4–5)

While clearly based on ideological rationality rather than empirical evidence, such statements were enormously influential.

Nevertheless, both the former National Housing Supply Council and the Productivity Commission attempted to identify empirical data to determine whether Australia's supply of serviceable land for housing development was adequate in the short and long term. Despite difficulties in obtaining comparable statistics from the state planning agencies, the available evidence (primarily plateauing land values) suggested that adequate reserves of serviced land existed in all jurisdictions (Productivity Commission, 2011).

Similarly, the National Housing Supply Council found that existing reserves of broad hectare (greenfield land) across the eight Australian capital cities were sufficient for more than a decade's total supply of dwellings (1,794,000), and, combined with redevelopment areas, amounted to at least fifteen years' supply of sites (from 2008), even allowing for considerable excess capacity (NHSC, 2009).

Thus, sluggish rates of new housing production did not seem to reflect insufficient land for development, despite strident lobbying to the contrary by the industry itself (Property Council of Australia, 2007). The more likely problem was that new house building had stalled *because of* affordability pressures. Under Australia's market-driven housing system, when house prices stagnate so too does new housing development, highlighting the dilemma faced by state governments dependent on the private sector to deliver housing supply. While there has been much policy emphasis on the need for rapid rezoning of land to enable housing development, often driven by the industry itself, rezoning does not mean that the sites will be developed in the short or even medium term. Many firms will prefer to release sites gradually, attracting a premium, or to wait until the market lifts, both options that are easily available to both larger developers with significant resources and to smaller landholders who have alternative uses for their land, such as market gardening (prevalent around the major cities).

At the same time, there has been growing disquiet over the demand-side effects of Australia's financial and taxation settings, which favor home ownership and property investment through generous grants, incentives, and concessions (Yates, 2010; Wood et al., 2012). Housing in central city areas appeared increasingly attractive (as the costs of commuting to work from far-flung car-based suburbs mounted) (Dodson & Sipe, 2008). Thus, the government's fiscal policy settings, which supported property investment, served to boost demand for housing overall without necessarily stimulating new supply. With investors seeking to maximize capital gains, they often favored existing dwellings in established blue-chip suburbs. Consequently, real estate values rose, increasing the wealth of existing property owners, who were able to draw on this equity to fund further real estate investment, exacerbating the barriers faced by aspiring home owners trying to raise a deposit. One consequence has been a growing disparity between the wealth of home owners and renters, raising the prospect of new intergenerational disadvantage based on housing tenure.

Overwhelmingly, by the end of the decade 2003–2013, the political consensus appeared to be clear: urban consolidation policies had combined with inefficient local planning processes and hefty infrastructure charges to reduce housing output, exacerbating affordability pressures. Such was the conclusion of the specially convened Housing Supply and Affordability Reform working party:

> The Working Party examined the cost that developers and builders face through seeking development approval for new land and dwellings. This includes direct costs such as local councils' assessment fees as well as the in-house and consultancy costs they incur in seeking land rezoning and development approval. Many of these costs that developers and builders incur typically lower the overall supply and delivery of housing to the market, thereby reducing housing affordability.
> (COAG Reform Council, 2012, p. 2)

However, by 2014 the conditions for housing development in Australia had undergone a sharp shift. A sudden drop-off in the mining sector meant that Australia's housing market was seen as an important mechanism to stabilize the national economy. With the Reserve Bank lowering interest rates to bolster investment and consumer confidence, house prices began to rise, particularly in the capital cities (aside from Perth, where the long resources boom was coming to an end). Along with rising prices, dwelling commencements also rose. The cycle of public discourse and property politics thus continued, with a new (conservative) Prime Minister in 2014 accusing the federal opposition of trying to bring down house prices (via its efforts to promote dialogue on tax reform), while then-Treasurer Joe Hockey infamously advised aspiring home owners to seek a well-paying job if they wanted to enter the housing market. Subsequent Commonwealth government pronouncements again centered on the need for state and local planning reform to boost housing production. For their part, the states—and in particular the state of NSW—were themselves seeking to address affordability concerns through increased new housing production, as discussed further in the next chapter.

Conclusions: Implications for Addressing Housing Affordability in the New Millennium

To what extent does Australia's particular approach to strategic planning, land supply, and housing provision influence patterns of housing development and affordability? As outlined, for Australia's white settlers in the first century of colonization, achieving home ownership—freedom from landlords, and economic independence—symbolized a dream that could not be realized in Great Britain or Ireland. The form of housing settlement that evolved first moved outward from the cities in defiance of regulation, and, later, as a consequence of suburban bylaws that delivered quintessential

Australian neighborhoods defined by detached houses on their own lots. The cultural meaning of this housing typology remains highly significant to some sectors of the community, with vocal resident groups mobilizing a very powerful rhetoric against planning policies to increase housing density within existing neighborhoods.

The provision of land and housing was, and remains, driven by private developers, with only a very small social and not-for-profit sector. Thus, the capacity for state and local governments to intervene proactively to secure public benefits from the planning process, such as affordable housing, has remained limited. The use of planning for delivering affordable housing is opposed both by residents who resist change in their neighborhoods and by the development sector, which perceives inclusionary housing models as a form of increased regulatory intervention, with direct cost implications and potential effects on the value of their property.

Political emphasis has focused on perceived new constraints to the market—such as the rise of environmental concerns in urban planning policy and implied effects on land supply—but these impacts do not seem supported by the available evidence. By contrast, far less attention has been placed on the more obvious cause of stagnant housing supply, including reduced capital for social housing provision and affordability constraints, which lock aspiring first home buyers out of the market. This implies that the role of planning in constraining the market and therefore reducing housing supply and affordability is likely overstated, influenced by internationally circulating policy ideas and local politics in favor of blame-shifting and the status quo. However, given the limited government funding for social housing provision and the increasing needs of low- and moderate-income groups, the question remains as to whether planning reform should enable more direct and systematic affordable housing inclusion in new development, or more direct intervention in the land development process.

Overall, Australia's new-millennium housing problem—concern about rates of housing production despite a long boom and relatively loose planning regimes—provide an interesting counterpoint for nations keen to liberalize their own planning systems in a bid to lift housing output. It also highlights the many layers of sociopolitical meaning imbued within notions of home and property, and the ways in which these notions may come to bind the policy imagination to fairer forms of government intervention in land and housing provision.

References

ACT Planning and Land Authority. (2010). *Australian Capital Territory Dual Planning Fact Sheet*. Canberra: ACT Government.

Austin, P., Gurran, N., & Whitehead, C. E. (2014). Planning and affordable housing in Australia, New Zealand and England: Common culture; different mechanisms. *Journal of Housing and the Built Environment, 29*(3), 455–472.

Australian Bureau of Statistics. (2015a). *6416.0 Residential Property Price Indexes: Eight Capital Cities, March 2015*. Canberra: ABS.
Australian Bureau of Statistics. (2015b). *8731.0 Building Approvals, Australia (March 2015)*. Canberra: ABS.
Australian Institute of Health and Welfare. (2013). *Housing Assistance in Australia*. Canberra: Australian Institute of Health and Welfare.
COAG Reform Council. (2012). *Housing Supply and Affordability Reform*. Canberra: COAG Housing Supply and Affordability Reform Working Party.
Davison, G. (2000). Colonial Origins of the Australian home. In P. Troy (Ed.), *A History of European Housing in Australia*. Cambridge: Cambridge University Press, pp. 6–25.
Davison, G., Gurran, N., Pinnager, S., & Randolph, B. (2012). *Affordable Housing, Urban Renewal and Planning: Emerging practice in New South Wales, South Australia and Queensland*. Melbourne: AHURI.
Development Assessment Forum. (2012). *Meeting Communiqué—26 June 2012*. Canberra: Development Assessment Forum.
Dodson, J. & Sipe, N. (2008). Shocking the suburbs: Urban location, homeownership and oil vulnerability in the Australian city. *Housing Studies*, 23(3), 377–401.
Ellis, L. (2014). *Space and Stability: Some Reflections on the Housing–Finance System, Address to the CITI Residential Housing Conference, Sydney*. Sydney: Reserve Bank of Australia.
Freestone, R. (2010). *Urban Nation: Australia's Planning Heritage*. Canberra: Csiro Publishing.
Groenhart, L. & Gurran, N. (2015). Markets, Rights and Power in Australian Social Policy. In G. Meagher & S. Goodwin (Eds.), *Markets, Rights and Power in Australian Social Policy*. Sydney: Sydney University Press, pp. 231–256.
Gurran, N. (2008). Affordable housing: A dilemma for metropolitan planning? *Urban Policy and Research*, 26(1), 101–110.
Gurran, N. (2011). *Australian Urban Land Use Planning: Principles, Systems and Practice*. Sydney: Sydney University Press.
Gurran, N., Austin, P., & Whitehead, C. (2014). That sounds familiar! A decade of planning reform in Australia, England and New Zealand. *Australian Planner*, 51(2), 186–198.
Gurran, N. & Blakely, E. (2007). Suffer a sea change?: Contrasting perspectives towards urban policy and migration in coastal Australia. *Australian Geographer*, 38(1), 113–131.
Gurran, N., Milligan, V., Baker, D., Bugg, L. B., & Christensen, S. (2008). New Directions in Planning for Affordable Housing: Australian and International Evidence and Implications. *AHURI Final Report Series*. Melbourne: AHURI.
Gurran, N. & Phibbs, P. (2014). Evidence-free zone? Examining claims about planning performance and reform in New South Wales. *Australian Planner*, 51(3), 232–242.
Gurran, N. & Phibbs, P. (2015). Are governments really interested in fixing the housing problem? Policy capture and busy work in Australia. *Housing Studies*, 30(5), 711–729.
Gurran, N. & Ruming, K. (2015). Less planning, more development? Housing and urban reform discourses in Australia. *Journal of Economic Policy Reform*, 1–19.
Lateline. (2006). *Howard Blames Land Shortage for Home Buyer Problems. ABC Lateline, 21/8/2006*. Sydney: ABC.

Local Government and Planning Ministers' Council. (2011). *First National Report on Development Assessment Performance 2008/09*. Adelaide: COAG Business Regulation and Competition Working Group.

McGuirk, P. & Dowling, R. (2009). Neoliberal privatisation? Remapping the public and the private in Sydney's masterplanned residential estates. *Political Geography*, 28(3), 174–185.

Major Cities Unit. (2010). *State of Australian Cities 2010*. Canberra: Major Cities Unit, Infrastructure Australia.

Marsden, S. (2000). The Introduction of Order. In P. Troy (Ed.), *A History of European Housing in Australia*. Cambridge: Cambridge University Press, pp. 26–41.

Moran, A. J. (2006). *The Tragedy of Planning: Losing the Great Australian Dream*. Melbourne: Institute of Public Affairs.

Murphy, L. (2014). "Houston, we've got a problem": The political construction of a housing affordability metric in New Zealand. *Housing Studies*, 29(7), 893–909.

NHSC [National Housing Supply Council]. (2009). *State of Supply Report 2008*. Canberra: Australian Government.

NHSC. (2011). *National Housing Supply Council State of Supply Report 2011*. Canberra: Australian Government.

NHSC. (2012). *Housing Supply and Affordability—Key Indicators 2012*. Canberra: National Housing Supply Council, Commonwealth of Australia.

NHSC. (2014). *2013 State of Housing Supply Report; Changes in the Way We Live*. Canberra: Treasury.

Paris, C. (1993). *Housing Australia*. South Melbourne: Macmillan Education.

Parliament of Australia. (2008). *A Good House is Hard to Find: Housing Affordability in Australia*. Canberra: Commonwealth of Australia.

Parliament of Australia. (2015). *Out of Reach? The Australian Housing Affordability Challenge, Senate Economics References Committee Inquiry Report*. Canberra: Parliament of Australia.

Phibbs, P. & Gurran, N. (2008). *Demographia Housing Affordability Surveys: An Assessment of the Methodology*, Sydney: Shelter NSW.

Productivity Commission. (2004). *First Home Ownership, Report No. 28*. Melbourne: Productivity Commission.

Productivity Commission. (2011). *Performance Benchmarking of Australian Business Regulation: Planning, Zoning and Development Assessments; Productivity Commission Draft Research Report*. Canberra: Australian Government.

Property Council of Australia. (2007). *Australia's land supply crisis; supply demand imbalance and its impact on declining housing affordability*. Sydney: Residential Development Council, Property Council of Australia.

Ruming, K. (2014). "It wasn't about public housing, it was about the way it was done": Challenging planning not people in resisting the Nation Building Economic Stimulus Plan, Australia. *Journal of Housing and the Built Environment*, 29(1), 39–60.

Ruming, K., & Gurran, N. (2014). Australian planning system reform. *Australian Planner*, 51(2), 102–107.

Ruming, K. Houston, D., & Amati, M. (2012). Multiple suburban publics: Rethinking community opposition to consolidation in Sydney. *Geographical Research*, 50(4), 421–435.

Sandercock, L. (1975). *Property, Politics, and Urban Planning: A History of Australian City Planning, 1890–1990*. Victoria: Melbourne University Press.

Searle, G. (2007). *Sydney's Urban Consolidation Experience: Power, Politics and Community, Research paper 12*. Brisbane: Urban Research Program, Griffith University.

Troy, P. (2009). The Commonwealth and National Housing Policy. *Paper presented at State of Australian Cities Conference*, 2009, Adelaide.

Troy, P. (2012). *Accommodating Australians; Commonwealth Government Involvement in Housing*. Sydney: The Federation Press.

van den Nouwelant, R., Davison, G., Gurran, N., Pinnegar, S., & Randolph, B. (2014). Delivering affordable housing through the planning system in urban renewal contexts: converging government roles in Queensland, South Australia and New South Wales. *Australian Planner*, 52(2), 77–89.

Wood, G., Ong, R., Cigdem, M., & Taylor, E. (2012). *The spatial and distributional impacts of the Henry Review recommendations on stamp duty and land tax*. Melbourne: Australian Housing and Urban Research Institute.

Wood, G., Ong, R., & Winter, I. (2011). Stamp duties, land tax and housing affordability: The case for reform. *Paper presented at conference on Australia's Future Tax System: A Post-Henry Review*, Sydney.

Yates, J. (2011a). *Housing in Australia in the 2000s: On the Agenda Too Late?* Sydney: Reserve Bank of Australia.

Yates, J. (2011b). Housing and tax: the triumph of politics over economics. *Presented at conference on Australia's Future Tax System: A Post-Henry Review*, Sydney.

3 Planning and Property Politics in Sydney's Urban Renewal and Growth Centres

Introduction

This chapter carries forward the national analysis of Australia's housing system and the politics surrounding planning and the housing market into key case studies of the development process. It focuses on Australia's largest city—Sydney—in the most populous state of New South Wales (NSW). In many ways, Sydney has been the epicenter of Australia's new-millennium housing affordability pressures and urban policy debates. The two case study sites—Green Square in Sydney's inner east and Rouse Hill in the outer northwest—epitomize attempts to improve housing supply and affordability through planned residential development catalyzed by new town centers. Both areas also exemplify the contradictions in Australia's housing and planning policy frameworks and delivery mechanisms, which rely heavily on the machinery of government in the guise of special purpose development corporations and legislation while emphasizing market-driven outcomes.

The formal elements of Australian planning as introduced in the previous chapter—land use zoning and development control processes—are also examined in practice through the discussion overall and the cases in Sydney in particular. Although Australia's federal system of government implies some operational differences in planning law and processes at state and local levels, the two Sydney cases highlight a number of common features of Australia's contemporary housing system and the interactions between politics, planning, and the housing market. These include: 1) the attempt to foster a new form of suburban housing development characterized by denser, more diverse dwelling styles around transport and centralized service centers; 2) new roles for government and the private sector in supplying and developing residential land; 3) shifting approaches to infrastructure funding and provision; and 4) ongoing contests over urban regulation in the context of deepening national affordability problems and a political climate of neoliberal reform.

The chapter begins by recapping Australia's policy shift in planning for residential development from detached homes in outer suburbia to a new emphasis on compact cities or urban "consolidation" within existing inner and middle ring areas. This shift—perhaps more rhetorical than real—coincided with the contraction of funding for social housing provision (which fell from around 15 percent in the early 1980s to between 1 and 2 percent by the turn of the new millennium), as well as a number of intense demand-side pressures on the housing market. Over the period, a change in approaches to planning and delivering new homes also emerged, with increasing emphasis on "master-planned" residential estates, initially in outer suburban locations and subsequently characterizing inner renewal contexts as well. The chapter then examines particular policy trajectories, development patterns, and outcomes in the Greater Sydney area. In doing so, it focuses on the NSW government's attempts to deliver new housing supply through "Growth Centres" in greenfield contexts and urban renewal areas in the inner city, using two landmark cases—"Rouse Hill" in Sydney's outer northwest and "Victoria Park/Green Square" in Sydney's inner east—for particular analysis. The concluding section of the chapter challenges the prevalent view of the role of planning in Australia's housing market. Rather than constraining the market and restricting supply, the story is rather of a system in thrall to market forces, with few provisions for sharing the benefits arising from public planning and infrastructure investment processes, and a growing socio-spatial sorting by housing wealth.

Australia's Changing Housing System, and the Role of Planning

The historical evolution of Australian settlement, as sketched in the previous chapter, reflects the dynamic interactions between speculative land developers, state infrastructure providers, and the content and stringency of urban regulation. Australia's early colonists arrived with a deep-seated aspiration for home ownership on the one hand and emancipation from landlords and wider authority on the other. This played into the distinct housing typology of detached cottages on their own plots of land that rapidly emerged following the introduction of rail in the mid-nineteenth century (Freeland, 1972). The close relationships between state and, subsequently, local politicians and land speculators influenced decisions around the siting of transport and other key urban infrastructure in the major capital cities. Over the past century the close circles of influence between land developers and state and local politicians have remained a recurring theme in explaining particular planning decisions that seem contrary to wider strategic objectives (Sandercock, 1975; Gleeson & Low, 2000a).

Nevertheless, and despite underlying tensions, Australia's housing system appeared highly successful in delivering a plentiful supply of high quality—and largely affordable—homes for a broad sector of the population until the latter years of the twentieth century, when house price inflation began to outstrip wages (Yates, 2011). The policy notion of "urban consolidation"

—reducing outward suburban expansion on "greenfield" estates by redeveloping underutilized sites and encouraging more intense housing in existing and planned release areas—also took hold in Australian metropolitan planning in the early 1990s, although in Sydney there were earlier attempts to arrest sprawl even in the 1960s (Searle, 2007). As noted in the previous chapter, the results of urban consolidation policies have been mixed. Despite a powerful policy rhetoric of urban consolidation and housing diversity, most Australian households still live in detached dwelling houses, and in Sydney the proportion remains at about 50 percent, while around 30 percent of new housing development continues in greenfield locations on the urban fringe. Nevertheless, industry lobby groups and developers have argued since the early 1990s that consolidation policies have led to land supply shortages and that new infrastructure charging regimes have pushed up development costs (Ruming et al., 2012; Troy, 2012) while residents of existing suburbs have mounted effective campaigns against higher-density housing. Overall, state governments have struggled to foster levels of higher-density development of a quality and scale sufficient to disrupt the prevailing pattern of housing provision, or to secure wider community acceptance of new housing forms.

However, significant renewal efforts led by government development agencies in each of the major state capital cities have been under way since the mid-1990s, while in outer release areas developers and government planners alike have attempted to "master-plan" new communities. Integral to these strategies have been the concepts of more sequential and planned programs of new land release (offset by the aforementioned emphasis on housing development sites within the existing urban area), as well as infrastructure funding arrangements that encourage a more efficient urban footprint. Much like the renewal efforts in inner city areas, state governments have experimented with new approaches to these outer "growth" areas, with corporatized state land developers playing a leading role, often overseen by special purpose development authorities established to coordinate the overall process.

Yet these efforts have not been sufficient to overcome the effects of an increasing centralization of urban opportunities, with jobs increasingly concentrated in central city areas (Major Cities Unit, 2010). With the renewal of inner city areas advantaged by strong public transport infrastructure, the price gradient between inner and outer metropolitan areas has steepened. In Sydney, transport funding decisions have tended to favor upgrades to the road system, and the majority of middle and outer ring suburbs are dependent on the private motor car. At the same time, the decline in manufacturing industries over the past few decades has meant fewer employment opportunities in outer suburban areas. While major infrastructure and facilities—hospitals, schools, police services, regional roads, and public transport—are provided by the NSW state government, funding allocation and decisions about the location and timing of provision are typically outside the remit of the land use planning process. Similarly, water and electricity services are also managed by quasi-independent organizations that are not beholden to the state planning authority. Local governments provide local roads, parks, and community facilities, and are able to levy development contributions to offset these costs. However, funding cuts since the 1980s have made local councils increasingly dependent on such charges, while the state has sought to extract special developer contributions toward regional infrastructure items (Gurran et al., 2009). Thus the direct costs of land and housing development have increased considerably in Sydney over the past two decades, as they have in other state capital cities (Productivity Commission, 2011).

Finally, as discussed in the previous chapter, Australian urban planning has been subject to ongoing rounds of regulatory reform since the 1990s (Gleeson & Low, 2000b; Ruming et al., 2014). In NSW, as in the other states, this has included successive rounds of "red tape" reduction to standardize and reduce local planning controls and increased centralization and "depoliticization" of local planning decisions, often through the appointment of expert "panels" to decide on more significant developments (bypassing locally elected politicians). Further, in NSW in particular, a number of reforms have paved the way for private-sector involvement in the assessment of planning proposals and in proposing and delivering major projects, including infrastructure developments, unhindered by local planning controls. While initially prosecuted under the banner of neoliberalism, these reforms became increasingly tied to concerns about sluggish rates of housing production in NSW and in particular in the capital city of Sydney (Gurran & Ruming, 2015). These overarching reform efforts and ongoing concern about levels of new housing production in Sydney provide background context for the two case study sites.

The Housing "Shortage" in NSW

Sydney, as the capital of NSW and the nation's largest city, had a population of around 4.8 million residents in 2015. The greater metropolitan region, which encompasses the regional suburban centers of Gosford/Wyong to the north, Wollongong/Illawarra to the south, and Parramatta to the west, straddles a total metropolitan area of 12,368 square kilometers. The eastern coastline and the World Heritage-listed Blue Mountains to the west provide a natural perimeter for the metropolitan area, within which substantial tracts of undeveloped rural and remnant bushland remain. Thus, although Sydney is considered Australia's major global city, its low population density of around 373 persons per square kilometer (compared to roughly 2,691 and 6,690 for London and Hong Kong respectively) is accommodated primarily in detached homes with private gardens.

Planning for the entire metropolitan region, which is divided into forty-three local government areas (and over 650 individual suburbs), has always been complex, and there have been a number of experiments with regional governance since the Second World War. In 1945, the County of Cumberland Council was established to provide a metropolitan-wide structure for coordinated planning in the post-war period, in the context of growing concern over urban sprawl, traffic congestion, and a looming housing shortage. The Cumberland Council included state-appointed members from the Sydney City local government administration and nine other elected members from other local municipalities. A draft metropolitan plan (instituting land use zoning, strategic land allocations for new settlements, and the designation of areas for roads, open space, and greenbelt) had been prepared by 1948, but a series of policy adjustments delayed its confirmation until 1951. The designation of a significant greenbelt—designed to contain Sydney's rapidly spreading footprint—was one of the most contentious elements of the County of Cumberland Plan, opposed by landholders who wished to develop their land, and by local councils, who resented restrictions on the future growth of their areas. Further, the failure of the Commonwealth to fund satellite towns created further pressure on the greenbelt during the intense population boom of the post-war period. Although it was intended that the plan be implemented through local town planning schemes (adjusted to reflect the County of Cumberland's specified zones), many councils resisted pressure to prepare modern zoning schemes, preferring to retain their existing discretionary powers over development proposals (Sandercock, 1975). Such struggles between state and local government over the implementation of metropolitan planning directives became an ongoing theme in Sydney's development.

The Cumberland County Council was dissolved in late 1963, and a State Planning Authority established in its wake. The Authority issued a new metropolitan plan (1968), following the Scandinavian model of development along rail corridors, and continuing efforts to manage outward urban expansion (Morrison, 2000). As part of this effort, state planning policy permitted three-story flats in general residential zones (Searle, 2007). However, the population of inner Sydney began to decline, with falling household sizes and motorway projects, which destroyed inner-city neighborhoods and facilitated further greenfield housing expansion. Subsequently, inner-city residents, concerned about ugly "six pack" apartments, campaigned for new planning provisions to protect the heritage character of existing residential areas. This resulted in the introduction of stricter development controls in residential zones, and the passage of two pivotal laws: the NSW Heritage Act 1974 and the subsequent Environmental Planning and Assessment Act 1979. Both Acts instituted contemporary processes for community consultation in land use planning, and heralded new merit-based criteria for development proposals.

At the federal level, the short-lived Whitlam (Labor) government established a Department of Housing and Regional Development in the early 1970s, which sponsored decentralization initiatives, including the establishment of regional "Growth Centres" in selected areas (Gleeson & Coiacetto,

2005; Troy, 2012). Designated infrastructure investment, alongside the relocation of public services, was intended to stem depopulation in rural areas and relieve Sydney from population pressures by attracting new private development to places such as Bathurst/Orange in regional NSW. To facilitate the planning of the Growth Centres, special-purpose state legislation—the Growth Centres (Development Corporations) Act 1974—was brought to statute. While the regional growth center model was largely abandoned in the years that followed, the legislation persisted, enabling the formation of special purpose development corporations to oversee the development of designated growth centers and to acquire land.

In the city, concerns over the long-term viability of car-dependent suburbia remained, and in 1980 and 1981 the state began to permit "dual occupancy" development. This entailed requiring local councils to permit two dwellings on a single block of land in residential zones, a measure which, under certain conditions, was subsequently extended to permit subdivision of the land into two separate titles. The dual occupation policy appeared to have little impact, however, while other attempts to permit medium-density housing across all residential areas attracted significant opposition by residents and their political representatives in local councils, concerned about the loss of green space and amenity, privacy and overlooking from apartments into backyards, and visual impacts on the streetscape (Searle, 2007). Local councils—governed by elected representatives—were able to use their planning powers to resist medium- and higher-density development in a number of subtle ways, thus subverting the intent of the state's metropolitan planning policies:

> Local council opposition to the policies took a variety of forms. Often it simply involved scrutinising development applications for non-detached housing more thoroughly and delaying their path to approval. In other cases, special development control provisions ... were placed on medium density developments which increased their costs ...
> (Searle, 2007, p. 3)

Recalling earlier strategies of resistance to the County of Cumberland Plan, councils also refused to implement state policies designed to encourage medium-density development by rezoning areas to enshrine smaller minimum lot sizes and/or to permit town houses and villas. However, a house price boom in the late 1980s (fueled by financial deregulation and increased international immigration) made the promise of urban consolidation—smaller lot and dwelling sizes, and lower infrastructure costs—seem more attractive.

Community opposition to the state's policy of dual occupation and rezoning for townhouses and villas was particularly strong in the city's well-heeled North Shore suburbs. For instance, organizations such as the vocal NSW-based resident action group "Save Our Suburbs" (SOS) emerged during this time and have long since campaigned to prevent intensification of housing development within existing neighborhoods:

> Sydney's beleaguered residents have been fighting an endless string of localised battles against increased density developments ("urban consolidation"). SOS supports residents in their struggle to save our city from overcrowding, traffic congestion, pollution and loss of bushland and heritage resulting from ill-considered planning impositions.
> (Save Our Suburbs, n.d., p. 1)

In outer areas, there was little resistance to increased housing density, but the construction of apartments in areas poorly serviced by employment and public transport raised new problems (Searle, 2007). Consequently, the government continued to identify outer greenfield areas for future urban release, and began to focus urban consolidation efforts on well-located sites in less contentious areas, including former industrial areas of the inner city. Pyrmont/Ultimo, to the immediate west of the CBD, was the first major renewal experiment, overseen by a specially formed City West Development Corporation. A regional plan prepared in the early 1990s fast-tracked the rezoning and development-control process, assigning approval powers to the Minister for Planning. This approach—the suspension of local powers via a state planning instrument and/or a special purpose development authority—became the model for major growth and renewal initiatives both in established suburbs and in new release locations.

By 2005, the state government was facing the tail end of another period of steep house price inflation (which raged nationally between late 1996 and 2004). In Sydney the boom ended with price stagnation—rather than absolute falls—leaving many first home buyers still unable to enter the housing market and a drop-off in new housing production. At national and state levels, industry lobby groups at the time blamed inadequate housing production for persistent affordability problems, calling attention to what they argued was a national crisis of land supply (Property Council of Australia, 2007). According to this narrative, new housing development was hamstrung by environmental "green tape" and heavy infrastructure charging in new release areas, and NIMBY home owners preventing higher-density development within existing suburbs (Property Council of Australia, 2006; Property Council of Australia, 2007). In Sydney, as in the other state capitals, these claims resonated, because of the sustained government emphasis on urban consolidation in metropolitan strategic plans—much to the opposition of residents in existing suburbs. There had also been sharp increases in development charges for infrastructure provision in greenfield locations, imposed by both state and local governments. But the steady increase in inner-city house prices reflected not so much a shortage of land for detached homes on the outer fringes, but rather a shift in market preference for locations offering greater accessibility and urban amenities, which buyers seemed increasingly willing to prefer, despite trade-offs in dwelling size and open space.

Sydney's 2005 metropolitan strategy, "City of Cities," reinforced the policy emphasis on urban containment, setting a target that 70 percent of housing supply now be delivered in existing urban areas through renewal of underutilized localities and piecemeal infill development. The plan also cemented provisions for new release areas, accommodating the balance of new growth, to be better planned and coordinated, with growth focused in designated areas. It was at this point in time that the North West and South West Sydney Growth Centres were declared, overseen by a special quasi-independent Growth Centres Commission (empowered to operate as a development corporation). The Commission was established by order of the Government Gazette (No. 81, 1/7/05), under the previously mentioned Growth Centres (Development Corporations) Act 1974. The Growth Centres were intended to be the focus for new greenfield development, accommodating between 30 and 40 percent of Sydney's future housing, providing a basis for more coordinated infrastructure and service provision (Department of Planning, 2005).

The Case Studies

These changing policy and administrative arrangements form the backdrop for the evolution of planning and development in the two case study areas. The Green Square/Victoria Park area is one of Sydney's flagship urban renewal projects. Situated about 3.5 kilometers from Sydney's city center and 4 kilometers from the airport, the area is surrounded by the former industrial suburbs of Beaconsfield, Rosebery, Alexandria, and Zetland, as well as one of Sydney's largest concentrations of public housing in the suburb of Waterloo. By contrast, the Rouse Hill Town Centre, located 42 kilometers from the CBD, has been a focus for master-planned greenfield housing development in the northwest. Both cases are shown in their regional context in Figure 3.1.

Green Square

Planning for the urban renewal of the Green Square area (which covers around 292 hectares) began in the early 1990s, following commitments to construct a rail line connecting the airport with Sydney's Central Business District (CBD). The site was initially projected to accommodate around 20,000 new homes and 40,000 residents by 2031, although this figure has undergone periodic upward revision.

The state's decision to construct a new train station at Green Square provided a focus for the renewal area, and the potential to use the station as a catalyst for a new town center. Critically, although the economic significance of Sydney's inner southeast industrial lands had declined

Sydney's Urban Renewal and Growth Centres 67

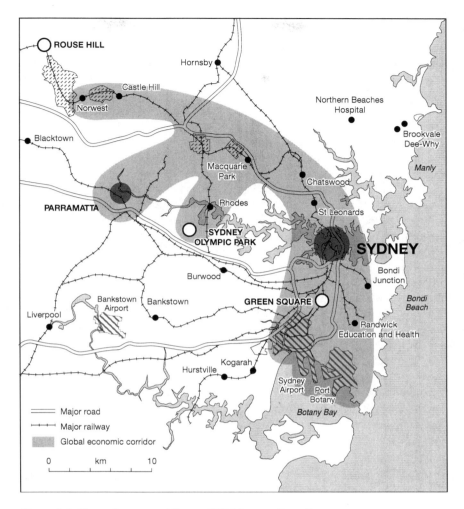

Figure 3.1 Green Square and Rouse Hill Metropolitan Context
Source: Adapted from NSW Planning & Environment, 2014, p. 13

following the departure of manufacturing industries to the outer suburbs in the 1970s, its strategic location between the central business district, Port Botany, and the airport, implied significant future economic potential.

The key players in the planning process were the former South Sydney City Council (later merged into a larger City of Sydney Council) and the NSW government. In 1996 the government established a special purpose development corporation to coordinate planning and delivery of infrastructure under the Growth Centres (Development Corporations) Act 1974. In 1997, a Development Control Plan was prepared by the South Sydney

Council, covering the whole area, as well as master plans for the two sites in single ownership ("Victoria Park," and a former glass factory site that had been acquired by the property developer Meriton Apartments). The government's land developer, Landcom, had carriage of the overarching development of the site, including the provision of open space and community facilities.

The Green Square Structural Masterplan (Stanisic Turner and Hassell Consultants) was released in 1998. It featured a diversity of land uses, building types, and housing, connected by a strong public domain and social and ecological infrastructure (through a network of naturally vegetated parks and street verges, community facilities, and a library). The site was to reinforce and demonstrate the potential for the new medium- and higher-density housing forms emerging in Sydney's former industrial areas to be commercially successful, while also winning over skeptical Sydneysiders as to the benefits of density "done well." The emphasis was on mixed uses, connectivity (for active transportation and a strong social realm), and a diversity of housing types, ultimately focusing on a walkable center providing a degree of self-containment through local shops and employment opportunities, exemplifying the new ideal for Sydney's future growth in self-contained high-density communities. At the same time, the plan recognized the existing traditional residential neighborhoods surrounding the area and retained key heritage elements. Key precincts of the Green Square Development Area are shown in Figure 3.2.

In 1999, the South Sydney Local Environmental Plan was amended, rezoning most of the area for mixed use but deferring the Green Square Town Centre pending a specific master plan. One of the critical elements of this instrument was an inclusionary zoning mechanism for affordable housing. This mechanism—which was to require that 10 percent of new housing development in the Green Square area be affordable to those on low and moderate incomes—was challenged by Meriton Apartments (the major private landholder), who brought an action to the NSW Land and Environment Court. The Property Council of Australia lent its support to the challenge, calling for a new state planning instrument to clarify the legal basis for affordable housing contributions, under very limited circumstances and confined solely to voluntary incentives (Williams, 2000). Meriton was successful in its legal challenge, but the Land and Environment Court found that the entire local planning scheme was invalid, meaning that the site in question reverted to its former industrial zoning. The impasse was broken by changes to the Environmental Planning & Assessment Act 1979, which clarified that local plans could provide for affordable housing. In practice this meant simply that affordable housing was a valid planning consideration capable of being addressed in the objectives of planning instruments and implemented through requirements for financial or in-kind contributions. However, the council was forced to reduce its original affordable housing requirements to a much smaller 3 percent of floor area

Sydney's Urban Renewal and Growth Centres   69

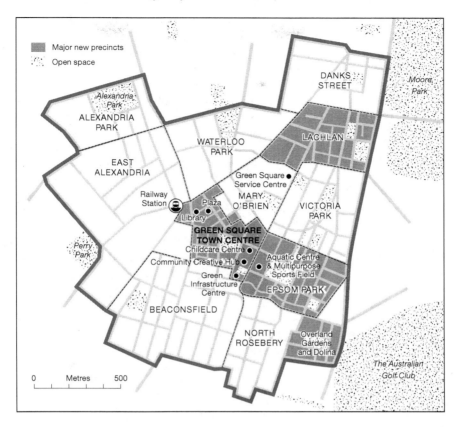

Figure 3.2 Green Square Development Area and Precincts
Source: Adapted from City of Sydney, 2015

for residential developments and 1 percent for commercial projects, provided as a cash payment. This story of attempts by local government to bring forward affordable housing schemes only to be rejected or curtailed by the state planning authority (typically influenced by the views of the property sector) became a common pattern in NSW and the other Australian jurisdictions (Gurran et al., 2008).

In the case of Green Square, the levy was provided to the special purpose affordable housing developer/provider, the City West Housing Company. However, the decision to permit a cash contribution—rather than provision of land or a proportion of completed units—meant that the affordable housing developer was forced to bid on the open market for sites. This approach had two drawbacks. First, when affordable housing companies are obliged to pay commercial rates for non-market housing development, their overall yield is reduced. Over time, this can lead to pressure for affordable housing developers to move to lower-value (and less accessible) areas of the city, where more dwelling units can be achieved for the same funds. Similarly, affordable housing developers may face barriers in purchasing sites or securing planning approval.

In this particular case, the City West Housing Company is required to use its income stream to develop homes within a defined geographical area (irrespective of the potential to gain a higher yield if their funds are expended on a cheaper site). This ensured that at least some housing in Green Square would be allocated for lower income groups with demonstrable ties to the area (such as local employees or long term residents). However, City West did face some initial barriers to securing access to land within the Victoria Park development. The government's own land developer, Landcom, was initially reluctant to sell a site to the affordable housing company, concerned about potential stigma affecting the price of their market offerings. The Planning Minister ultimately intervened to enable the sale, but the first affordable housing project in Victoria Park was constrained by a site specific set of controls, which limited its height, dwarfing the development and rendering it overlooked by surrounding private apartments (Bebbington, pers. comm.). In another indication of Landcom's orientation toward delivering a commercial return to government, the corporation declined to maximize its own permitted density and yield, using generous open space and landscaping treatment to achieve a price premium.

Nevertheless, a few years later and in the context of a slow market, Landcom was much more amenable to selling to the affordable housing company City West, which promptly constructed a prize-winning apartment building on O'Dea Avenue. By 2015, around 104 units of affordable rental housing had been funded under this scheme, against a total target of 330 by 2035.

The South Sydney Development Corporation was disbanded in 2005, but the state government developer, Landcom, continued to shepherd the area (itself becoming a Development Corporation in 2013, when Landcom was merged with the Sydney Metropolitan Development Authority to become Urban Growth NSW). While Victoria Park, with its generally consolidated pattern of ownership, was progressively developed, the Green Square Town Centre was hamstrung by complex landownership constraints, challenging infrastructure requirements, issues of land contamination (and clean-up costs), and unresolved questions of flood risk affecting the site. A consortium involving Landcom, Mirvac Projects, and Leighton Properties was formed in 2009 to resolve these issues. The group submitted a new planning proposal to the Sydney City Council, proposing a significant increase in permissible development intensity in order to address viability issues, and this proposal was adopted.

By 2012, the area covered by the Green Square and "City South Village" (as the areas surrounding the Green Square Town Centre were named), accommodated over 20,100 residents (an increase of 36 percent from 2006).

Figure 3.3 provides an indication of the differential levels of population growth in the different parts of the development area, including adjoining suburbs and growth over the decade between 2001 and 2006.

By 2015, detailed planning for the area indicated that around 11,000 new dwellings had been constructed, with another 16,368 anticipated by around 2022, to accommodate a total of around 53,778 residents (City of Sydney, 2015). Thus, despite complex planning arrangements and institutional difficulties between state and local governments, the project continued to proceed.

Nevertheless, while the entire Victoria Park precinct has been completed, residents have waited over a decade for neighborhood retail facilities. The promised Green Square town center remains a construction site, but the area boasts strong social services, including a library and community center. Recognizing that high-density living on such a scale is a relatively new form of housing for Australian-born residents, the City of Sydney is undertaking ongoing efforts to support community building activities. Yet serious questions are emerging about the sustainability of Sydney's burgeoning "strata" communities (where land and overall building structures are held in common ownership, but individual dwellings owned on a "strata" title deed).

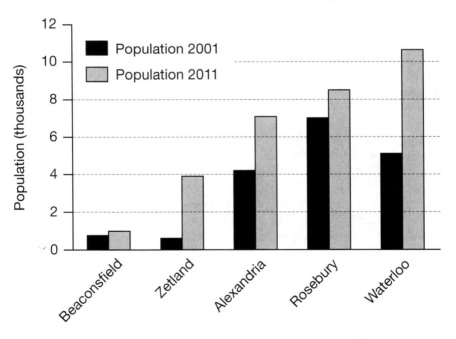

Figure 3.3 Population Growth, Green Square and South Sydney Villages, 2001–2011

Source: ABS Census, 2001, 2006 Basic community profiles

Figure 3.4 Mixed Residential and Commercial Development under Construction Surrounding the Green Square Train Station
Source: Sam Phibbs, 2015

Complex management arrangements and the need for owners of strata properties to deliberate over day-to-day operational decisions, as well as more significant questions about long-term maintenance, repairs, and, potentially, redevelopment, have introduced what some have described as a privatized "fourth tier" of urban governance with uncertain implications (Easthope & Randolph, 2009).

Despite the significant housing yield achieved to date in the South Sydney area (Table 3.1), very little of this stock has been affordable for lower-income groups. Beyond the dedicated affordable housing units financed by the inclusionary zoning scheme, which have currently yielded around 103 apartments (less than 1 percent of the total housing delivered to date), there is little evidence that the project will contribute affordable housing supply to meet the needs of Sydney's lower-income renters, and even moderate-income aspiring home owners will find few opportunities in any of the Green Square schemes. As discussed further below, median monthly mortgages and rents are well above that of the Sydney median as a whole, while the significant public investment in the area—particularly the rail line—has only reinforced patterns of gentrification. Although Landcom as the government land developer had an opportunity to moderate price pressures, for instance by maximizing dwelling yields in Victoria Park as per the original scheme, emphasizing more modest strata developments with lower management fees,

Table 3.1 Completed and Projected New Dwellings, Green Square and "South Sydney Villages", 2015

Neighborhood precinct	Built (2015)	Proposed	Total (2025)
Danks Street	2,500	1,100	3,600
Alexandria Park	657	240	897
Lachlan	1,059	2,003	3,062
Waterloo Park	1,003	535	1,538
Mary O'Brien	535	640	1,175
Victoria Park	4,050	—	4,050
East Alexandria	614	97	711
Green Square Town Centre	—	3,308	3,308
Epsom Park	—	2,877	2,877
Beaconsfield	135	2,331	2,466
North Rosebury	354	3,237	3,591
Total	10,907	16,368	27,275

Source: City of Sydney, 2015

and/or offering some affordable home purchase opportunities subsidized by rising values across the entire development, the requirement to deliver a commercial return to government seems to have made such strategies appear unviable.

In its new incarnation as "Urban Growth NSW" (formed in 2013 to incorporate Landcom and various other special purpose development corporations), even the rhetoric of affordable housing appears to have been lost in plans to maximize housing density on the site. The ongoing development contribution framework for affordable housing assumes a modest revenue stream will continue to finance around two hundred additional rental properties for low- and moderate-income groups. This will amount to around three hundred affordable homes—1 percent of the total 27,275 dwellings anticipated for the site.

A similar story emerges in the very different context of Rouse Hill, in Sydney's northwest.

Rouse Hill

Like the Green Square area, planning for Rouse Hill preceded its development by many years. The northwest sector of the city was slated for future urban expansion in the 1968 Sydney metropolitan plan, but detailed planning did not begin until much later (Forsyth, 1997). In the early 1980s, the state government purchased 122 hectares in the area for the purpose of eventually developing a regional center. Rather than artificially creating the center, however, the government's intention was to introduce it when the market conditions indicated demand. Thus, a regional plan was prepared covering the local government areas of Blacktown and Baulkham Hills (the Sydney Regional Environmental Plan 19—Rouse Hill, in 1989). The regional scheme enabled the Minister for Planning to declare land for urban release, expediting a process usually driven by local councils. The scheme also specified matters to be included in the local zoning instrument, including provision for a minimum residential density of ten dwellings per hectare (double the prevailing norm) and a requirement that medium-density apartments be permissible across the residential zone (consistent with state planning policy at the time). The plans were also to include an objective "... to provide affordable accommodation to meet the needs of households of all types with a variety of housing in type, tenure, price, and location" (Sydney Regional Environmental Plan—19 Rouse Hill, s7(a)(b)(a)).

By 1991, around 1,500 hectares had been rezoned to enable housing development in the Blacktown and Baulkham Hills local government areas. However, the development that followed was fragmented, particularly in the Baulkham Hills area, making it difficult to service. The predominant development model at the time was for infrastructure and services (such as schools, shops, and transport upgrades) to be provided once a threshold population was achieved. In the case of Blacktown, where the release areas were contained and contiguous to existing neighborhoods, infrastructure followed housing development by the late 1990s (S. Driscoll, speaking to Heimans, 2007). But, in the case of Baulkham Hills, services took longer to arrive. Former Baulkham Hills Shire Council Planner Peter Lee recalled that the haphazard development of the Rouse Hill release area was dictated by Sydney Water, which operated to enable or prevent development without reference to sequencing for strategic planning or infrastructure provision:

> ... you had areas out at Rouse Hill or pockets of subdivisions occurring all over the areas where it wasn't coordinated by the Council. It was coordinated by Sydney Water in the provision of infrastructure. The problem that caused is that there were pockets of residential land being released and the roads were not being upgraded because the Council didn't have the funds to coordinate the road infrastructure with that. The problem that created for the Council was the areas were being developed, people were moving in without the community facilities without the other services they needed to service the release area.
> (Peter Lee, in interview with Heimans, 2007)

In part to address this problem, a consortium involving private developers and the State Department of Housing formed the "Rouse Hill Infrastructure Consortium" to facilitate development by arranging private finance for water infrastructure (Forsythe, 1997). Nevertheless, according to former planner Peter Lee, local councils continued to face other barriers to infrastructure provision, associated with the haphazard process of land acquisition following rezoning:

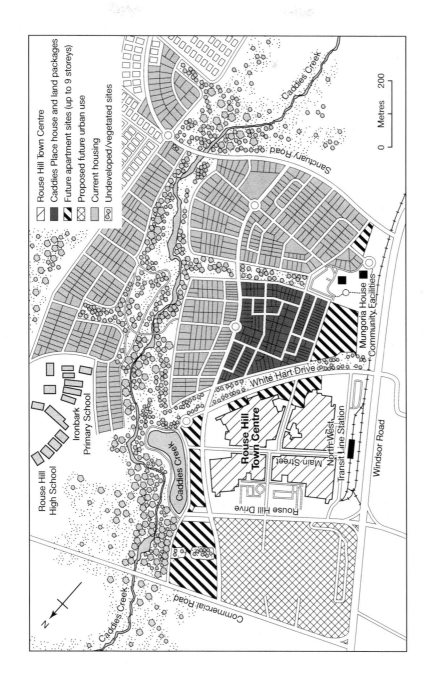

Figure 3.5 Rouse Hill
Source: Adapted from Landcom (n.d.)

> When the area was released prices of land changed significantly from a rural paddock of land to a residential block of land. The price of land was a three hundred percent increase and so the Council then had to buy land for parks and reserves, community centres with a significant increase of price going with that as well.
>
> (Peter Lee, in interview with Heimans, 2007)

By this time, a range of groups had become interested in the development of the northwest, and plans for the Rouse Hill area began to attract intense scrutiny and debate (Forsyth, 1997). Although greenfield development was seen as less constrained by local resident views, Ann Forsyth (1997) documents intense debate over the area's future during the early 1990s, with conservation and environment groups concerned about environmental impacts and the perpetuation of Sydney's urban sprawl. By contrast, developers and so-called "expansionists" (those critical of the "compact city" agenda) were strongly in favor of the area's growth and viewed Rouse Hill as an opportunity to achieve a "new city" offering "egalitarian" homes for all, in line with the prevailing Australian suburban ideal:

> ... expansionists believed that the government should support homes for "people" of a particular sort, nuclear families, and in a particular form of "reasonable surroundings," low-density suburban dwellings.
>
> (Forsyth, 1997, p. 49)

Over much of this period the council advocated strongly for the area's transport services to be upgraded, and, crucially, for commitment to a new heavy rail service. Ultimately a "transit way" (a dedicated off road bus lane) connecting the area with Blacktown–Castle Hill and Parramatta centers was introduced, while heavy rail to connect to the City transport network (the North West Rail Link) was finally announced in the early 2000s (it is currently under construction).

The state government, as a major landholder in the area, was also waiting for the critical mass of residents to make the regional center economically viable. By the late 1990s, there was sufficient development in the northwest to commence detailed planning. Joint studies were undertaken by the NSW Department of Urban Affairs and Planning and the Baulkham Hills Shire Council in 1998, leading to the rezoning of the Rouse Hill Town Centre in 2001. The total area covered by the Town Centre plan was around 120 hectares, eleven of which were earmarked for a mixed retail, commercial, and residential precinct.

The state planning department as landholder approached the government's developer Landcom to partner in the process, and in 2002 expressions of interest were invited to engage the private sector, with the international firm Lend Lease appointed for the residential component and a commercial shopping center developer for the retail/commercial project selected as the preferred tenderers. A mixed-use regional Town Centre, comprising supermarkets, 200 smaller shops, a public library, and community facilities formed the nucleus of the master plan, which sought to include a mix of dwelling types, decreasing in density according to distance from the town center. Initial planning envisaged 1,800 dwellings, of which 500 were to be sold as sites for commissioned homes. The balance was to be sold as completed town houses, terraces, and apartments, including shop top apartments in the very center. Walkability and high-quality open space were key features of the master plan, with all homes within a ten-minute walk of the Town Centre and transit way, and new primary and secondary schools within walking distance for all homes.

The distinctive innovation of the Rouse Hill Town Centre was the construction of the regional retail and commercial area—alongside the full provision of a library and community facilities up front—before the arrival of residents. This innovation was intended to address the problems of social isolation and car dependency which had plagued the Australian suburban housing development of the late twentieth century. However, the model was only possible with significant state government involvement as the primary landowner of the site. Thus, the capacity to influence the outcomes and patterns of new growth was strictly limited to the site in government ownership. Consequently, the Town Centre and its immediate surrounds are situated within a wider semi-rural context, punctuated by piecemeal housing estates dissected by major roads. Soon after the opening of the Town Centre, journalist Michael Duffy observed:

> If you go out along the Windsor Road today you'll see a gleaming mini-city has appeared in the rural landscape. The new Rouse Hill Town Centre opened last week. It's not really a city but it is enormous, particularly striking because it is still surrounded by fields, like something just created in the computer game SimCity. Unusually in the history of Sydney's expansion, the town centre has been created before the town.
>
> (Duffy, 2008, p. 1)

Critical to the new Town Centre was a decision to incorporate both retail and residential accommodation from the outset. This meant that the large retail center had an immediate clientele, with significant porosity between the retail "mall," community realm, and residential areas. Within the residential areas there is also significant urban design and landscape innovation. Another departure from the residential subdivisions of the 1970s and 1980s was the emphasis on natural and cultural heritage elements in the landscape, and the commitment to retaining the existing topography of the site (rather than levelling undulations for ease of development) (Heimans, 2007).

However, permeability beyond the self-contained new suburb is poor, with the area ringed by busy arterial roads that present major barriers to walking and cycling. Large swathes of undeveloped land surrounding the suburb also limit the walking and cycling catchments, in a development pattern that is highly typical for the North West and South West Growth Centres and Sydney's outer suburbs more widely.

The provision of diverse housing types in and around a new town center marked a radical departure from the prevailing approach to suburban housing development in Australia, and remains relatively unusual. Interviews with planning officers involved in the process suggest that the capacity for the government developer—Landcom—to assume the risks in creating what was essentially an untested housing market was critical to the implementation of more diverse housing styles in Sydney's outer suburbs. The seniors' housing in particular, which is situated above the retail precinct but designed to provide semi-private open space at elevation, struggled to find a market, and profitability was low. Over time, however, the area has become increasingly popular and the high-quality public domain and attractive retail facilities have consolidated the area as an important regional center.

Current planning for the North West Rail Link reveals the state government's expectations to capitalize on this new demand. The state government anticipates that an additional 950 dwellings can be achieved in the area by 2036, predominantly through increased three- to twelve-story apartments and smaller lot residential dwellings by rezoning sites surrounding nearby housing development areas (NSW Transport, 2013, p. 5).

Comparison of Housing Outcomes in Case Study Areas

Overall, it is difficult to truly compare the housing outcomes in the two case study areas and in relation to the other strategic sites examined in this book. Certainly, both projects had a long and uncertain gestation, hamstrung by institutional and political complexities at times, and by market conditions at others. Undoubtedly, those closest to the projects—the state and local planners, land and housing developers, community based groups, and, ultimately, residents, will offer mixed views regarding the extent to which original aspirations or promises for the sites have been achieved. Yet, it would be difficult to identify better examples of planned greenfield and urban renewal projects in the Australian context. After slow starts, original housing supply expectations have been met or are on track to be exceeded, while urban design, accessibility, and environmental and heritage conservation objectives have largely been achieved. Further, both cases epitomize distinct but complimentary choices in planning for Australia's new housing supply—in designated, self-contained new release areas that are well connected to larger centers but offer qualities of urbanity usually associated with the inner city (Rouse Hill)—or within intensely developed renewal precincts where private space is traded for accessibility, but environmental infrastructure and open space sustain connections to the natural realm.

Comparing both Rouse Hill and the Green Square/South Sydney development areas, these differences flow through to the composition of new housing supply. Despite the rhetoric of housing choice and diversity, housing in the Rouse Hill area remains as predominantly low-density detached homes, in comparison to the high-density housing forms in Green Square (Figure 3.7), and this trend has been reinforced over the past decade. Thus, the origins of the Rouse Hill development as a last frontier for the quintessentially Australian new town—planned "expansion" rather than density and containment (Forsyth, 1997)—have persisted. Dwellings in Rouse Hill and Green Square are larger and smaller, respectively, than in the Sydney metropolitan area overall, with the majority of homes in Rouse Hill boasting four or more bedrooms. Yet, arguably, in both cases the housing outcomes are of a very high standard indeed—with Rouse Hill offering walkable urbanity but within a suburban context, and Green Square/Victoria Park providing intensive housing density that is nevertheless embedded within a network of quality private and public open space.

Unfortunately, where both case studies align is in the failure to deliver housing opportunities that are affordable to moderate- and lower-income earners. Somewhat surprisingly, despite the perception that greenfield housing development offers more affordable housing opportunities, average mortgage and rental payments exceed that recorded for the Greater Sydney region and the Green Square/South Sydney area (Figure 3.10) and one-fifth

Figure 3.6 Apartments and Open Space, Victoria Park/Green Square
Source: Sam Phibbs, 2015

80 Sydney's Urban Renewal and Growth Centres

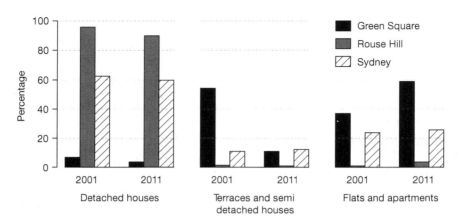

Figure 3.7 Comparison of Dwelling Stock, 2001–2011, Green Square Renewal and Rouse Hill Development Areas

Source: ABS, 2012

Figure 3.8 House under Construction, Rouse Hill

Source: Sam Phibbs, 2015

Sydney's Urban Renewal and Growth Centres 81

Figure 3.9 Apartments Surrounding the Library and Central Square, Rouse Hill Town Centre
Source: Sam Phibbs (2015)

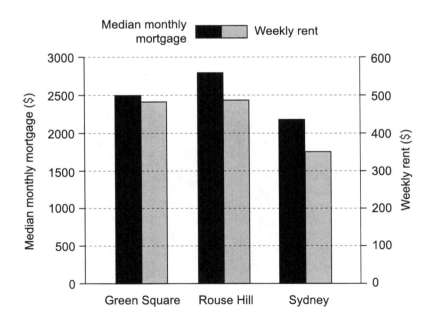

Figure 3.10 Mortgage and Rent Payments, Green Square, Rouse Hill, and Sydney (2011)
Source: (ABS, 2012)

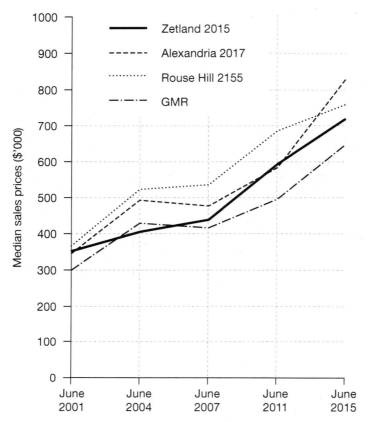

Figure 3.11 Median Sales Prices, All Dwellings, 2001–2015

Source: Compiled from NSW Government Rent and Sales Reports (September Release, June Quarters, 2001–2015)

of households in Rouse Hill are paying more than 30 percent of their income on mortgage repayments (double the national rate) (ABS, 2012).

House prices have increased in line with the Greater Metropolitan Region, but in both places price increases have exceeded the median for Sydney, again highlighting missed opportunities to secure affordable housing as part of the planned development process (Figure 3.11). In short, while both Green Square and Rouse Hill development areas could be regarded as examples of well-planned communities, with strong public investment in the design process, as well as in the provision of local and regional infrastructure, the major beneficiaries seem to have been private-sector developers and initial home buyers and investors.

There is little evidence to suggest that these developments have either improved affordability outcomes overall or delivered a significant supply of new homes to lower- and middle-income earners in particular. Thus, the two case study sites reflect the politics of property ownership and development writ large across Australia's largest metropolis, bypassing established areas in favor of outer greenfield sites and designated inner-city areas, with the risks and costs borne by government, and the profits gleaned by landholders, developers, and investors. State and local government relationships suggest that the state's significant resource capacities can create demand for new residential communities, but the lack of levers to capitalize on this public expertise and investment—despite the existence of government land developers—suggests that Australia's "market-supportive" model of housing provision is no longer able to offer opportunities for younger generations of aspiring home purchasers.

Conclusion: Property Politics, Planning, and Constraints to Affordable Housing Supply

The two case study sites examined in this chapter, and the wider case of planning for housing in Australia, provide a real-world insight into scholarly debates about the impacts of land use regulation on the housing market. As noted in the introduction to this book, these debates often center on whether planning systems constrain greenfield land supply through urban containment policies (implemented by state governments) or prevent more diverse housing development (through local development controls preventing higher density homes). This chapter shows how, in theory, both conditions—of planned (or constrained) greenfield land supplies in new release areas and local government/home owner resistance to increased development within established areas in particular—appear to apply to the case of housing development in Sydney, Australia's largest and most expensive city, since at least the 1990s.

Thus, the theory of land supply constraint and resident opposition appear plausible explanations for Sydney's high house prices, which lead the nation and indeed are among the most expensive in the world. But closer analysis of the interplay between the planning process, private residential development, and wider policy settings through the two case studies, challenge any simplistic notions about the impacts of regulation in constraining new housing supply. In fact, recalling the historical evolution of Australian cities and the role of speculative developers and political sponsorship in the siting of infrastructure and the release of land, contemporary processes appear to perpetuate a planning culture that is permissive rather than punitive, at least in relation to major development projects. Rather than constraining the supply of new housing (which in Australia seems fully dependent on the market), the planning system could be blamed for neglecting questions around the distribution of housing opportunities and the other benefits associated with public infrastructure investment and private amenity. While in both of the cases planning and public investment in urban infrastructure have supported new housing development and generated considerable value, these benefits have not been evenly shared. Rather, the planning process has arguably exacerbated inequalities between existing home owners and those seeking to enter the market, by failing to secure wider community benefits from public planning processes. Similarly, the lack of programs to include affordable housing development as part of wider market processes reinforces underlying processes of socio-spatial disadvantage.

In this way, the Sydney case studies reviewed here show how planning processes can reinforce dual disadvantages arising from: 1) increasingly unequal levels of property owning wealth, and 2) access to employment and other urban opportunities. Australia's urban policy settings will need to confront these dual pressures—tenure-based and locational disadvantage—in the years ahead. If policy makers remain complacent, captive to the mantra of supply at all costs, widening social disparities between home owners and those increasingly forced to remain in unstable rental tenure may finally unsettle the nation's entrenched politics of property ownership and investment.

References

ABS [Australian Bureau of Statistics]. (2012). *2011 Census QuickStats*. Canberra: Commonwealth of Australia.

City of Sydney. (2015). *Green Square Infrastructure Strategy and Plan (Draft March 2015)*. Sydney: City of Sydney.

Department of Planning. (2005). *City of Cities: A Plan for Sydney's Future*. Sydney: Department of Planning.

Duffy, M. (2008, March 15). New City in Modern Times Shows Best and Worst of Design. *Sydney Morning Herald*.

Easthope, H., & Randolph, B. (2009). Governing the compact city: The challenges of apartment living in Sydney, Australia. *Housing Studies*, 24(2), 243–259.

Forsyth, A. (1997). Five images of a suburb: Perspectives on a new urban development. *Journal of the American Planning Association*, 63(1), 45–60.

Freeland, J. L. (1972). People in Cities. In A. Rapoport, (Ed.), *Australia as Human Setting; Approaches to the designed environment*. Sydney: Angus and Robertson, pp. 99–123.

Gleeson, B., & Coiacetto, E. (2005). Public land agencies in Australia: The key to positive planning? *Urban Research Program Research Paper*, 5, 8–13.

Gleeson, B. & Low, N. (2000a). *Australian Urban Planning: New Challenges, New Agendas*. Melbourne: Allen and Unwin.

Gleeson, B. & Low, N. (2000b). "Unfinished business": Neoliberal planning reform in Australia. *Urban Policy and Research*, 18(1), 7–28.

Gurran, N. & Ruming, K. (2015). Less planning, more development? Housing and urban reform discourses in Australia. *Journal of Economic Policy Reform*, 1–19.

Gurran, N. Milligan, V., Baker, D., Bugg, L. B., & Christensen, S. (2008). New Directions in planning for affordable housing: Australian and international evidence and implications. *AHURI Final Report Series*. Melbourne: AHURI.

Gurran, N., Ruming, K., & Randolph, B. (2009). *Counting the costs: Planning requirements, infrastructure contributions and residential development in Australia*. Macquarie University: ResearchOnline.

Heimans, F. (2007). *Baulkham Hills Shire Oral History Project: The New Rouse Hill*. Sydney: Baulkham Hills Shire Council.

Landcom. (n.d.). *The New Rouse Hill Masterplan*. Sydney: Landcom.

Major Cities Unit. (2010). *State of Australian Cities 2010*. Canberra: Major Cities Unit, Infrastructure Australia.

Morrison, I. (2000). The Corridor City: Planning for Growth in the 1960s. In S. Hamnett & R. Freestone (Eds.), *The Australian Metropolis: A Planning History*. Sydney: Allen & Unwin, pp. 131–149.

NSW Planning & Environment. (2014). *A Plan for Growing Sydney*. Sydney: NSW Government.

NSW Transport. (2013). *North West Rail Link; Rouse Hill Station Structure Plan; A vision for Rouse Hill Station Surrounds*. Sydney: NSW Government.

Productivity Commission. (2011). *Performance Benchmarking of Australian Business Regulation: Planning, Zoning and Development Assessments; Productivity Commission Draft Research Report*. Canberra: Australian Government.

Property Council of Australia. (2006). *Reasons to be fearful? Government taxes, charges and compliance costs and their impact on housing affordability*. Sydney: Residential Development Council, Property Council of Australia.

Property Council of Australia. (2007). *Australia's land supply crisis; supply demand imbalance and its impact on declining housing affordability*. Sydney: Residential Development Council, Property Council of Australia.

Ruming, K. J., Gurran, N., Maginn, P. J., & Goodman, R. (2014). A national planning agenda? Unpacking the influence of federal urban policy on state planning reform. *Australian Planner*, 51(2), 108–121.

Ruming, K., Houston, D., & Amati, M. (2012). Multiple suburban publics: Rethinking community opposition to consolidation in Sydney. *Geographical Research*, 50(4), 421–435.

Sandercock, L. (1975). *Property, Politics, and Urban Planning: A History of Australian City Planning, 1890–1990*. Victoria: Melbourne University Press.

Save Our Suburbs (n.d.). *Save Our Suburbs NSW—For Sustainable Living (assorted web material)*. Sydney: Save Our Suburbs.

Searle, G. (2007). *Sydney's Urban Consolidation Experience: Power, Politics and Community, Research paper 12*. Brisbane: Urban Research Program, Griffith University.

Troy, P. (2012). *Accommodating Australians; Commonwealth Government Involvement in Housing*. Sydney: The Federation Press.

Williams, P. (2000). Inclusionary zoning and affordable housing in Sydney. *Urban Policy and Research*, 18(3), 291–310.

4 Power and Democracy in the English Planning System

Introduction

This chapter and the next provide an account of apparent "development inertia" and the "housing crisis" in England, which has its epicenter in London. The current chapter aims to localize the broad framework set out at the beginning of this book, examining those aspects of the English planning system that we might reasonably expect to impact on housing supply: the power and scope of planning per se, the roles of different actors within the "governance" of planning, and the system's treatment of, and impacts on, land supply. The broader analysis provided here sets the scene for a case study-based examination of development outcomes in the next chapter, which drills down to significant housing schemes that can be used to exemplify the challenge of development inertia in England and its broader, and more deeply constituted, housing crisis.

The English planning system has undergone seemingly radical reform over the last fifteen years, with the pace of that reform noticeably quickening under the Conservative–Liberal Democrat coalition between 2010 and 2015. In the run-up to the 2015 General Election, devolution of all sorts of powers, including planning powers, to cities and to communities was an important battleground. Prior to the 2010 election, David Cameron had committed the Conservatives to what appeared to be a radical devolution of power to communities, promising a "control shift" in the level of decision making in England, putting communities in control of a range of planning decisions (Conservative Party, 2009). The Labour Party spent the coalition years playing catch-up on this fast-developing agenda, with the then leader, Ed Miliband, eventually promising further devolution of power to towns and cities, "the like of which has not been seen in living memory" (Planning Resource, 2014). However, the electorate seemed to have greater trust in Conservative strategies and was swayed by the criticism of Labour as a party with centralizing tendencies. In the northwest of England, the pledge to create a "Northern Powerhouse," with a far-reaching devolution of powers to the Manchester city region, proved particularly appealing and saw Labour lose political ground in one of its traditional heartlands.

Planning, as a key instrument of public policy, has been center stage in this race to empower the grass roots. One might be forgiven, in light of the sheer volume of recent rhetoric and policy pledges, for thinking that major shifts in the locus of power in England have been confined to (or at least concentrated in) the last few years. But this is not so. Since its inception, the comprehensive planning system in England has been subject to episodic power shifts. It began life as part of a broader package of post-war welfare reforms that saw the empowerment of the state to deliver a range of public goods, through the comprehensive regeneration of bomb-damaged inner urban areas and the planning and delivery of free-standing New Towns over the next thirty or so years. The local authorities (or development corporations for the New Towns) were handed significant power and autonomy: to plan and deliver new urban fabric (John, 1990). But, in the seventy years after 1947, power has gradually ebbed away from the local state to private enterprise and now, it might seem, to community actors who are able to shape and direct planning outcomes. In this chapter we will provide the fuller narrative of the changes summarized above, while unpacking some of the key features of planning in England.

But, first, an explanatory note: since devolution of power away from London to Cardiff, Edinburgh, and Belfast in 1999, it is no longer possible to talk of a United Kingdom or British planning system. There are, of course, commonalties, political and fiscal, across the different parts of the UK, but the planning systems of the nations of the UK display ever-greater difference and nuance. Even the planning system in London is substantively different today from that of the rest of England, being directed in part by the mayor's office, which is a level of strategic oversight no longer exercised in the rest of the country following the revocation of Regional Strategies from 2010 onward. However, London and the rest of England remain subject to the same overall planning legislation and policy framework. Therefore, the "English planning system" is treated as a single entity.

Power and the Scope of Planning

The principal concern in this chapter is with power in the planning process: the power to deliver outcomes through decision making, either by directing change positively, or through an inertia that confirms continuities. Lukes (1974) contends that power is wielded by those individuals or agencies able to make decisions that alter the trajectory of—in this case—development, or choose to do nothing and therefore deliver continuity or other outcomes borne of inaction. Power is exercised by those with choice. It is also relational, in that it will restrain the choices of others, creating a situation in which some agents have power "over" others (Clegg, 1989), who find themselves in a subordinate position. Planning is centrally concerned with the exercise of power, bestowing rights on individuals (e.g. the right to develop land) or restricting those rights. But this power is circumscribed by laws that provide the foundation of the planning system. The scope of planning in England was debated during the Second World War and then set out in the Town and Country Planning Act 1947. Subsequent legislation (including the Localism Act 2011, which we will examine in due course) has not altered the basic approach to planning in England or changed the balance of power in the planning system.

Local authorities had been directed to produce town planning schemes for development in their areas of jurisdiction in 1909, but few did so (Ashworth, 1954). The reason was that they had no actual control over urban change. Development rights remained with private owners, who were able to develop land or alter buildings as they wished, subject to building controls. Some restrictions on these rights were introduced in the 1930s, notably to control ribbon development in 1935, but, in broad terms, the owners of land remained free to profit from the development of their land. Local authority control was limited, and without that control planning powers were extraordinarily weak.

The war prompted a radical rethink of the role of the local state in the control and planning of development. Gordon Cherry (1974) and Andrew Gilg (2005) have produced extremely useful overviews and critiques of comprehensive post-war planning in England. They both highlight the importance of reflection on the likely scale of post-war reconstruction, mixed with a radical social agenda that began to emerge from the late 1930s onward. In terms of planning, debates during the war (which underpinned the Scott, Uthwatt, and Barlow Reports) culminated in a consensus around the need to protect non-urban land, plan for the future distribution of industry, and create a comprehensive planning system through a nationalization of development rights, which would allow the local state to exercise direct control over land use change. This consensus provided a firm foundation for post-war planning, but was made more potent by its alignment with the social objectives of the 1945 Attlee government and its vision of an enlarged system of public services, including a National Health Service and an expansion of public housing provision. The vision of a government more centrally concerned with delivering key public goods (in stark opposition to the Keynesian thinking of the Conservatives) sat well with the nationalization of development rights, and planning came to be seen as part of the radical Beveridge agenda. The New Towns Act 1946 seemed to confirm that development, planned and delivered by the state, should be seen as part of a wider social welfare package.

It was in this context that the Town and Country Planning Act 1947 emerged. It established what came to be known as "comprehensive planning," setting out a requirement for all local authorities in England (and Wales) to produce a land use plan, which would thereafter become the basis for planning control, exercised by elected council members on the advice of officers of the local authority. A key aspect of planning in England is the degree of power and "discretion"—to interpret national policy in a way that is judged locally appropriate and acceptable—wielded by local politicians. Politicians are supported by professional advisors—trained planners who have gained "chartered" status and other local experts—but it is still the politicians who weigh the advice given against other considerations (including pressure to respond in particular ways to political situations) and make the big decisions, sometimes delegating less important decisions to planning officers. The nationalization of development rights in 1947 delivered significant power into the hands of locally elected politicians.

In turn, landowners (whose rights were curtailed) were compensated "once and for all" (Cullingworth & Nadin, 2006, p. 23), and a system of planning permits (permission) was created, operated at first by county councils or county borough councils (covering urban areas). Government, through its local authorities, came to own the development right (except in cases of "permitted" agricultural development) and hence assumed a powerful position within the development process. It became the gatekeeper. Owners suddenly required a "development permit" from their local authority, the receipt of which would re-confer the right to develop. The effective "demarcation" (but not simple "zoning") of areas where housing, commercial, or industrial uses would be permitted created areas of (effectively) retained rights (subject to policy compliance and at the discretion of planning authorities); outside of these demarked areas (indicated on "proposals maps" forming part of the development plans), rights were denied. This created a new spatial reality, of winners and losers and of concentrated land value. The introduction of a comprehensive planning system changed fundamentally the economics of planned development in England and also prompted episodic attempts to capture land-value uplift, from "current use value" to "planning use value" on the receipt of planning permission. National attempts to tax land value uplift eventually evolved into a locally controlled system of procuring affordable housing, and other infrastructure contributions, through the planning system. We return to this issue in later sections.

· But the simple "zoning" of areas for development has never been a feature of comprehensive planning in England. Rather, local authorities assumed two key functions in 1947: development planning and development control. They were tasked to draw up plans in compliance with primary legislation and then take development control decisions that broadly respected those plans. But, unlike zonal planning systems elsewhere in the world, England's comprehensive planning system did not simply stipulate fixed legal criteria that, once met, would allow development to proceed. Rather, aspirations for an area would be described in policy attached to a particular place or, at a more fine-grained scale, a particular parcel of land. Moreover, general area-based policies would articulate a broader development strategy. All of this was to be interpreted by the local authority, which was then able to "judge" whether a particular planning application was right for an area, aligned with broader development aspirations, and offered the best deal in terms of contributing to wider policy objectives. In other words, the granting of planning permission was discretionary (emerging from the local political process outlined above) rather than compliance-based and automatic. Planning authorities wield discretionary power circumscribed by a local interpretation of national planning policy. They have the discretion to grant or not to grant permission, to act to facilitate change, or to block development in support of existing continuities: power in the sense described by Lukes (1974).

But, in the long history of planning in England, other bodies have come to share in that power. The system as constituted in 1947 concentrated power in the hands of local authorities (the counties and borough counties). However, that same power was redistributed to the New Town Development Corporations in some instances after 1946, which were conferred with significant powers of land assembly in order to facilitate the planning and delivery of New Towns. Thereafter, these Development Corporations built new, free standing settlements on their own "municipalized" land, connecting them to existing urban centers for the purpose of planned overspill. But more significant in terms of general planning was the separation of strategic from development planning powers. Governments after the war became increasingly concerned with the strategic direction of development and subregional infrastructure planning. A way needed to be found to join together local plans, and this was eventually achieved through the separation of "structure" from "development" planning. The Labour government's Town and Country Planning Act 1968 envisaged these two activities occurring within the same authority. But, following the party's General Election defeat in 1970, further legislation was introduced in 1971 (another Town and Country Planning Act) and 1972 (a Local Government Act), which handed Structure Plan responsibilities (dealing with county-wide issues and broad priorities, for example in relation to infrastructure) to the counties and dropped development planning to district and borough authorities. Thereafter, strategic decisions were taken at a level higher than development decisions, constraining the development choices of the authority closest to apparent point of impact, as the content of local plans needed to be "in compliance" with the strategic framework provided by these "Structure Plans."

This separation was perhaps a critical moment in the history of planning in England, as it triggered what has become a perennial debate over planning's claim to democratic accountability. In the years after the war, planning decisions were taken by locally elected representatives, directly serving a local electorate, and were not framed by a separate tier of strategic oversight. There was supposed to be a measure of public input into those decisions. The fact that this remained modest and largely underdeveloped for several decades was less problematic than one might imagine, largely because local decision making affecting strategic and developmental outcomes stayed within a single tier and was relatively close to community interest. However, the advent of structure planning in the 1970s sawthe beginning of a drift upward of strategic decision making, and greater distance between direct community interest (in issues of development and development impact) and the level at which representative democracy was exercising its executive power. It started with county-level strategic planning from the 1970s, but by the 1980s loose affiliations of counties had begun to plan at subregional and regional levels (e.g. SERPLAN), and by the late 1990s experiments in regional planning became institutionalized through the creation of Regional Planning Bodies (RPB) in the form of the Regional Assemblies, which began preparing "advisory" regional planning guidance that became a material consideration when drawing up the Structure Plans with which local plans needed to be compliant. Within five years, in 2004, the Structure Plans had been abolished and Regional Spatial Strategies had become England's only strategic planning framework. The race to the top that had started with the 1971/1972 legislation appeared complete and England was left with a planning framework that, to some, appeared increasingly distant from community interest. Much of what was now happening at the level of development planning, especially housing development and the insertion of subregional infrastructure, was being directed at a regional level. And, yet, the power of the regions over development planning was curtailed by county representation and by internal resistance to the imposition of housing targets by central government. Rather than simply distributing targets to the local authorities, regions became the arena for debating these targets; they became melting pots of conflicting opinion and political grandstanding.

Prior to the 2010 General Election, the Labour and Conservative Parties arrived at very different solutions to the regional impasse in planning. Labour decided to strengthen regional planning by moving it from the Assemblies to its Development Agencies, unshackling it politically from the lower tiers; the Conservatives, on the other hand, decided that they would dismantle the regional machinery in its entirety and return to a planning system closer to the post-war settlement, albeit with a larger element of community input. In terms of power over planning decisions, what has been witnessed over the last seventy-plus years in England was a gradual weakening of local authority control as national governments sought to take strategic control over development outcomes, followed by an abrupt return of some powers "to the town halls," which became a rallying call of coalition policy between 2010 and 2015.

Decision Making and the Governance of Urban Planning

However, this is far too simple a descriptor of the contouring of power in English planning. Government has, since 1947, been grappling with the "strategic dilemmas integral to *governing*" (Davies, 2008, p. 11). As well as confronting the issue of strategic oversight and control, it has also been faced with questions of democracy and local involvement. Governing is about more than achieving a desired outcome. It is also concerned with the manner in which decisions are made, or the "art" of government (Foucault, 1991). This concern was supposed to be integral to the design of the planning system in 1947 but became lost during the early years of strong intervention and then forgotten as planning assumed a more regulatory role relative to the growing power of private development interests in later decades (Gilg, 2005); this is a discussion that we return to later in this chapter. By the time of the Skeffington Report in 1969, participation in the planning process was at a low point and now undermining confidence in planning outcomes. However, the rescaling of planning described in the last section continued unabated, compounding the challenges of local accountability and trust. The creation of a tier of structure planning, noted above, pushed large parts of decision making (for example, the allocation of major strategic development) further from local interests, and the strengthening of regional planning at the end of the 1990s extended this distance further. Even by the 1980s, there was a growing sense that planning was being "uprooted" from its local base and decision making was becoming ever more distant from the impact of those decisions. This was one of a number of reasons why the first Thatcher governments were hostile to the idea of planning control: it sought to achieve false social goals, undermined personal freedoms, and needed to be reoriented toward "market support" (Griffiths, 1986, p. 5). The "vivid anti-planning rhetoric" (ibid., p. 3) that defined the 1980s, however, did not survive into the following decade. Quickly, the Major government moved in 1994 to establish a "real governmental locus away from Whitehall" (Cullingworth & Nadin, 2006, p. 58), a move that precipitated the rise of regional planning later in that decade. But it balanced its support for central planning policy and intervention with the rhetoric of "local choice" (Stoker & Young, 1993), a rhetoric that became more audible with the arrival of the first Blair government in 1997. What we see in the 1990s and 2000s is a struggle with those "strategic dilemmas integral to governing" by governments that, unlike the first Thatcher administrations, demonstrated some belief in the value and power of local planning to create sustainable places.

This struggle took the form of a balancing act aimed at delivering housing and key infrastructure (the 1992-based projections of housing growth in England famously predicted that a further 4.4 million extra households would form over the next twenty-five years, which was a considerable step up from previous forecasts) while also restoring a degree of trust in the sensitivity and democratic credentials of the planning system. So, in the 2000s, while the Labour governments were seeking to strengthen the hand of regional planning by scrapping Structure Plans and requiring that Local Development Frameworks (LDFs, Labour's local plans) became compliant with the content of Regional Spatial Strategies (see above), they also embarked on significant local government reforms, ostensibly aimed at putting "communities in control" of the "spatial planning" of services and future infrastructure (Morphet, 2011). They did this by creating Local Strategic

Partnerships comprising key stakeholders from the public, private, voluntary, and community sectors. These partnerships were charged with the drawing up of a community strategy for their local area, which would become a framing document, or "plan of plans" (Morphet, 2004), that would set out future aspirations for planning, development, and service delivery. Land use plans (contained in the local development framework) would henceforth need to be compliant with these community strategies. This, it was suggested, would give communities a shaping hand in future development, empowering them to take control of the local planning system. However, the system created through a series of local government acts during the 2000s became increasingly complex, comprising multiple plans and strategies, which gave the planning system an opaque quality that communities ultimately found to be difficult to engage with (Gallent & Robinson, 2012). Moreover, community representation on the local strategic partnerships was confined to the chairs of official community groups, often bodies established to represent local networks and community councils. These were accused of being disconnected from the communities they sought to represent and failing to give genuine voice to community interests (ibid.). England was washed over by a powerful tide of community rhetoric during the 2000s, but most communities were underwhelmed by government promises and saw instead the growing power of regional planning to determine local outcomes from distant regional offices. This was certainly the experience in southern England (Gallent et al., 2013), where distrust of regional planning reached a zenith by the end of the 2000s.

This failure gave the Conservatives the platform they needed to launch a withering attack on the "steering centrism" of the Labour governments. They were able to portray the key tenets of Labour planning—stronger regional control after 2004 and the removal of ministerial control over major infrastructure applications after 2008, and thereafter the transfer of planning powers to the Regional Development Agencies from 2010—as antidemocratic. Their remedy for all of this lost democracy was a localization of the planning process, involving a dismantling of the regional planning apparatus and a return of power to town halls and to communities, in the form of "neighbourhood planning" (Gallent & Robinson, 2012). Essentially, they would be righting the wrongs of the Labour governments and resolving seventy years of failure in development planning, erasing the post-1968 mistakes and re-establishing the local focus of the post-war years, albeit with substantially strengthened community input into statutory planning.

The election of a Conservative–Liberal Democrat coalition government (the first coalition since the war) seemed to herald a radical departure from the top–down planning of the previous decade. But the reality is that the coalition struggled with the strategic/local dilemma in much the same way as its predecessor. The Conservatives' 2009 Planning Green Paper, "Control Shift," promised a radical rescaling of planning, suggesting that future development planning would be pieced together from local aspirations set out in formalized "community-led plans" and that local plans would reflect these aspirations. Communities would be able to take control of the planning system for the first time since 1947 and shape it according to their own needs. The Conservatives borrowed the term "open source" (Conservative Party, 2010) from the world of software development as a descriptor of this new approach to planning. However, a fracture soon appeared in the government between those wedded to the ideals of local control and decentralization and those who prioritized, first and foremost, the need to deliver major infrastructure projects and deliver a step change in housing growth. When the Localism Act 2011 eventually prescribed the parameters of Neighbourhood Development Planning in England, the power of communities to direct change was heavily circumscribed by the primacy of local plans. All community aspirations, over the level of housing growth, the siting of new homes, and even their design, would need to be in conformity with the local plan. Localism seemed to be fundamentally about the empowerment of local councils, not local communities. And even that level of devolution was tempered by the government's broader aspirations for planning, set out in the National Planning Policy Framework (NPPF). Greg Clark MP, Minister for Decentralisation (until 2012 and Secretary of State for Communities and Local Government from 2015), had previously argued that the choices and empowerment handed communities by Neighbourhood Planning would turn a "nation of NIMBYs into a nation of IMBYs" (wanting development "in their back yards"), because community opposition to development (derided by Kate Barker in 2004 as pure parochialism) had never been opposition to the actual outcomes of planning but to the manner in which planning decisions were taken—behind closed doors and without proper recourse to community interest. But the NPPF seemed to open the door to development, in all its potential forms. The Localism Act and Neighbourhood Planning would require that developers enter into early negotiations with community forums or parish councils, but the NPPF seemed to stack the cards in favor of developers as long as they were able to demonstrate the "sustainability" credentials of their proposals. Neighbourhood Planning in England gives communities a potential platform on which to negotiate some of the details of development with the private sector, but it seems not to alter the fundamental balance of power between private and community interests.

What we have seen in England for the past fifteen years is an attempt to renew a sense of local democracy while achieving strategic development outcomes. This resulted in a dualism in the planning process under Labour, of "communities in control" and stronger regional planning, and a similar dualism under the coalition, of "neighbourhood planning" juxtaposed with the apparent open door to development offered by the NPPF (there have, as yet, been no changes to this arrangement following the election of a Conservative majority government in May 2015). And, throughout this episode, there have been periodic reminders that power remains with the state. Planning decisions are constantly "called in" by the Secretary of State for Communities and Local Government (the Planning Minister), who is often "minded" to approve developments otherwise rejected by local planning committees: a reminder perhaps that in response to "the strategic dilemmas integral to governing," government frequently chooses to exercise its executive power.

In relation to local actors, it is clearly the case that central government is able to exert its will on the planning and development processes. It is also able to devolve powers from the center, to the regions, to local authorities and downward to community and private actors (adjustments to "permitted development rights" in England, freeing private householders from certain planning restrictions is a recent example of this). The history of planning in England could simply be presented as the center bestowing power on the different levels of government, experimenting with alternative institutional arrangements, and demonstrating its ultimate control of development outcomes. This would be a largely false and partial presentation of power in the planning system.

Running parallel with the periodic rescaling of planning control is another narrative, one in which the planning system in England came to assume a more regulatory role relative to the growing power of private development interests after the initial phase of public sector-led reconstruction and New Town Development following the Second World War (Gilg, 2005). The aspiration for planning in 1947 was that it should deliver direct public benefit, in much the same way as the creation of the NHS (National Health Service) and the acceleration of public house building would deliver direct public goods. It would work in tandem with public development (of housing and nationalized industries and infrastructure) and have direct delivery power. The immediate post-war years are sometimes viewed as a golden age for planning in England. It played a delivery role in urban renewal and, as part of the New Towns program, in the master-planning and advancement of major new settlements. Rather than (merely) regulating private activity, planners at the time were working to deliver major areas of planned development and did so (arguably) successfully at places such as Milton Keynes and Stevenage. Planning was a positive and proactive force in rebuilding England, and the rest of the UK, following five years of war. A generation of architect–planners—the successors to Unwin and Abercrombie—was leading on major development schemes, all funded by the taxpayer, and (by the late 1950s) were rebuilding large parts of England's major cities according to the Modernist vision.

But this golden age did not last. Large-scale public housing development was not without its social and environmental problems, and it was also very costly to fund (Holmes, 2006). There was therefore a steep decline in the number of public projects relative to private schemes after the 1960s, and by the 1970s private housing development by a shrinking number of large commercial and residential developers (Wellings, 2006) had become the dominant development model in England. This shift changed fundamentally the role and power of public planning. A system designed to facilitate and deliver urban change was left only with the power to regulate that change. The power to deliver became the power to regulate. And, as private enterprise grew its volume share of development activity, it also expanded its corporate influence, via bodies such as the House Builders Federation (now the *Home* Builders Federation), over the design of planning policy and planning targets. During the 1990s and into the 2000s, this influence was particularly apparent in the arena of regional planning, leading some critics to suggest that both housing targets and locations for future housing growth were being influenced by a handful of large and powerful companies (Valler et al., 2013). But, even in the absence of regional planning today, the corporate influence of the private sector is felt locally and in the design of national policy. The government's recent "red tape challenge" (a move to cut bureaucracy and regulation) and its streamlining of planning policy (Atkinson & Maliene, 2015) are unashamedly "pro-business," not in the sense of nurturing a partnership with the private sector, but rather giving the sector free rein to pursue development opportunities when and where it wishes.

A simple observation at this stage is that public planning has greater potency when it is aligned with the power to deliver development. That alignment existed in 1947 and has since disappeared. The power of planning, in its delivery mode, is most apparent through the New Towns program. Advocates of reinvigorated planning today often argue for a reconstitution of the New Town Development Corporations (or a modern equivalent), with powers of land assembly, as a means of delivering a new generation of garden cities (which all the major political parties have shown tacit support for). Ownership and control over land would give planners direct power over development outcomes. The potency of this type of planning has been demonstrated in the German city of Freiburg, which has become a place of pilgrimage for many disillusioned (or, at least, disappointed) English planners, and was held up by Peter Hall in 2013 as a prime example of what good planning can achieve: a "city of short distances" comprising a diversity of high-quality residential neighborhoods in proximity to jobs and services, brought together through excellent public transport.

But Freiburg is a world away from the average housing development outcome in England. Without control over land (except in a few instances where public land is opened up for private development, often during periods of economic downturn and as a means of kick-starting house building: Madeddu, 2013), planning is confined to a regulatory function. Whether or not development proceeds is down to the deal struck between landowners and aspiring developers. Where there is a public-sector desire to see that development proceed (perhaps in a more fragile market), planning is relegated to the status of bystander, often exerting its influence over the nature and scope of development cautiously, not wishing to jeopardize the progress of a scheme. It will have greater power, however, to shape outcomes where the market is strong and where developers may be more amenable to accepting the influence of local planning by agreeing the delivery of significant planning gains. It was noted earlier that the nationalization of development rights in 1947 resulted in a spatial concentration of land values, generating significant uplift in areas allocated for development. In order to capture this uplift, or "betterment," government imposed a 100 percent "development charge" on the rise in land value from current to planning use. The basic idea was that owners should not benefit from the unearned income generated simply by the granting of planning permission. They would (and should) continue to benefit, however, from the development of their land and from the sale of a developed asset. But, in the fragile and uncertain post-war economic situation, the imposition of this land tax was viewed by many as a brake on essential development and economic growth. The 1947 change/tax was abandoned, as were two further attempts to impose a national tax on betterment before the end of the 1970s: the 1964–1970 "betterment charge" and the 1974–1979 "development land tax." Critics of this form of tax saw it as a further erosion of property rights and also argued that landowners and developers should be seen as partners in the development process, not simply as beneficiaries to be squeezed at every opportunity. It was perhaps no coincidence that governments returned to the land tax question at times of economic downturn, seeking to raise new revenues to counter fiscal austerity. Following the second failed attempt to tax betterment, the national approach started to give ground to local negotiation. Section 52 of the Town and Country Planning Act 1971— updated by Section 106 of the Town and Country Planning Act 1990 —established a mechanism whereby local authorities could enter into agreements with developers to secure "community gains" from the granting of planning permission. Despite criticism of this approach in the 1980s (Barlow & Chambers, 1992) and into the 1990s—with some commentators claiming that it instituted the "buying and selling of planning permission" (Ennis et al., 2002)—it became the primary means of mitigating the costs of development (e.g. the infrastructure costs otherwise borne by the local state) and securing broader gains including a range of contributions toward housing, healthcare, education and so on. The approach has since been set alongside a tariff-based Community Infrastructure Levy (based on a local calculation of future infrastructure costs, and the imposition of a fixed charge per unit or per square meter linked to that calculation), but Section 106 agreements remain the key mechanism for procuring affordable housing contributions through the granting of planning permission. And the amount and value of affordable housing generated in this way is a key indicator of the regulatory power of planning in different market conditions. It was noted above that local planning will have greater power to shape outcomes where the market is strong (and rising) and where developers are more willing to accept the influence of planning by agreeing planning gains. This reality has been demonstrated very clearly in the studies by Tony Crook, Christine Whitehead, and colleagues, during the 2000s. They have shown that by far the largest proportion of community gains from the planning system have been generated in London and the surrounding regions. Far less has been generated in other parts of England (Crook & Monk, 2011). Planning's power in this respect is determined by the market, delivering very particular spatial outcomes and varying levels of planning gain, of course, through the market cycle.

But as well as signaling the variability of local planning's power relative to landowners and developers, the broader land tax question also says much about the corporate influence of the development lobby, alongside major landowners. Planning creates wealth, but not for planners (of course!) and not generally for the communities persuaded to accept additional development (though various incentive schemes have been brought forward in recent years, the most recent being the coalition government's Homes Bonus, with the government promising to match local council tax receipts for homes built above a local authority's plan target). Landowners have been successful in retaining much of that wealth since 1947. They will part with some of it where planning agreements are entered into, but the cost of those agreements will be shared with developers and, in many cases, owners will secure significant returns from the development of their land (thereafter losing a proportion through personal taxation). Who profits from planning and from the development process must surely be an important indicator of where power lies in the planning process; much of that power remains in the private sector, which has successfully resisted all attempts at fairer distribution for more than seventy years. Patterns of landownership—and the power of landowners—in England mean that there is little chance of Freiburg-type developments coming forward any time soon, and also explains why such nostalgia surrounds the New Towns program and its use of Development Corporations with their key powers over land assembly. As noted above, planning has greatest power in its "delivery mode," where there is alignment between regulation and landownership. Although not on the scale of Freiburg, the Prince of Wales's development at Poundbury illustrates what can be achieved where a strong vision combines with control over land and development (Hardy, 2006).

It seems likely that those who reflect today on the power of planning are primarily concerned with its influence over the framing of development decisions. This is certainly the case in England, where the power of planning to deliver change is heavily constrained by landownership, by corporate interest and, to a lesser extent, by community interest and action. Land and corporate influences have been instrumental in shaping the planning framework and in limiting its powers; community interest has become more important as a material and political consideration in local development decisions since the 1970s. This last point has been most strongly and clearly articulated by Rittel and Webber (1973) who have characterized the socio-spatial problems of planning as "wicked" problems, defying resolution in a pluralistic society in which one person's benefit is another's potential loss. Rittel and Webber argued that increasing social complexity makes it very difficult, if not impossible, for planning to pursue a singular public good. Everything is contested and different communities are now looking for government to deliver a diversity of outcomes, suited to particular local situations and needs. This reality, combined with sustained critique of post-war government as distant "administration" (Foucault, 1982) unable to deal with social pluralism, has given impetus to informal community action (Gallent & Ciaffi, 2014) and normative attempts to reconnect to community interests through a rescaling of planning, decreased reliance on representative forms of democracy, and a pervasive "governance shift" (Bailey, 2003). This has certainly happened in England, and accounts for the journey toward localism and neighborhood planning recounted above. Practically, it has resulted in a planning system that is more sensitive to community input, partly because that input has become more audible and partly because local political systems have adjusted in response to a crisis in representative democracy (measured in falling voter turnout), and seek to legitimize outcomes continually rather than at periodic elections.

Although the power of community interest has been constrained by governments' attempts to retain strategic focus (see the earlier discussion on this subject), there have been an increasing number of cases in England of community action defeating major development proposals. One notable example, retold by Hewson (2007), is that of a development proposal at the village of Wye in Kent. The local authority signed a concordat with a landowner-cum-developer (actually, a well-known London university) to build 5,000 houses on the edge of the village. Details of the concordat were leaked to members of the village's parish council, who then went on to mobilize the community—and influential friends of the community—against the development. The proposal was withdrawn within nine months and the village was "saved" (ibid.). Similar community-led actions have become relatively commonplace in recent years, causing a stalling of major development schemes at Stevenage in Hertfordshire (Gallent, 2008) and at numerous other locations in southern England (Haughton & Counsell, 2004). Community action is now more regularly a deciding factor in development outcomes, and many local authorities now acknowledge that decision making behind closed doors is unlikely to ease the path of development. Officers of the local authority responsible for the Wye concordat appear to agree that they "got it badly wrong" (Gallent & Robinson, 2012) and have since opened up their decision making to greater public scrutiny. There has been a noticeable shift toward greater transparency in policy design, and subsequent decision making, since the end of the 1990s, in part triggered by the various local government reforms of the Labour administrations and extended by the coalition's localism agenda. Even if there is not total agreement with Greg Clark's suggestion, noted above, that a more open planning process is likely to lead to greater acceptance of development, the manner of decision making in planning has become increasingly important, especially in a world where information, and misinformation, spreads so easily.

Urban Planning and Land Supply

What does all the above—corporate influence, planning operating in a regulatory mode, and enhanced community interest, meshed together within a new governance reality—mean for the supply of land for development? Land supply, particularly for housing development, has become a perennial debate in England. The planning system is not allocating enough; developers are hoarding too much, profiting from speculation on rising land values rather than house building; and community parochialism, led by a well-housed majority, is constraining both the supply of land and of new homes. These are all regularly voiced concerns underpinning the political debate surrounding housing and house building. Each of these key accusations had been tested almost *ad nauseam*, and the evidence for each has been found to be wanting. Despite often hostile local politics, a great deal of land in England has been allocated for new housing. Developers have in many cases signed option agreements to develop it, but are waiting for the arrival of the local market's "sweet point": when it will be viable to do so, and whether likely returns will satisfy investors. And, although community actors now take greater interest in the land allocated for development, this seems not to have reduced the pace and volume of allocations. The revocation of Regional Strategies, however, does seem to have affected local delivery targets and therefore the allocation of land for future development. When the coalition came to power in May 2010, the incoming Secretary of State moved almost immediately to remove Regional Spatial Strategies by ministerial decree. After various wranglings in the courts, he was judged to have exceeded ministerial powers. Officially, government needed to wait for Parliament to pass its Localism Bill before revocation, following on from necessary sustainability appraisals, could proceed. But, in the meantime, all Chief Planning Officers in England received a letter from London telling them that the intention to revoke the strategies should be treated as a material consideration in all planning decisions, leading many to commence early plan reviews with the aim—in many cases—of revising targets and reviewing allocations made within local plans. Research by Tetlow King Planning on behalf of Policy Exchange (2012) revealed that targets across England fell by nearly 273,000 homes between 2010 and December 2012.

We can conclude from this that planning and the politics guiding the planning system have a huge impact on land supply. National policy is particularly important. A decade before the RSS revocation saga, a stronger emphasis on the use of "previously developed land" for housing (which emerged from the Report of the Urban Task Force, 1999,) set out in planning policy guidance for housing (in the form of a new PPG3 in 2000), prompted a review of many local plans across England, with councils deleting allocations on greenfield sites and trying to replace those allocations with urban infill or land recycling opportunities on former industrial land. In some instances, councils put almost all their allocations on previously developed land, some of which was contaminated and failed ultimately to attract development interest. The sites were neither attractive to the market nor viable. In Stevenage, one of two councils (North Hertfordshire and Stevenage Borough) working together to bring forward an urban extension at Stevenage West withdrew its local plan on the back of the issuing of revised guidance, causing the whole development to stall (the full Stevenage story is retold in the next chapter). Again, these central edicts are important.

But, generally, it is a primary duty of the planning system, and of local authorities, to allocate sufficient land for housing development. The first circular issued on planning for housing, in 1984, stated clearly that *sufficiency* in land supply for housing is planning's top priority. And this has been restated in every new version of planning guidance since that date. Of course, some of the detail has changed and there has been a gradual broadening of policy concerns, to embrace design, affordability, and the mix of housing types. But perhaps the most significant change came in 2006, following on from a 2004 government-commissioned review into housing supply. The Barker Review posited that allocations were insensitive to market realities and housing delivery is constrained where planning is unconcerned with the achievability of development on allocated land. Sufficiency is not enough; planning must concern itself with the deliverability of housing on allocated sites. After 2006 (and the issuing of a new PPG3 in that year), policy emphasis was placed on the responsiveness of planning to market signals, and regional planning was tasked to undertake subregional market analysis as a basis for strategic planning for housing. Furthermore, authorities were required to actively manage the supply of land for housing, maintaining a "rolling supply" and adding new allocations to the existing pot once land was developed. With the exception of the regional focus, these principles were carried forward by the coalition government. The National Planning Policy Framework issued in 2012 tasks planning authorities to "identify and update annually a supply of specific deliverable sites" (Para. 47). Authorities must demonstrate that the identified sites are *available* (free from ownership constraint), *suitable* (free from physical constraint), and *deliverable* (meaning specifically that there is a realistic prospect of the site being viable for development within five years of allocation).

There has been a thirty-year journey in thinking on land supply in England. This began in 1984 with the simple reminder to planning authorities that they should be allocating a sufficient number of sites for development against assessed need. In the 2000s, this focus shifted to embrace responsiveness to the market. Today, emphasis is placed on the likely *viability* of development on allocated land. It is accepted that viability will change through the market cycle, that allocation of a site may not happen at the "sweet point," and that there may need to be a "maturation of circumstances" (Goodchild & Munton, 1985) before development can proceed (in other words, land will remain undeveloped in the planning system for a number of years, such is the nature of local markets). This shift in thinking is reflected in the evolving mechanics of the allocation process and in the roles that different actors, public and private, are now playing in that process. In the 1980s and 1990s, local authorities undertook either "urban capacity" or "land availability" studies. These involved cataloging potential sites for development, discounting obviously unsuitable land, assessing potential ownership constraints, and conferring with private partners on the likely "marketability" of the land: its attractiveness to development interests. But viability of development under different market conditions was not tested. The "marketability" assessment amounted to "best guess" and was undertaken by officers of the local authority, often untrained in any methods of valuation or viability testing. As well as talking to local developers, a range of assessed constraints—ownership, contamination, infrastructure, access, and planning—were simply used as a proxy for viability, without any testing of that viability against possible development briefs, comprising a range of forms of development, housing types, and densities. The process was public sector-dominated and imprecise.

This situation has gradually changed since 2006. A system of "strategic housing land availability assessment"—or SHLAA—emerged from mixed local practice to become at first the preferred and then the mandatory form of pre-allocation assessment. This ten-stage approach, which begins with the sifting of possible sites and ends with an evidence base for *"informing* the 5 year supply of deliverable sites" has viability testing at its core. The local authority must work with partners to estimate the housing potential of each site and to consider when and whether sites are likely to be developed. The Royal Institution of Chartered Surveyors (RICS) has worked with private- and public-sector partners to arrive at guidance on viability testing in planning (RICS, 2012), which can be used by authorities to test development viability during allocations and when negotiating Section 106 agreements (see earlier discussion). Viability has moved to the heart of the allocations process, which means a bigger role for the private sector in determining the distribution of land supply, locally and through representative bodies such as RICS. But others still retain a powerful influence over this process. There is no obligation on landowners to release land for development, therefore ownership constraints may become a determining factor in land supply, even constraining major development sites where owners are unwilling to sell, or hang on to (ransom) strips of land, access across which is essential for development to proceed. Given the high value of land for development use—compared to its agricultural use value—such situations are unusual, but not unheard of.

But it is, of course, local politicians who hold greatest sway over the pattern of land supply, influenced by political and electoral interest. Local council members across England regularly oppose allocations in their own wards, responding to the concerns of their constituents. The SHLAA process delivers only an "evidence base" to inform site allocations; it is still the politicians who decide where land will be opened up. This means that community and political influences are strong, and perhaps stronger still since the revocation of the Regional Strategies. Required compliance between local plans and regional plans meant that the "principle" of strategic development sites could not be contested. Councils were supposed to work toward their delivery. But, in the absence of this strategic steer, councils are free to produce completely independent evidence bases, focusing on local need rather than the strategic, cross-boundary pressures addressed by regional planning. Cooperation across boundaries is still required, but today's framework is generally thought to be weaker than it was when the RSSs were in place (Gallent et al., 2013). The only external pressure on local authorities comes from government-appointed planning inspectors, who are, at Local Plan Inquiries, charged with testing the evidence base produced by local authorities and the sufficiency and viability of planned allocations relative to that base. The government's hand is strong in this process, and the evidence so far is that Inspectors will reject local plans that deal ineffectively with the issue of land supply for new housing.

Overall, the normative planning process has a key role in determining the spatial distribution of land for development, and good planning tends to enjoy the support of government inspectors. The advent of Neighbourhood Planning in England has added a new layer to this process. While local plans continue to define the need for development over the next five years (and beyond), along with the quantum of land that will be required to satisfy that need, some authorities are working with parish councils and neighborhood forums to decide which land will be allocated. Because the local plans retain their primacy in decision making (Neighbourhood Development Plans need to be compliant with them), a spatial vision (setting out whether, for example, development is to be concentrated at urban extensions or distributed to key settlements) will already have been determined, but where the realization of that vision requires development within particular neighborhood jurisdictions (e.g. parishes) the local authority may have the opportunity to devolve some decision making (against the evidence base) to community actors. In the best examples to date in England, communities have worked with planning consultants, landowners and prospective developers to determine where land might be allocated. This rescaling of the processes appears to have worked well in some instances, silencing some Neighbourhood Planning doubters and confirming that the manner of decision making is indeed important in building consensus around necessary development. Still, all this happens in the shadow of hierarchical power: government and local authorities take framing actions that determine planning outcomes, and the private sector—

with its control over land, finances, and other resources—will ultimately determine development outcomes.

There has been a gradual rescaling of planning in England over the last fifteen years. This process was not started by the coalition government, but it took it to a new level. The Labour Party, in opposition, signaled its intention to maintain the coalition's direction of travel if returned to power in 2015, and neither step back from Neighbourhood Planning nor reinstitute regional planning in its previous form. The prospect of a Labour victory in 2015 did not suggest any radical changes to local planning, and the Conservative majority actually achieved appears to mean that decisions over land allocation and supply will remain a matter for local negotiation between public, private, and community actors. Even major developments, perhaps including a new generation of garden cities (with a minimum of 15,000 new homes), will be a matter for local decision making (unless the intervention of a development corporation is deemed necessary). But, while it may be a fairly straightforward task to build consensus around relatively small schemes, major developments will always be contentious. This is why a great many have become stuck in the planning process over the last fifteen years. Localism has not kick-started these major developments. The same conflicts have continued and many schemes—including Stevenage West, examined in the next chapter—seem to have no greater prospect of delivery today than they did five or ten years ago. In instances of conflict, two forces are likely to come into play. The first is the presumption in favor of sustainable development contained in the NPPF, which is likely to support schemes that substantively meet housing needs and can demonstrate a range of sustainability credentials. The second is the Secretary of State. Call-in powers, turning a local refusal into a consent, still provide a powerful riposte to the "strategic dilemmas integral to governing." Despite criticism that the use of such powers runs contrary to the spirit of localism, there seems to have been no reduction in the number of times that the Secretary of State has overturned local development refusals since 2010. Moreover, government likes to remind both the private sector and local authorities, every now and again, that development is both desirable and essential.

It will also support that development through the distribution of capital funding to pay for necessary infrastructure and transport investments. This now generally comes from the government's Growing Places Fund, with a budget determined by the periodic Comprehensive Spending Reviews. Specific funding for education or health can be provided from departmental budgets, as part of capital investment programs. And, yet, finding the resources to fund the transport and other infrastructure necessary for development to go ahead is never easy. Much of the responsibility rests with the local authority, which will need to calculate the costs of that infrastructure and seek contributions through the Community Infrastructure Levy (CIL) and on-site negotiations based on Section 106 agreements. The problem then is that these contributions are payable only when development has been completed. Therefore, it is local authorities that will need to forward fund infrastructure through local revenue receipts, government capital funding, and anticipated developer contributions. The required up-front funding can be borrowed, with the debt then serviced from future CIL or Section 106 contributions. In some situations, developers will offer up-front investment in some key infrastructure (if matched funding from the public sector is made available) in order to allow development to proceed. During the preparation of the South East England Regional Spatial Strategy in the mid-2000s, the consultants Roger Tym and Partners calculated that a £38,260,000 investment in infrastructure would be needed for every 1,000 new homes to be delivered (Roger Tym and Partners, 2005, p. ii). This included the cost of all additional blue-light services, education, health care, and newly arising demand for affordable housing and transport. The transport component alone was £21,400,000. A couple of years later, the 2007 Comprehensive Spending Review allocated £1.7 billion for all of the government's major growth areas and growth points over a three-year period. Assuming the government achieved its then target delivery of 240,000 homes per annum, this would mean capital funding for infrastructure of just over £2,350 per dwelling (assuming all homes in all areas and all development contexts attracted the same funding), leaving a per-dwelling shortfall of roughly £36,000, to be borrowed and then recouped from planning contributions and general revenue sources.

Even in a strong market, the need to procure significant contributions toward infrastructure from the planning process would have affected the location of development, confining it to the most profitable places and requiring cross-subsidy for development elsewhere. In a weaker market, far greater central investment is needed in infrastructure if development is to proceed. In many instances, a falling market will mean that developers seek the renegotiation of Section 106 agreements (now possible under the Growth and Infrastructure Act 2013), attempting to maintain basic viability by reducing planning costs. This may be possible where development comprises small infill schemes not requiring any significant additional investment in enabling infrastructure. But major schemes may become stuck in the same falling market, as any renegotiation of Section 106 contributions would threaten investment in the new access roads, and so on, that would make the development possible. There would simply not be enough value in the land to realize the development without significant up-front public investment.

Planning has a regulatory, framing power in the development process. But this power is circumscribed by market conditions. It was noted above that the power of planning, in its regulatory mode, is greatest in a rising market. This is when development planning, operated primarily by local authorities, has greatest influence. The prospect of running a significant profit gives momentum to development; owners and developers will work with the planning system's objectives of procuring affordable housing and achieving enhanced design quality—objectives repeated in all recent planning guidance in England—in situations where development remains viable: that is, where there is enough value in the development to deliver these objectives *and* make money.

But planning's influence over the quantity and price of housing in England is less easy to assess. House prices have risen rapidly over the last thirty years. England has experienced the steepest price rises, and greatest volatility in prices, of any country in Europe (Cooper et al., 2013). Critics of the system argue that planning has constrained land supply in areas of greatest need and demand, particularly in London and southern England. Price pressure has then rippled out to the rest of the country. Statistics show that house prices for first-time buyers in London are 7.5 times greater than earnings (Nationwide, 2013). Few people would deny the existence of a housing affordability crisis in London. There are affordability pressures across the whole London metropolitan area (with only a few "affordable locations"). These pressures then extend to commuter-belt towns and villages, many of which are washed over, or bounded, by London's greenbelt. Other more distant towns, including Oxford and Cambridge, have their own greenbelts to contend with. Although there is land in the system for development, across England as a whole there appears to be a shortage of developable land in the south and this magnifies price inflation in the general context of high housing demand, driven by domestic and overseas investment pressure. There may be a case for reviewing planning constraint —particularly greenbelt boundaries—in some instances, and this is currently happening. But is planning solely responsible for rising house price pressures and for the unaffordability in the south? Danny Dorling (2014) has recently argued that England has more than enough housing for its population, but a significant portion of that housing has been swallowed up by investors—domestic and international—and now sits empty, much of it on the banks of the Thames in London. Over the last decade, thousands of riverside apartments have been built on the Thames, from Fulham down to, and beyond, the Isle of Dogs. Other luxury areas away from the river—in Westminster, Kensington and Chelsea, Hammersmith, and now in less likely parts of north London—have also become destinations for high-end development and investment in existing property. It has also been argued, though empirical evidence is scarce, that many apartments on the Thames are now merely "piles of safe deposit boxes" for international investors, for the laundering of "dirty Russian money" and for "Chinese gambling" on rising property values (Rees, 2014). Planning authorities should perhaps have acted sooner to deal with this problem, granting fewer permissions for luxury development and insisting on a great many smaller apartments, suited to the needs of London workers. But this is not an easy nut to crack. These developments generated significant planning contributions; some were used, off site, to develop affordable housing in other parts of London. Other contributions were used to pay for infrastructure upgrades, the irony being that the upgrades were supposed to address transport and education needs, and so on, in areas where few people (i.e. the investors) might actually live. Simon Jenkins recently observed in the Evening Standard that Westminster once had a serious parking problem. Residents had hoped that the council would find ways to get rid of the cars. But, instead, it got rid of the residents (Jenkins, 2014).

Planning—the national framework and local implementation—affects land supply and property prices. It may not allocate enough land for development in areas of greatest demand; or, when it does allocate, development may be contested, causing significant delay to the introduction of new housing supply to areas experiencing high demand. The planning system has not always been responsive to market pressures, often focusing in the past on the absolute scale of allocations rather than their spatial logic, relative to the contours of the market. This has changed in the last few years and there is now greater concern for the achievability of development. However, after five years of relative economic stagnation, England's housing bubble has started to inflate again. Prices in London rose by 18.2 percent in the year to mid-2013, slowing to 11.3 percent to mid-2015, according to the ONS. But, despite yearly fluctuations, Oxford Economics has predicted a doubling of house prices in the next fifteen years, bringing the London average to £1 million (Elliot, 2015). It is too early to say whether market-responsive planning will be able to vent this growing pressure. The construction industry needs to regain the capacity lost during the crisis years, but, much more importantly, it needs to be acknowledged that this is no normal bubble. It is centered on a world city, generally regarded as a safe haven for international investment at a time of political and social upheaval across much of the Middle East and the former Soviet Union. There is a steady flow of investment into London, which will continue to push up prices and drive a broader housing crisis, irrespective of local planning responses.

Conclusions: Power and Influence in Planning and Development

This chapter has reflected on the scope and evolution of planning in England, unpacking a seventy-year narrative in which there have been key shifts in the locus of power and an extension of local democracy. At the beginning of this period, planning was operating in a delivery mode; it was leading urban change. But, midway through, it switched to a regulatory mode as the volume of direct public investment was eclipsed by private development. In this regulatory mode, the key power of planning has been to lever public goods from the development process, a power derived from its control over development rights but which diminishes during low points in the economic cycle. Regulatory mode planning in England is strongest in rising markets.

Over the same period, top–down government has gradually been substituted by more localized patterns of governance. On the one hand, an up-scaling of planning began with the division into development and structure planning and then continued with the institution of formal regional planning. On the other hand, parallel down-scaling pressure began in the 1970s with growing concern for social pluralism and planning's failure to connect with diverse communities. This pressure precipitated a general governance shift, which came to embrace planning as an important tool for achieving place- and community-specific social and environmental goals. From the 1990s onward, successive governments attempted to connect to local aspiration while maintaining a focus on broad strategic goals. Neighbourhood Planning in England is the latest of these attempts.

As well as elucidating this broader narrative, this chapter also unpacked some of the key features of planning in England. In terms of the *scope of urban planning*, it has shown that:

1. Despite the transition to regulatory-mode planning, elected local authorities retain strong discretionary control over planning outcomes. This control is framed by national policy and sometimes limited by central government interventions. A rescaling of planning to embrace neighborhood ambition suggests some loss of power from local authorities, but the latter's plans retain primacy in the local planning process. There is evidence, in very recent development planning practice (e.g. in the allocation of land for development) of the public sector devolving decision making to community groups; and also, in the context of development planning that is more sensitive to the market, of a sharing of power with private-sector partners. There are early signs that rescaled development planning (resulting from the revocation of regional strategies and a new Neighbourhood Planning framework) could result in a different manner of decision making, and a different way of exercising power, which could calm some conflicts and result in the more regular achievement of consensus-based outcomes. But, ultimately, most development outcomes are delivered by the private sector and all are determined by market conditions.

In terms of decision making and the governance of urban planning:

2. The switch from a post-war delivery mode to an eventual regulatory mode has changed the balance of power in planning. Planning is less potent a force for urban change when it is not allied with landownership. The New Town Development Corporations possessed powers that are now the envy of many in England's planning community. Similar powers are retained elsewhere in Europe and have helped planning in cities such as Freiburg deliver comprehensive urban change that England's "comprehensive planning system" is unable to emulate. That is not to say that government in England does not have significant power to alter planning and development outcomes. Despite a recent

localization and down-scaling of the system, central government–in the guise of the Secretary of State—often steps in to force particular outcomes. Government is able to influence all stages of the planning process, from plan making to development control. Recent changes to the planning framework in England—set out in the National Planning Policy Framework—potentially strengthen the hand of development interests in planning appeals and plan reviews, giving developers the opportunity to argue that development in almost any form is "sustainable" and should be approved. The transition to Neighbourhood Planning in England appears to give communities greater influence over these same processes, but that influence is circumscribed by the Local Plan. Neighbourhood Planning devolves *responsibility* to communities to work with the local authority toward the delivery of its Core Strategy. If that Strategy allocates additional housing in, for example, a particular parish or defined urban neighborhood, then the parish council or Neighbourhood Forum must work with the authority on the detail of the allocation and thereafter with developers on shaping their proposals for specific sites. The public gains some influence, but also a great deal of additional *responsibility*; although arguably within a far more transparent decision-making process.

And, finally, in terms of urban planning and land supply:

3. Planning has a key responsibility for supplying land for development though a local allocations process. That responsibility was established in primary legislation in 1947, but it was not until 1984 that it was set out in policy guidance (in the form of a government circular) to local authorities. They were tasked to provide sufficient land for housing through the planning process. For the next two decades, authorities were preoccupied with the overall level of allocations and there was often inadequate concern for the achievability of development on allocated land. This has changed and authorities must now test the viability of allocations. The normative planning process is, however, used only to deliver an evidence base in support of decision making and it is local politicians who take land allocation decisions. These allocations will be influenced by community feeling, perhaps by pressure from landowners, and by the input of development interests. The latter will have a corporate influence over national policy determining land supply and over local estimates of the achievability of development at specific locations. The same set of interests will influence changes of land use, planning applications and the detailing of schemes, including development intensity, although intensity (and density) will be largely determined by calculations of viability. The recent NPPF makes it clear that achievable density is a matter for the local market, which is a departure from previous policy guidance, which always maintained that

density aspirations should be set within local plans. At the present time, as England's economy returns to stronger growth, there is political pressure to support development. But although the NPPF is "pro-growth" and pro-development, local authorities face great challenges in funding the infrastructure to enable development and support growth, which is largely achieved through local funding sources including the procurement of developer contributions. And, finally, planning has a significant impact on land supply and property prices, through the normative allocations process and the political decisions that follow.

But, in England today, high prices rippling out from London need to be seen not only as a consequence of local planning decisions (framed by national policy), but also a result of the city's attractiveness to domestic and international investment. London has a dual housing market—one for investors and one for homebuyers—but this is not reflected in the planning system or in the way land is released for development. The safeguarding of private property rights (if not development rights) makes it impossible to draw a distinction, but at least this reality reminds us that not all of England's housing problems are on the supply side, or resolvable by planning.

References

Ashworth, W. (1954). *The Genesis of Modern British Planning*. London: Routledge and Kegan Paul.
Atkinson, I. & Maliene, V. (2015). Challenges of English Town and Country Planning Policies: Regeneration and Sustainable Communities. In E. Hepperle, R. Dixon-Gough, R. Mansberger, J. Paulsson, F. Reuter, & M. Yilmaz (Eds.) *Challenges for Governance Structures in Urban and Regional Development*. Zurich: vdf Hochschulverlag AG an der ETH Zürich, pp. 235–249.
Bailey, N. (2003). Local strategic partnerships in England: The continuing search for collaborative advantage, leadership and strategy in urban governance. *Planning Theory and Practice*, 3, 443–457.
Barlow, J. & Chambers, D. (1992). *Planning Agreements and Affordable Housing Provision*. University of Sussex, UK: Centre for Urban and Regional Research.
Cherry, G. (1974). *The Evolution of British Town Planning*. Leighton Buzzard, UK: Leonard Hill.
Clegg, S. (1989). *Frameworks of Power*. London: Sage.
Cooper, C., Orford, S., Webster, C., & Jones, C. B. (2013). Exploring the ripple effect and spatial volatility in house prices in England and Wales: Regressing interaction domain cross-correlations against reactive statistics. *Environment and Planning B: Planning and Design*, 40(5), 763–782.
Conservative Party. (2009). *Control Shift: Returning Power to Local Communities*. London: Conservative Party.
Conservative Party. (2010). *Open Source Planning: The Conservative Planning Green Paper*. London: Conservative Party.
Crook, T. & Monk, S. (2011). Planning gains, providing homes. *Housing Studies*, 26(7–8), 997–1018.

Cullingworth, B. & Nadin, V. (2006). *Town and Country Planning in the United Kingdom* (14th ed). London: Routledge.
Davies, J. S. (2008). Double-devolution or double-dealing? The local government white paper and the Lyons review. *Local Government Studies*, 34(1), 3–22
DCLG. (2012). *National Planning Policy Framework*. London: DCLG.
Dorling, D. (2014). *All that is Solid: The Great Housing Disaster*. London: Allen Lane.
Elliott, L. (2015, May 14). London House Prices Could "Double in the Next 15 Years to £1m." *The Guardian*.
Ennis, F., Healey, P., & Purdue, M. (2002). *Negotiating Development: Rationales and Practice for Development Obligations and Planning Gain*. London: Routledge.
Foucault, M. (1982). The subject and power. *Critical Inquiry*, 8(4), 777–795.
Foucault, M. (1991). Governmentality, translated by R. Braidotti and revised by C. Gordon. In G. Burchell, C. Gordon, & P. Miller (Eds.) *The Foucault Effect: Studies in Governmentality*. Chicago, IL: University of Chicago Press, pp. 87–104.
Gallent, N. (2008). Strategic-local tensions and the spatial planning approach in England. *Planning Theory and Practice* 9(3), 307–323.
Gallent, N. & Ciaffi, D. (Eds.) (2014). *Community Action and Planning: Contexts, Drivers and Outcomes*. Bristol, UK: Policy Press.
Gallent, N. & Robinson, S. (2012). *Neighbourhood Planning: Communities, Networks and Governance*. Bristol, UK: Policy Press.
Gallent, N., Hamiduddin, I., & Madeddu, M. (2013). Localism, down-scaling, and the strategic dilemmas confronting planning in England. *Town Planning Review*, 84(5), 563–582.
Gilg, A. (2005) *Planning in Britain: Understanding and Evaluating the Post-War System*. London: Sage.
Goodchild, R. N. & Munton, R. J. C. (1985). *Development and the Landowner: an Analysis of the British Experience*. London: George Allen & Unwin.
Griffiths, R. (1986). Planning in retreat? Town planning and the market in the eighties. *Planning Practice & Research*, 1(1), 3–7.
Hall, P. (2013). *Better Cities, Better Lives: How Europe Discovered the Lost Art of Urbanism*. London: Routledge.
Hardy, D. (2006). *Poundbury: The Town that Charles Built*. London: Town and Country Planning Association.
Haughton, G. & Counsell, D. (2004). *Regions, Spatial Strategies and Sustainable Development*. London: Routledge.
Hewson, D. (2007). *Saved: How an English Village Fought for Its Survival, and Won*. Leicester, UK: Troubador.
Holmes, C. (2006). *A New Vision for Housing*. London: Routledge.
Jenkins, S. (2014, March 25). Only a New Tax Will Prevent this Being a Ghost Town. *The Evening Standard*.
John, P. (1990). *Recent Trends in Central-Local Government Relations*. London: PSI.
Lukes, S. (1974). *Power: A Radical View*. Basingstoke, UK: Macmillan.
Madeddu, M. (2013). Housing quality and the rescue of failed private housing schemes in England: a policy review. *Journal of Housing and the Built Environment*, 28(3), 567–578.
Morphet, J. (2004). *RTPI: Scoping Paper on Integrated Planning*. London: Royal Town Planning Institute.

Morphet, J. (2011). *Effective Practice in Spatial Planning*. London: Routledge.
Nationwide. (2013). House Price Index: 2013 Reports and Data. Available at: www.nationwide.co.uk/about/house-price-index/headlines, accessed on Feb 28, 2015).
Planning Resource. (2014, April 8). Miliband to Pledge "Radical" Devolution to Towns and Cities. *Planning Resource Online.* Available at: www.planningresource.co.uk/article/1289311/miliband-pledge-radical-devolution-towns-cities, accessed on February 28, 2015.
Rees, P. W. (2014, May 31). Londoners "Priced Out" of Housing Market: Interview with the BBC. Available at: www.bbc.co.uk/news/uk-england-london-27628579, accessed on February 28, 2015.
RICS. (2012). *Financial Viability in Planning—RICS Guidance Note*. London: RICS.
Rittel, H. W. & Webber, M. M. (1973). Dilemmas in a general theory of planning. *Policy Sciences*, 4(2), 155–169.
Roger Tym & Partners. (2005). *South East Plan: Regional Assessment of Urban Potential—Stage Two*. London: Roger Tym & Partners.
Skeffington Report. (1969). *Report of the Committee on Public Participation in Planning: People and Planning*. London: HMSO.
Stoker, G. & Young, S. (1993). *Cities in the 1990s: Local Choice for a Balanced Strategy*. Harlow, UK: Longman.
Tetlow King Planning. (2012). *Updated Research on the Impact of the Impending Revocation of Regional Strategies on Proposed and Adopted Local Housing Targets across England*. Research prepared for Policy Exchange. London: Tetlow King Planning.
Urban Task Force. (1999). *Towards a Strong Urban Renaissance*. London: UTF.
Valler, D., Tait, M., & Marshall, T. (2013). Business and planning: A strategic-relational approach. *International Planning Studies*, 18(2), 143–167.
Wellings, F. (2006). *British Housebuilders: History and Analysis*. London: Blackwells.

5 Delivering New Homes on Major Development Sites in England

Introduction

The previous chapter had two substantive foci. The first was the development over recent decades of planning in England and important changes in the *power and scope of planning* (from 1947 onward and the transition away from a system vested with core responsibility for delivering development to one that exercises power largely through regulation), the evolving *governance arrangements for urban planning* (and periodic rescaling, the most recent episode being the turn to localism), and the ways in which planning has dealt with the issue of *land supply*. The second was planning for housing and how power shifts, governance arrangements, and land supply affect housing outcomes in terms of supply and prices. These two foci were set within a single narrative in which the power of planning to deliver direct outcomes (by framing and facilitating public-sector projects, including post-war urban renewal and New Towns) gave way to a regulatory power.

It was shown that planning has both land use and spatial aspects; it is concerned with regulation and control of development and with broader spatial policy and outcomes. In its land-use aspect, regulatory power is about the granting and denying of development permissions and procuring public goods (through value-capture mechanisms) from the planning/development process. In its spatial aspect, it is a power to facilitate and coordinate urban transformations, working with multiple actors to deliver major infrastructure and place-shaping. In the final sections of the previous chapter, we alluded to a housing crisis in England that can be partly, but not entirely, attributed to tensions in the planning system affecting housing supply. That crisis has many drivers, with significant demand pressures (underpinned by demographic trends and a tax structure that incentivizes arguably excessive investment in housing—see below) coming together with a supply shortage to cause sharply rising prices, especially in London and the wider southeast. It is in these locations that housing supply targets (set out in the London Plan) have been regularly missed and where housing investment pressures are greatest.

Planning in its regulatory mode seems to have failed to facilitate the delivery of enough housing to meet need and market demand. And this supply shortage, as Kate Barker (2014, pp. vii–viii) has recently noted, has "exacerbated some underlying problems." Barker attributes undersupply to opposition to housing in areas, especially the southeast, where economic activity is now concentrated but where many local authorities are failing to "produce up-to-date plans." Regulatory and political obstacles have of course been made worse by the financial crisis, by falling land values (causing some developments to stall), by the loss of many small and medium-sized building firms, and by a weakening of the "skills and materials base" for the house building industry (ibid., p. viii). Prices have risen, creating a "big incentive for those who can afford it to invest in housing, while others get left further and further behind" (ibid., p. ix).

Edwards (2015) highlights a number of drivers for the current situation, which predate and postdate the recent financial crisis. The loss of "non-commodity" (public or social) housing from the 1980s onward precipitated far greater reliance on private enterprise to satisfy all housing needs and demands. The expectation that the market would provide has proved ever more unrealistic over the last thirty years. It is currently delivering 124,000 new homes annually (DCLG Live Table 209) against newly arising demand for 220,000 (DCLG 2012-based Household Projections). Many in the industry now believe that this is its maximum capacity and that speculative house building by volume producers needs to be augmented by other forms of delivery: SMEs (some of which were lost in the recent crisis—see above) and self-builders working with smaller sites and direct public house building on a scale that has not been seen since the 1960s. Rising demand is exceeding industry capacity because of both demographic pressures (unforeseen in the 1980s but which really set in during the 1990s, driven by the trend toward smaller households and international migration fueled by the expansion of the EU) and of "asset accumulation" becoming an obsession (ibid.) for domestic and international investors. More and more money is being pumped into housing because of both its highly favorable tax treatment (see also Barker, 2014). Local council tax is extremely low relative to current values, as rates are based on property valuations that are more than twenty years old. Capital Gains Tax (CGT) is not charged on the unearned income from price inflation on first homes, and the way in which Inheritance Tax (IHT) is calculated and paid means that there is significant intergenerational transfer of housing wealth. The tax treatment of housing is critically important: it encourages investment in housing over other forms of investment, with knock-ons for the wider economy, and it incentivizes trade-up (asset accumulation) through the market irrespective of household need. Both the undertaxed pot of private wealth invested in England's housing stock and housing demand are growing, while supply is failing to keep pace.

Yet, while the financial drivers of the market are undoubtedly important, how much new housing is being built is another crucial part of the jigsaw. Edwards (2015) notes that local planning processes and patterns of landownership (affecting value capture and infrastructure investment) are as critical to housing supply as broader capacity issues in the house building industry. Indeed, housing supply has played a major part in what has become an urgent social and political problem in England. We alluded, in the previous chapter, to numerous barriers to housing supply, including the following:

- The withdrawal of direct state investment in housing and the demise of major public house building projects from the 1960s onward.
- Difficulty in capturing the value uplift on large potential housing sites in private ownership owing to the failure of different land and development charges (and the demise of public sector-led New Town projects) and the piecemeal approach based on planning obligations, leading to considerable difficulty in delivering the infrastructure needed to catalyze major development.
- The uprooting of planning in the 1990s from its local base, and growing opposition from then onward to imposed housing targets (and, more generally, to the manner in which strategic planning decisions are taken).
- Opposition to speculative house building, partly because of the monotony of much of it (owing to routinized building processes and standardized products aimed at capturing the benefits of economies of scale), partly because of the difficulties in delivering necessary infrastructure and fear of excessive pressure on existing services, and partly because of concerns among nearby home owners that high-volume new-builds would threaten existing property values.
- Opposition rooted in the belief that private interests (speculators and landowners) benefit disproportionately from development that then delivers insufficient public gain.
- Inconsistencies in policy approaches and planning frameworks (and some sudden changes) resulted in a heightened sense of regulatory risk (e.g. the turn away from greenfield land allocations in the 1990s and the revocation of regional strategies in the 2010s).
- Historic misalignment between closeted planning processes and market signals, leading to the allocation of land for housing in some curious locations and a lack of concern for the viability and achievability of development. In short, a planning system lacking commercial awareness.
- Key challenges for strategic sites owing to center-local and region-local tensions and critical difficulties in working across jurisdictional boundaries (i.e. between local authorities). Cross-boundary working has been a key challenge, especially for major housing development (Hamiduddin & Gallent, 2012), and expresses deeper political tensions in many areas.
- Planning that is unresponsive to market shifts, with many smaller housing sites becoming "stuck" during the last five years because of planning obligations (requests for infrastructure and affordable housing

- contributions) that do not fit the changed economic reality and were difficult (until the Growth and Infrastructure Act 2013) to renegotiate.
- But, more broadly, such renegotiation of key infrastructure is not possible for large sites where that infrastructure is critical to the progress of a scheme. The real problem in those instances seems to be that value uplift was not adequately captured up front, when land was sold, and therefore doubts over infrastructure persisted, causing the developments to stall.

Generally, planning can impact negatively on housing supply where decisions are oriented to addressing a political situation rather than the actual need for housing. Planning is contested and private landowners have unreasonable expectations of retaining a high proportion of the value uplift generated by planning consent, significantly reducing what is available to pay for infrastructure. This in itself can cause developments to stall. The local environment for planning professionals is not always a happy one. With their powers weakened during recent decades (see the previous chapter), their ambition can also be curtailed, and they may lack the capacity (because of underfunding and government cuts) to dedicate sufficient time to the driving forward of major housing schemes, and it is development "at scale" that is needed if housing supply is to significantly increase.

In this chapter, our aim is to exemplify how these barriers undermine efforts to accelerate housing supply using three case study sites. Although these are all immensely important sites in southern England (receiving a considerable amount of media and political attention), individually they are unable to illustrate the full range of planning challenges; but, taken together, they provide important insights into all the barriers listed above, showing how these develop and sometimes take on an intractable quality.

The Housing Crisis and Major Sites

The fate of major sites, and their importance, needs to be understood in the context of an evolving housing crisis in England centered on London—where prices are currently rising at more than 20 percent per annum—and the wider southeast. There have been many housing crises of one type or another in England over the last hundred years, linked to economic cycles, migration, and two world wars. At different times, the demand for housing has far outstripped available supply, usually triggering a drive to build more public ("council") housing. This was the answer to the supply/demand mismatch for much of that hundred-year period, but not after 1980. Major public investment in housing, which had begun in earnest with post-war reconstruction and the New Towns, was replaced with a neoliberalism that favored market responses to housing needs and demand, and cross-sector innovation to deliver the "affordable housing" needed for the anticipated minority of households unable to access home ownership and whose needs could not be met within a revitalized private rented sector. With public housing all but obliterated (nothing new was built and the existing stock was gradually privatized), the regulatory power of planning was called upon to procure affordable housing—usually to be managed by a voluntary sector comprising a range of housing associations, trusts, and societies (Cope, 1999)—through local agreements with the developers of private schemes. The ambition to "innovate" affordable housing solutions in this way was set out in 1987 (HM Government, 1987) and the mechanisms for doing so in 1991 and 1992 (Department of the Environment, 1991, 1992).

The 1980s had seen a major shift in the housing system, away from public-sector provision to far greater reliance on private enterprise, increasingly dominated by a small number of "volume" producers (Wellings, 2006). The decade ended with a recession, further restructuring of the private housing industry (due to the bankruptcy or acquisition of many smaller companies) and a new approach to providing affordable housing, based not on public subsidy but on negotiation with the private sector. The housing system had changed and, in hindsight, it had lost much of its previous capacity. That change coincided with major social shifts revealed in the 1992-based housing projections (Breheny, 1996). These pointed to a sharp reduction in average household size and a commensurate increase in the number of households expected to form in England over the next twenty-five years. Political debate refocused on how the private sector would step up to the challenge of meeting increased demand and how it might be supported by the planning system in general, and eventually by facilitating development at scale.

However, throughout the 1990s housing supply failed to keep pace with newly arising demand, prompting debate on all aspects of planning's treatment of the housing question, from strategic oversight (through

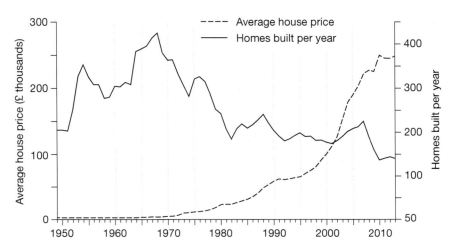

Figure 5.1 House Prices and Houses Built in England

regional planning) to local processes leading to the allocation of land for development and the regulatory costs being imposed on private enterprise, affecting site viability and leading to delay. Toward the end of the decade, and following a change of government in 1997, there was a growing appetite for strategic development at scale to be delivered in the form of new settlements and urban extensions, to be framed by stronger regional planning. The impetus for this approach grew in the 2000s. House prices continued to rise sharply, underpinned by supply and demographic fundamentals and by a rising tide of domestic and foreign investment in the London housing market. Between 2000 and 2007, house prices rose constantly. Between 2007 and 2011/12, they fell back in some parts of the country but remained flat in London. After 2011/12, prices continued on their upward curve.

The appetite for strategic development at scale can be seen as one component of a broader narrative. Because of overinvestment in housing (which is now viewed by some observers as *the* fundamental driver of a much more pervasive social crisis; see Dorling, 2014), the build-out of major development sites during the 2000s would not, on its own, have resolved the supply dilemma or general crisis of housing affordability facing England (see Figure 5.2). "Stuck sites" (Hall, 2014; Hall & Ward, 2014) are not failed solutions to the housing crisis, but the inability to deliver housing at scale in the 2000s must be seen as part of a wider policy failure (stretching from planning to the tax system) and one of the multiple causes of the current situation.

Strategic Planning and Major Sites

The various plans, policies, and initiatives forming and dissolving during the 2000s have been reviewed many times over. Useful overviews are provided by Swain et al. (2013) and Allmendinger (2011). The general narrative is this: regional planning enjoyed a renaissance in England during the 1990s, with new regional governance structures being established first by the Conservative government led by John Major between 1992 and 1997, and then the first Labour government led by Tony Blair between 1997 and 2001; plans for major housing development at strategic sites emerged from the new interest in strategic spatial planning. In the wider southeast, sites for concentrated development to the north of London, in the Thames Gateway, and in Kent were contained in RPG9 (Baker & Wong, 2013). These were given weight by a broader government strategy published in 2003 to address housing overspill and undersupply in southern England, and market restructuring and failure in the Midlands and north. The "Communities Plan" was championed by the Deputy Prime Minister, John Prescott, and published from his office. Four major "Growth Areas" were designated —Milton Keynes and South Midlands, London–Stansted–Cambridge (the M11 Corridor), the Thames Gateway, and Ashford (Office of the Deputy Prime Minister, 2003, p. 54)—which reflected previous regional planning

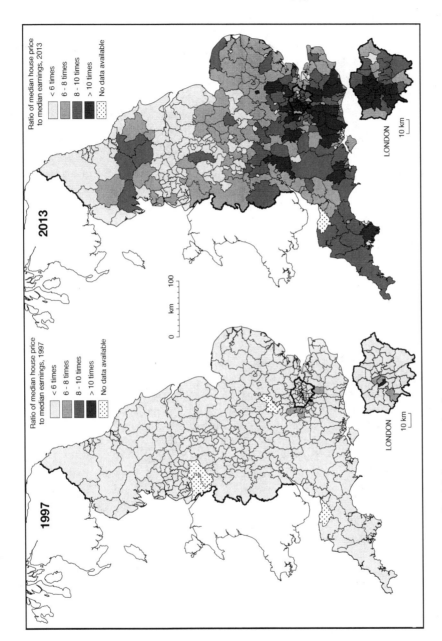

Figure 5.2 Housing Affordability in England

ambitions to rejuvenate the Thames Gateway and concentrate housing at key transport nodes just beyond the Metropolitan Green Belt. All of the designated Growth Areas contained housing sites with complex prior planning histories. The aim of the Communities Plan was to concentrate effort and resources on those sites, sometimes by setting up "special delivery vehicles" and also by making regional development funds (for infrastructure upgrading) available to the Growth Areas. More broadly, government sought to bring about a step change in housing supply—at the Growth Areas and many other "Growth Points" around the country—through concerted and concentrated effort.

But actual housing delivery at those sites has fallen well short of expectation. The broader reasons for this were suggested above. How key challenges around infrastructure, community opposition and politics, policy uncertainty, local-center tensions, landownership, and assembly all played out at actual sites is the focus of the next part of this chapter.

Case Study Sites

The three case studies presented here have each been controversial in different ways and have presented local planning with a variety of challenges. They represent two broad types of development site: urban extension onto greenfield land and the regeneration of ex-industrial land. They were selected to represent a broad range of development challenges and because they share many similarities with comparable sites found across England. Although these all have long site histories, in their recent manifestations they share a common root in either Structure Planning or Regional Planning from the 1990s. The principle of development at Stevenage West—the first of the sites examined—was set out in the 1998 Hertfordshire Structure Plan, being a county-level response to growing housing need in the area and reflecting a desire to concentrate development, rather than disperse it across the county, parts of which are within London's Metropolitan Green Belt. But, like the sites at Ashford and Ebbsfleet—the second and third cases—the principle of concentrating development along the M11 corridor was set out in Regional Planning Guidance (and in the Regional Spatial Strategy after 2004: see Baker & Wong, 2013) and thereafter in the 2003 Communities Plan. In the same plan, Ashford was said to be the "gateway to Europe," being situated on the high-speed rail link that was then due to open in 2007 (Office of the Deputy Prime Minister, 2003, p. 55). The Borough Council and its partners had identified capacity for at least 31,000 new homes by 2031, delivery of which would be dependent on building a new junction on the M20, receiving funding for town center redevelopment and regeneration, and dealing with issues of water supply and flood management. And, finally, the Ebbsfleet development, at the heart of the Kent Thameside, received outline planning permission in 1998; this was envisaged as a scheme "based upon mixed use, high density living with intensification of activities around the station [sitting

England: Major Housing Development Sites   123

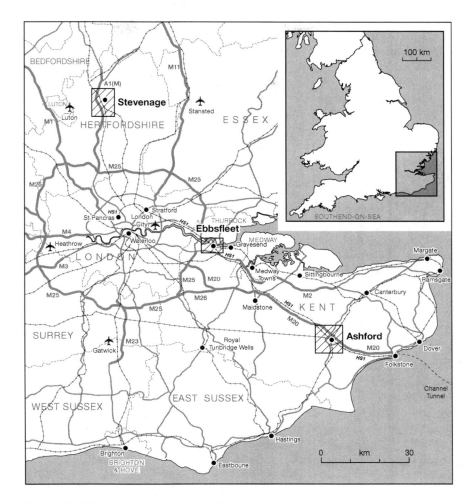

Figure 5.3 Three Study Sites, England

on the same high-speed line as Ashford, 80 kilometers to the southeast]" (Lock, 2000, p. 43). Ebbsfleet and the Eastern Quarry were assessed to have capacity for about 10,000 homes, all situated in a walkable development within reach of the new international station (Office of the Deputy Prime Minister, 2003, p. 53). The big difference between this site and the other two presented here is that all the land to be built on was formerly industrial and previously developed.

The narratives set out here draw on a number of past projects examining strategic development sites (see Gallent, 2008a, 2008b; Hamiduddin & Gallent, 2012) and community responses to housing growth (Gallent & Robinson, 2012; Gallent et al., 2013). Each case study follows the same structure: short notes on development origins and evolving planning context for the sites are followed by a general presentation of the narrative. The narratives are followed by reflections on seven key issues:

1. Challenges around value uplift, negotiating planning obligations and delivering enabling infrastructure.
2. Opposition to top–down strategic planning and externally devised targets.
3. Insufficient public gain and concerns relating to the overloading of existing infrastructure.
4. Inconsistencies and sudden shifts in policy (national and local), increasing the "regulatory risk" for developers.
5. Issues of market shift and viability affecting major development sites.
6. The flexibility of planning in accommodating those shifts, for instance through ongoing negotiation around planning gain.
7. Regional–local tensions and the difficulties of working across local government boundaries.

Stevenage, Hertfordshire

Origin and Context

Stevenage is considered by many to be an "unfinished New Town." It is situated to the east of the A1(M) (motorway) and is on the East Coast Mainline, about 40 kilometers north of London, in the county of Hertfordshire. Between 1962 and 1965, various proposals were brought forward by the Stevenage (New Town) Development Corporation to extend the town onto 586 hectares of agricultural land to the west of the motorway. The proposals faced stiff public opposition. A decade later, in 1972, central government commissioned proposals for an even larger development (of 1600 hectares) at the same location. The weight of public opposition was such that the proposals were abandoned before the planned Public Inquiry in 1974. Five years later, the land around Stevenage became designated greenbelt.

Stevenage is an "under-bounded" town: it is larger than its administrative area and bordered by land subject to policy constraint (Hamiduddin & Gallent, 2012). Nevertheless, it has significant development potential owing to its ideal location on key road and rail routes, its well-developed infrastructure and its proximity to the overheating London housing market. The New Towns were intended to vent London housing pressure, and that pressure has never been greater than it is today. Hence, there has been a continual revisiting of development opportunities at Stevenage. Yet, clearly, plans to resolve housing pressures that are not Stevenage's own—on open countryside within the greenbelt, overlooked by a number of small villages—has provoked strong public opposition. This opposition is a key feature of the Stevenage story, as is the struggle faced by an under-bounded town attempting to grow into neighboring authorities.

The Stevenage West Narrative

Building on earlier efforts, in 1998 the principle for a large strategic housing allocation west of Stevenage was established in the Hertfordshire Structure Plan. The allocation was for 5,000 homes in total, 3,600 of which would be completed by 2011. The site, at 281 hectares, was smaller than both the 1962 and 1972 proposals, but, like the earlier proposals, it crossed into neighboring North Hertfordshire District. Stevenage Borough itself was to take 1,000 homes on 93 hectares in the initial period and North Hertfordshire the remaining 2,600 homes on 188 hectares of greenbelt land. There appeared to be sufficient support for the development within the two neighboring planning authorities; they had a similar political make-up, and seemed committed to working with each other and with the County Council on the task of translating the broad strategic allocation into more detailed local plans. Indeed, there was enough certainty for a development consortium to form. The consortium produced a master plan for the site by early 1999. However, broader opposition to the development remained and local government elections later that same year saw a transfer of power in the county to groups opposed to significant development at Stevenage West. Those groups immediately sought to withdraw the Structure Plan, but were prevented from doing so by legal impediment. Undeterred, the new council began an early review of the Structure Plan, making its intention to delete the allocation very clear. The collapse of political support created an uncertain environment for the planning authorities and for the consortium, and this was compounded by the issuing of a revised "PPG3: Housing" in March 2000.

The new policy guidance emphasized the need to prioritize urban infill over greenfield development. Stevenage Borough had too few infill sites on which to meet its housing requirement, but North Hertfordshire—which was feeling the brunt of local opposition to the scheme (all the overlooking villages were in its jurisdiction)—saw the new guidance as a way out of a difficult political situation. On the basis of their interpretation of PPG3, and legal advice, North Hertfordshire's Local Development Plan was withdrawn, just at the point when a chapter and policy on Stevenage West was about to be inserted. Rather than continuing with the preparation of the current plan, the local authority decided to undertake an urban capacity study, and thereafter commence work on a new plan. These decisions reflected growing local opposition to the development, underpinned by concerns over the loss of local amenity were the development to go ahead, the undoubted impact on open countryside and also the probable effect on existing property prices. Concerns also related to the stress that might be placed on local services, although the aim of concentrating development at a single strategic site was to maximize planning gain contributions and integrate the scheme into existing infrastructure on the other side of the A1(M). The consortium now faced a completely uncertain situation, although neighboring Stevenage Borough Council seemed never to doubt the logic of the scheme. Its plan was retained despite the new guidance and it continued with its plan review, ahead of the second deposit stage, working up the details of the Stevenage West allocation but undertaking an urban capacity study in tandem with this process.

However, progress on the planning stages of the scheme depended entirely on the two authorities pursuing the same goals. They effectively separated in 2000 and took alternate paths, driven by very different needs and political pressures. The Campaign Against the Stevenage Expansion (CASE) became a focus for local opposition, drawing much of its core support from North Hertfordshire. It challenged the Stevenage West scheme at all stages and continued to do so throughout the 2000s. In 2001, the consortium (with encouragement from Stevenage Borough) submitted a revised master plan as part of a full planning application. Because the County Structure Plan remained in force (despite the ongoing review), the two authorities were obliged to consider this application, despite one of them now being expressly opposed to it in principle. They of course failed to reach agreement. North Hertfordshire saw reasons for refusal where Stevenage Borough saw none. Additional phasing master plans were submitted by the consortium, but these lacked detail as the various companies involved were unwilling to commit substantial resource given the uncertain political environment. How much and what type of affordable housing would be delivered on the site, through a Section 106 agreement, became a particular bone of contention. It was impossible to agree a formula and in May 2004 questions of phasing, design, and affordability were put before a public inquiry, which then reported to the Secretary of State in November.

At the same time, something really huge happened nationally. The Communities Plan (Office of the Deputy Prime Minister, 2003) had been published the year before and this confirmed the government's desire to see substantial growth in the M11 corridor (which stretches west to Stevenage). In 2004, the Planning and Compulsory Purchase Act was passed by Parliament. This paved the way for the abolition of Structure Plans and the creation of a new system of Local Development Frameworks, of which new Regional Spatial Strategies (RSS) would be an integral part, setting out strategic housing targets that would need to be planned for locally. By 2005, the East of England Regional Assembly was in the process of translating its old advisory Regional Planning Guidance into an "East of England Plan," which reaffirmed the need to build 8,500 houses to the north and west of Stevenage. It was in this context—and following on from the public inquiry—that the Secretary of State indicated that he was "minded to approve" Phase 1 of the Stevenage West scheme.

This gave the consortium enough confidence to reformulate its 2001 application. This was submitted in 2006 and, once the detail had been

England: Major Housing Development Sites 127

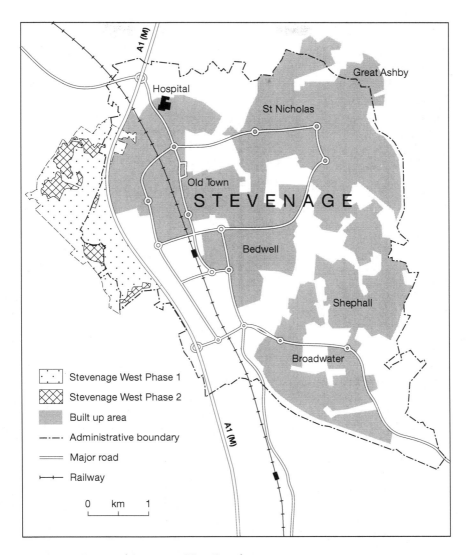

Figure 5.4 Proposed Stevenage West Development

worked through, permission was finally given in December 2009. Irrespective of their differences, the two authorities (which by then had begun work on a Stevenage and North Hertfordshire Action Plan, or SNAP) granted joint permission because of the strategic requirement set out in the East of England Plan. But the narrative then took another twist, which had an effect similar to the reissuing of PPG3 in 2000. The change of government in 2010 resulted in a letter being sent by the new Conservative Secretary of State to all Chief Planning Officers in England, stating the government's intention to revoke all Regional Spatial Strategies. This was the second "get out of jail free" card for North Hertfordshire, given that the Stevenage West site remained politically toxic. In June of that year, it suspended work on SNAP. Stevenage Borough, on the other hand, saw no reason to down tools (Hamiduddin & Gallent, 2012). There was great controversy over the sudden use of ministerial power to dismantle the planning system and it looked like the issue was heading to the courts, which indeed it did. However, after various difficulties, the government formally revoked the East of England Plan in January 2013. The Phase 1 planning application was withdrawn in August of that year. In a counter move, which is emblematic of the failing relationship between Stevenage Borough and North Hertfordshire District, the former commissioned a review of "green belt around Stevenage." That review was published just after the RSS revocation in 2013. It concluded that greenbelt land to the west of Stevenage did not make a "significant contribution" to greenbelt purposes (Amec, 2013, p. vii). But whatever the arguments for and against residential use, there has been no development at Stevenage West in the *fifty-three years* since it was first proposed.

The Impediments

The Stevenage West narrative is illustrative of four of the seven impediments: opposition to "remote" strategic decision making, disputes around public gain from development, policy shifts and regulatory risk, and the political and pragmatic challenges of cross-border working. Potential means of overcoming such impediments are discussed toward the end of this chapter, but here it is worth noting that negative reactions to "housing targets" have been represented as evidence of a "democratic deficit" in the planning system (Department for Communities and Local Government, 2011; Sturzaker, 2011), rather than mere NIMBYism. The fifty-three years of conflict in Stevenage tracks the periodic resurgence of stronger strategic planning and separation of target setting from local (democratic) planning control. In the 1960s, proposals for the extension were being led by the Development Corporation. In the 1970s, a combination of government intervention and the separation of county from district planning seemed central to the conflict, which was also the apparent impediment at the end of the 1990s. In the 2000s, the strengthening of regional planning added to a sense of external imposition—that imposition seemed acceptable to an urban authority desperate to grow but incensed a rural neighbor that was expected to absorb a major part of that growth. In that context, disputes around public gain from the development (relative to the huge profits to be made by private landowners), were little more than window dressing. Issues of infrastructure and planning gain—critically important on many large sites—joined a longer list of reasons for refusal. Critically, Stevenage Borough Council seemed convinced that developer contributions were sufficient to avoid overloading its own services and accepted, throughout the process, that concentration of development at a single site would deliver maximum community gain.

Policy shifts clearly played a huge part in the unfolding narrative, but they have to be seen in the context of local opposition. The reissuing of PPG3 in 2000 and the change of government ten years later provided an unwilling partner with a reason to walk away from an unpopular development. Sustained political support is crucial to the delivery of new homes on major development sites. Political shifts, resulting in significant changes to policy, reduce developer confidence. It is impossible to commit the resources needed to navigate planning and associated legal processes. But uncertainty (and opposition) in the case of Stevenage West was fundamentally about working across a difficult border. Stevenage, as noted above, seems to be an absolutely ideal location for substantial development. With its excellent road and rail connections, and the apparent ease by which new development to the west could be integrated with existing infrastructure, it is no wonder that, time and again, it has been highlighted as a site with strategic development potential. But, politically, it is the worst of locations. The under-bounded town is surrounded by greenbelt land, high-grade agricultural land, small villages, and neighbors who find it politically impossible to accept substantial overspill. Pragmatically, regional planning seemed to provide the necessary direction for joint working (planning permission was granted five years after the arrival of the integrated LDF–RSS system), but the political tensions were never resolved.

Ashford, Kent

Origin and Context

Ashford is a historic market town in the county of Kent, southeast England. It sits within its own rural borough so does not suffer the same boundary constraints as Stevenage. But, like Stevenage, it has been earmarked for expansion since the beginning of the 1960s, largely because of its proximity to London (about 98 kilometers away) and its location on the M20 and key rail routes. In the late 1950s, negotiations with London County Council led to 5,000 new homes being built in South Ashford as part of an overspill strategy. A few years later, in 1967, the Buchanan Report identified Ashford as a target location for future growth (Colin Buchanan and Partners, 1967). Since then, the opening of an international railway station in 1994 (serving High Speed One services from 2007) has given significant impetus to Ashford's growth.

Ashford's narrative is part of the wider story of economic growth in London and the southeast. By 2007, the southeast region was contributing £187.9 billion to the UK economy: 15.1 percent of total GDP (Office for National Statistics, 2008). At the same time, the ratio between average household incomes and average house prices had risen to 12:1 (National

Housing Federation, 2009). Population was growing by more than 60,000 people per annum (South East England Development Authority, 2006), so housing affordability problems were predicted to worsen without a significant supply response. Worsening affordability would be a serious constraint on economic growth, with a national impact. This narrative had been fairly constant from the mid-1990s onward and had underpinned regional planning objectives for the wider southeast. RPG9 (1994) settled on a strategy of redirecting growth pressure away from the western corridor (from Reading to London) toward Essex and Kent. Once transposed into the 2003 Communities Plan, Ashford became one of four principal "Growth Areas" and came to be viewed by government as an important "hub of activity":

> ... there is a network of cities and towns where most employment, leisure, retail and cultural activity in the region will gravitate, by virtue of their more developed transport networks and their wide mix of services combined with demand from accessible populations. As dynamic "hubs of activity", they are the logical areas within the South East within which the various components of growth will need to be focused and coordinated to help deliver more sustainable forms of development. A major part of this approach will be reducing the need to travel through closer alignment of local labour supply and demand
> (Government Office for the South East, 2009, p. 18)

Narrative: Ashford's Urban Extensions

In the case of Stevenage, debate has focused (mainly) on the potential of a single site to accommodate future growth. Ashford, on the other hand, has enjoyed a broader array of options. South Ashford and Kennington were built out in the early 1960s. Since then, attention has shifted to opportunities for expansion on the southwest and southeast corners of the town. In 2001, the Regional Assembly engaged consultants to undertake a study into Ashford's capacity to absorb additional growth. That study concluded that employment growth of 18,000 additional jobs and population growth of 35,000 residents would be possible during the next fifteen years (Halcrow & Ashford Borough Council, 2002, p. 17). Ashford's designation as a Growth Area two years later (Office of the Deputy Prime Minister, 2003) was followed, in 2004, by the drawing up of a Greater Ashford Development Framework (GADF), which examined strategic options for delivering against Growth Area objectives. That Framework envisaged 31,000 additional homes and 28,000 new jobs being delivered on 16 square kilometers of land between 2001 and 2031 (Urban Initiatives et al., 2005, p. 77).

Not all of this growth was to be attached to Ashford; some of it was to be distributed across the wider borough. But the last iteration of the South East Plan (Government Office for the South East, 2009) restated the case

England: Major Housing Development Sites 131

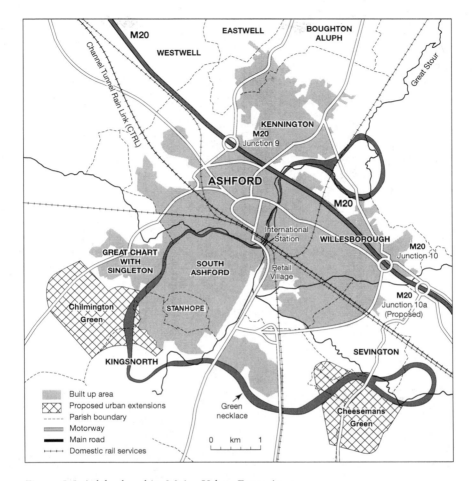

Figure 5.5 Ashford and its Major Urban Extensions

to concentrate nearly 50 percent (or 22,700 homes) of the East Kent and Ashford subregion's additional dwelling requirement in the Growth Area. Capacity studies have shown that a third can be delivered through urban infill, but the remainder—15,500 new homes—will need to be built on greenfield sites (some on the extensions described below and others elsewhere).

Ashford is surrounded by a number of picturesque Kentish villages, the residents of which have little appetite for substantial housing development. It is simply viewed as inappropriate and a threat to environmental amenity (Gallent & Robinson, 2012). They would certainly not wish to see development "smeared" across the district and so generally favor its concentration close to the town of Ashford. However, new extensions either side of the old South Ashford (and Kennington) extension have not been without their critics. Inevitably, the extensions will mean a loss of landscape amenity for communities situated just beyond the town's existing border. But the political situation has been very different from that of the Stevenage expansion. In that case, the scheme had no political support in the recipient district. But, in Ashford, there is general acceptance (given rates of employment growth—see below) that more housing is needed and political support has been strong outside of those wards that will be directly affected by development.

It was in this context that the borough's Core Strategy (2008) identified two major expansion sites, at Chilmington Green on the southwest edge of the town and at Cheeseman's Green and Waterbrook to the southeast. These extensions were presented as contexts for coordinating the delivery of new homes, employment space, and infrastructure while preserving the special character of nearby outlying villages. A good level of political support in the planning authority and a lack of primary constraint—either environmental or physical—seemed to make these locations prime candidates for expansion. It was thought that development on these sites could be readily integrated with existing infrastructure, linking them by public transport back to Ashford's center. In 2008, the Chilmington Green development was presented as a "new mixed-use urban community" that would be built out in two phases: 3,400 homes and 600 jobs by 2021 and a further 3,300 homes and 400 jobs between 2021 and 2031. A similar vision was offered for

Figure 5.6 New Housing in the Ashford Growth Area, 2010
Source: Nick Gallent 2010

Cheeseman's Green, though it would be separated from the town by an ancient coppiced hornbeam-oak-ash woodland and would be less "mixed" with distribution uses concentrated on the Waterbrook part of the extension and housing and other employment uses on Cheeseman's Green itself. Critically, development was already permissioned on Cheeseman's Green. Therefore, a more rapid Phase 1 was envisaged, followed by a smaller Phase 2: 4,300 homes and 1,475 jobs by 2021, and then 2,200 more homes and 750 additional jobs over the following decade. In total, 6,700 homes at Chilmington Green and 5,775 at Cheeseman's Green would be built.

The Ashford expansion plans were very much a product of government's wider growth strategy, which was adversely affected by both the economic downturn and by opposition to imposed "targets" that appeared, to some residents, to be insensitive to local situations and needs.

Cheeseman's Green

The vulnerability of long-run schemes to the market cycle is illustrated at Cheeseman's Green. A key difference between this site and the other, at Chilmington Green, is that because of existing permissions it seemed likely that development here would be brought forward in parcels by individual house builders rather than as a single scheme by a consortium of companies. Two years before the Core Strategy—in January 2006—an outline planning consent had been granted for 1,100 homes, 180 live/work units and 70,000 square meters of business floor space. This consent was based on the existing Borough Local Plan allocation and by the time the new Core Strategy was adopted it was expected that work would commence in 2009. However, the progress of the scheme was dependent on the construction of a new junction (10A) on the M20 motorway, which would provide the access needed to the site for the volume of additional traffic envisaged. The original Section 106 agreement required the developer—Crest Nicholson—to pay for the junction. But, because of the changed economic situation post-2007, it claimed that it was unable to meet the cost and progress the scheme. Although the original agreement could not then be changed, the Borough Council and the developer reached a compromise: Crest Nicholson would pay for an interim upgrade of the existing junction (10) to enable the first phases of the scheme to proceed (Phases 1 to 6 of the fourteen envisaged, comprising 700 homes).

Reflecting on this decision in the 2008 Core Strategy, concerns were raised that the fragmentation of the development (with no clear view as to when the next stages might be viable or what might be located on various parts of the larger Cheeseman's Green site) could undermine its cohesiveness and integration across its parts. There was still no clear view, for example, on where the main community facilities might be located (Ashford Borough Council, 2008). It was simply hoped that these questions would be resolved in the Area Action Plan for Cheeseman's Green.

Two factors conspired to produce this situation of piecemeal, fragmented development: first, the way in which infrastructure is paid for, and, second, the toughening economic conditions. The delivery of "growth assets" (which largely meant enabling infrastructure) was delegated to an arm's-length company in 2003: "Ashford's Future" (a "special delivery vehicle") was tasked to coordinate infrastructure delivery, working with the local authority, with developers, and with the Homes and Communities Agency. While it was able to access some grant support (and coordinate European bids), it had no powers of land assembly or purchase and therefore worked within the constraints of the Section 106 approach, with resources to deliver infrastructure being part of the viability calculation of the overall scheme, and vulnerable therefore to market shift. The greater value of the site had already been lost to (or was destined for, once the treaty agreement on the land sale took force) the landowner and therefore the resources to pay for infrastructure had already passed into private hands. If government now wanted the development to proceed (and accepted the developer's claim of non-viability) then it would need to step in with taxpayers' money to rescue the scheme.

Because of the ongoing and deepening crisis, nothing happened on the site for four years. Then, in April 2012, Crest Nicholson was awarded £2.3 million from the coalition government's rescue package for "stuck sites": the so-called "Get Britain Building Fund." That fund was intended to provide development finance to kick-start building on permissioned sites, with the taxpayer "stepping in" to share some of the risk with the private sector (Department for Communities and Local Government, 2011b). The funding did effectively unlock the site while the market was still recovering, and by October of that year building work had begun on the site that Crest Nicholson had now rebranded as "Finberry." By now, the press had started to refer to the "former Cheeseman's Green" site, envisaging "up to 1,800" homes by some unspecified future date, depending on viability and depending on the receipt of future planning permissions for different parts of the site.

The Borough Council was keen to stress in 2008 that Cheeseman's Green and Waterbrook should be viewed as a single extension. However, there were immediate concerns that integrated "place-making" on the site would be difficult given the market situation and doubts over infrastructure delivery. Ultimately, these factors resulted in a scaling back of the initial ambition and a scheme that struggled to overcome infrastructure constraint, only doing so with government support. Further comment is provided at the end of this section, but the key question here is surely why a prime development site in an economically prosperous region stalled in the way that it did. While the extended timescales of such schemes make them susceptible to market shift, the fundamental problem here seems to have been the failure to capture value from the increase in land values back in 2006 or before "hope value" had ballooned to the point that the value uplift had been entirely lost.

Chilmington Green

The Chilmington Green story is different in many respects. It quickly became embroiled in local politics and, while opposition to the development did not ultimately bring the project to a halt, that opposition raised important questions around the planning processes and infrastructure needs that are prerequisites to major housing development.

Reports of local opposition to the Chilmington Green extension began in 2010. Residents of Chilmington Green hamlet (a total of forty of them, occupying fourteen houses, many of which are "listed") started a petition against the extension. The petition had attracted 700 signatures by September of that year, which was claimed to be "90% of the population" (exactly which "population" was unclear: Kent Online, 2010). This was a year before formal consultation on a possible planning application was due to commence, with that application not expected until 2011/2012. At this point, the Borough Council leader said that too much work had gone into the scheme to stop it, but that the council would be willing to look at "density, shape and the number of houses." Local unrest attracted the attention of the national media, with *The Express* (2011) wading in with the claim that the scheme would "transform a peaceful idyll into a bustling extension." By now (March 2011), the petition had attracted 3,500 signatures, with the main argument against the extension being that Ashford was simply not growing and therefore additional housing was not needed. That argument was countered elsewhere by figures showing that employment growth in the Borough (at 3.6 percent) was twice the English average, with new housing needed to support and sustain that growth. Opponents of the scheme had looked at the possibility of launching a legal challenge against the allocation, but there was no clear basis for that challenge.

Therefore, an alternative strategy was devised: to field candidates in local elections and attempt to defeat the ruling Conservative group (six were elected, not enough to change the balance of local power). As well as employing the "not needed" argument, opponents claimed that the allocation was a hangover from the 2003 Communities Plan, with the Core Strategy a product of the previous government's housing targets and its soon-to-be-defunct (and extremely "high-handed") Regional Spatial Strategies. They also pointed to the low level of community gain relative to the massive financial windfall to two local landowners, accepting the reasons why farmers would sell land for housing but drawing attention to the injustice of these skewed benefits. On the first issue, there was some hope that changes to national planning policy, and the arrival of the draft NPPF (DCLG, 2011c), would undermine the basis of the development. But Chilmington Green was unaffected by the new planning framework. On the issue of benefits, it was further argued that the scheme would cause additional overloading of infrastructure and there was simply not enough money to pay for essential upgrading. The issue of finance for infrastructure became crucial during the consultation on the Chilmington Green Area Action Plan (AAP) in 2012. That consultation ended on June 11 and, in anticipation of the development being given a green light, opponents handed their petition (now with 8,000 signatures) to 10 Downing Street on that same day.

Ultimately the arguments were very simple: the extension at Chilmington Green was either unnecessary or essential and would or would not cause infrastructure stress. Eventually, the appointed planning inspector sided with the Borough Council, but this did not dampen opposition and the council needed to engage in a PR campaign in support of the extension. The opportunity to do so came with the publication of the final version of the NPPF (May 2012), which lent support to a new generation of "garden cities." Within a couple of months, it was announced that the council would seek the support of government for a garden city at Chilmington Green. In August, plans were submitted for a "5,750-home" suburb; the application was prepared by various consultants on behalf of a development consortium comprising Hodson Developments, Jarvis Homes, Pentland Homes, and Ward Homes. The council and the consultants quickly adopted a common language for Chilmington Green; now varyingly called a green suburb and a garden city, it was claimed that the development would "re-invent Ebenezer Howard's Garden City principles for the 21st Century" (Construction Index, 2012).

Opposition continued: "Keep Chilmington Green" organized a referendum on the development at the end of 2012, securing an 85 percent "against" vote on a 33 percent turnout. But opponents of the extension seemed to have reached a dead end. A two-day examination of the AAP in May 2013 judged it to be "sound," paving the way for development. The inspector said that he understood the reasons for local objection but that objections alone, unless founded on valid planning reasons, were not a reason for rejecting a plan. He added that the merits of the urban extension (weighed against disbenefits) had been thoroughly explored at the Core Strategy stage in 2008. Opponents conceded that they understood why it had passed the technical tests but reiterated that the development was not needed.

One similarity with Cheeseman's Green at this point was the need for government to step in and support infrastructure delivery. It became one of a number of sites given access to Local Infrastructure Funding (in June 2013), again raising questions over how much had been captured through the planning permission, versus how much might have been levied from the land sale (land values were estimated to have risen from £5,000 to £10,000 per acre at previous use to £500,000 per acre at intended use). Yet, despite some of the costs of infrastructure upgrading having to be met by the taxpayer, the scheme was still lauded as exemplary "place making" (Planning, 2014). In previous periods, the place making associated with garden cities had been linked to the compulsory purchase of land at agricultural value, with value uplift captured and used to fund necessary capital projects: roads, community facilities, and so on. Revenue for maintenance of infrastructure was thereafter raised through leasehold tenure and the payment of ground rents. None of these mechanisms features in the "reinvention" of garden cities for the twenty-first century, with government unwilling to prescribe the form these should take or the ways in which they might be delivered. It is perhaps for this reason that local opposition to development has not been quelled by the transformation of speculative housing (rather than trust-led) schemes into garden cities. In the case of Chilmington Green, Ashford Borough's Planning Committee voted (ten in favor and two against) to grant outline planning permission on October 15, 2014. In what was reported to have been an emotional debate, opponents continued to highlight the inadequacies of infrastructure contributions, calling the development a "hideous carbuncle" and threatening to "lie down in front of the diggers."

While opponents can be dismissed as mere NIMBYs, claims over limited community benefit (and the unfair flow of windfall to landowners) were not without foundation. As well as having to step in with external infrastructure funding, the scheme was ultimately given outline permission with a much-reduced affordable housing contribution: 10 percent of the first 1,000 homes, against a Local Plan requirement of 30 percent, and with agreement that later contributions would depend on viability.

The Impediments

The extensions at Ashford needed to overcome five of the seven impediments to major development: challenges around (the means of) value capture, opposition to "distant" strategic planning, the inadequacy (and perceived "injustice") of community benefit, market shifts affecting long-run projects, and the flexibility needed to address those shifts. Both narratives raise questions over the adequacy of current approaches to value capture, though neither scheme manages to resolve these questions. In the two cases, after permissions were granted (and land sales completed), issues arose around the costs of infrastructure upgrading. In the case of Cheeseman's Green, the development stalled on the inability of the developer to meet its obligation to pay for a new road junction, and at Chilmington Green there appears to have been insufficient value in the scheme to meet basic infrastructure costs. This is in a location where the value of land allocated for housing is up to 10,000 percent greater than that of land in agricultural use. The perception (and arguably the reality) of an unfair windfall flowing to landowners—that neither planning nor the Treasury was able to capture—linked ultimately to (justified) concerns that community benefits would be stunted. In both cases, government stepped in to underwrite the costs of infrastructure provision and, in the case of Chilmington Green, the developers' contribution of affordable housing was reduced. In neither case was this issue of early value capture resolved, and this is of course a national issue to which we return at the end of this chapter.

Relating to the above, market shifts have a profound effect on the progress of major schemes. In the case of Cheeseman's Green, it was arguably those shifts that prevented investment in a new road junction (although a disproportionate windfall to the landowner also played its part) and caused the development to stall. In this instance, local planners found a way to overcome this barrier, reaching a compromise with Crest Nicholson and placing the agreement in abeyance until such a time as the market improved. It was agreed that less-costly upgrades to an existing junction would be sufficient to allow the first phases of development to proceed. However, the depth of the crisis meant that nothing could happen on the site for a further four years, irrespective of the flexibility demonstrated by local planning.

Finally, opposition to the extension at Chilmington Green reached rapid "maturity" (Dear, 1992), with initial amenity-based arguments (the simple loss of views and agricultural land) being replaced with a sophisticated commentary on infrastructure overloading, value capture, and the democratic inadequacies of regional planning. The change of national government in 2010 raised the expectation that allocations underpinned by regional planning would be deleted. This was the de facto outcome in Stevenage, where the framework of cross-border working was lost. Yet, in Ashford, however despised the regional imposition had been, its removal did not give cause to reverse prior planning decisions at this important "hub of activity."

Ebbsfleet, Kent

Origin and Context

Although located in the same county as the Ashford extensions, the Ebbsfleet site could not be more different, being part of an ex-industrial landscape in the Thames Gateway. Peter Hall (2014) notes that the Ebbsfleet sites (see below) have a common origin with a number of East Thames sites, including the Stratford Olympic Park and Barking Riverside (ibid., p. 62). Regional Planning Guidance 9a (Department of the Environment/Thames Gateway Taskforce, 1995) proposed "huge mixed-use developments ... around the two stations that had been located on the Channel Tunnel Rail Link, later to be renamed High Speed One: Stratford and Ebbsfleet" (Hall, 2014, pp. 62–63). That guidance offered a development framework for the area that envisaged a "discontinuous development corridor more than 40 miles (60km) long, based on the high-speed train link from London to the Channel Tunnel, with concentrations of employment around planned stations, with dense local rail travel in between" (Department of the Environment/Thames Gateway Taskforce, 1995, cited in Hall & Ward, 2014, p. 187). The framework became the basis for early local plan allocations and development briefs. In January 1997, Gravesham Borough Council produced a development brief for land west of Springhead Road, predicting that the private market would see the Ebbsfleet area in a "different light" (that is, less negatively) with the opening of the international rail station and wider government efforts to regenerate the Thames Gateway. Indeed, the entire

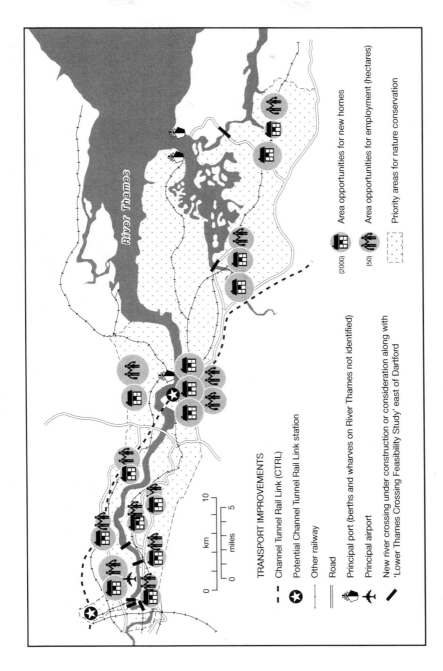

Figure 5.7 Thames Gateway Development Corridor

vision for the Gateway was predicated on unprecedented infrastructure investments, creating "two major anchors for employment and activity" (Hall & Ward, 2014, p. 188) at Stratford and at Ebbsfleet, the latter also being close to the M25 Dartford Crossing.

The story of Stratford has now become strongly associated with the successful 2005 bid to host the Olympic Games. In the preceding decade (from the time of the Thames Gateway Strategy), Stratford saw a great deal of development owing to the Jubilee Line extension and other investments. In the ten years after 2005, it became the showpiece of regeneration efforts in east London, culminating in the 2012 Summer Games and the subsequent reuse of Olympic infrastructure (including the Athletes' Village at what is now the Queen Elizabeth Olympic Park). But the Ebbsfleet narrative—focused on land around the new station and at the Eastern Quarry, which is situated just to the south of that station—is unquestionably more complicated than either the Stevenage or Ashford cases presented in this chapter, and arguably more so than Stratford, as it lacked the catalyst of the "Olympic bonus" (ibid., p. 196).

The Ebbsfleet narrative stretches out neatly over a twenty-year period, from the Gateway Strategy in 1995 to a small amount of current on-site activity in 2015. Generally, it is a story of unprecedented ambition, as yet unrealized. But it is also a complex narrative comprising a mix of sites, large and small, which have come to be collectively viewed as the Ebbsfleet Valley development area. Because the narrative is complex, involving a number of stops and starts and incidental small developments over the twenty-year period, we focus attention on efforts to bring forward development at Ebbsfleet itself and the Eastern Quarry (see Figure 5.7). This was the focus of Peter Hall's (2014) account of "stuck" sites in the Gateway and is now at the center of renewed effort by the government to accelerate housing supply in the area, through the designation of the first Urban Development Corporation in England for a decade.

Narrative: Ebbsfleet and the Eastern Quarry

Ebbsfleet comprises four "quarters" around the international station, while the Eastern Quarry, just to the south, is divided into two parts—Eastern Quarry 1 and 2. Outline permission for Ebbsfleet was granted in 2002. A combined permission for the whole Eastern Quarry was granted in 2003. The latter ran into difficulties and was renegotiated in 2007 just for Eastern Quarry 2. In 2008, Dartford Council resolved to grant outline planning permission at Northfleet West substation (Eastern Quarry 1) once the necessary planning obligations and supporting strategies were finalized. The sites have been "advanced for development" (cleaned and leveled) by Land Securities.

Following on from the 1995 Thames Gateway Framework and the Springhead Road development brief two years later, David Lock Associates (DLA) produced a master plan for the four development quarters

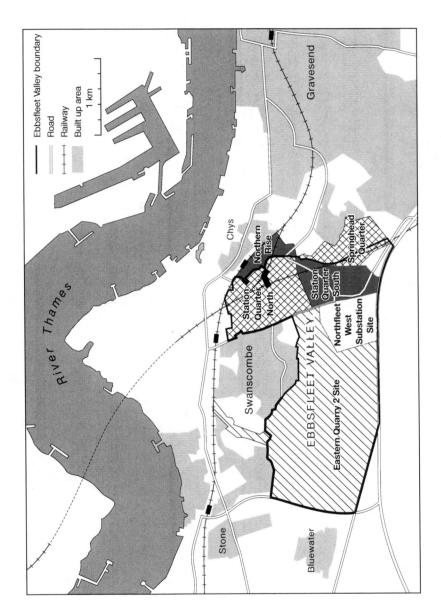

Figure 5.8 Ebbsfleet Valley Development Sites

(i.e. "Ebbsfleet," comprising 152 hectares) around the international station in 1997 (Lock, 2000, p. 43). That master plan was prompted by the publication of "Looking to the Future" (a consultation document examining the development potential of damaged land between Dartford and Gravesham over the next twenty-five years: Kent Thames-side Partnership, 1995) and a subsequent Ebbsfleet Development and Environment Framework, jointly produced by Dartford Borough Council, Gravesham Borough Council, and Kent County Council and adopted in June 1996 (Dartford Borough Council et al., 1996). This local framework responded to the RPG9a vision for the Thames Gateway in advance of a full review of local plans (which all predated the wider vision). The DLA master plan was drawn up for the "Thames-side partnership," which comprised the three authorities, Blue Circle Properties, and the University of Greenwich. That plan sought outline permission for 789,500 square meters of mixed-use development surrounding the international railway station on behalf of Blue Circle Properties. DLA then went on to produce development frameworks for each of the main development areas at Stone and Greenhithe, at Swanscombe Peninsular, at Northfleet Riverside, at Eastern Quarry, and at the London Science Park at Dartford. Blue Circle's involvement in the site stemmed from its ownership of 1,100 hectares of land (including the land for the new station) at Ebbsfleet and the Eastern Quarry, the base for its former cement works. It secured the outline planning permission for the station quarters, following negotiations around various phasing issues and legal agreements, in November 2002. It was envisaged that the development here would be rolled out over a twenty-five-year period. The four quarters comprised the Station Quarter North (920 dwellings), Northfleet Rise (number of dwellings unspecified), Station Quarter South (nearly 2,100 dwellings), and Springhead (again, number of dwellings unspecified).

To the south of the station, the Eastern Quarry is divided into two parts, known as Eastern Quarry 1 and 2. The narrative of this site is picked up again by Peter Hall (Hall & Ward, 2014, p. 196). Outline approval for a mixed-use development was submitted in January 2003 (Dartford Borough Council, 2010, p. 18). The application here was for 7,250 homes and 280,000 square meters of business and leisure space. This application was described, in 2010, as "live" but "unlikely to be implemented" (ibid., p. 18). Four years later, another application—this time just covering Eastern Quarry 2 (that is, the quarry site but excluding the Northfleet West substation, otherwise known as Eastern Quarry 1)—was submitted for 6,250 homes and 231,000 square meters of business and leisure use. The key features of that development were to be:

- Primarily residential, with the creation of a market center within the central village and local centers at the two remaining villages.
- A lake at the southern boundary within the cliff shadow.
- A major urban park along the northern boundary.

- Some mixed-use and employment areas.
- Encouragement of public transport and reducing reliance on the car through the provision of an east–west Fastrack route through the site and development oriented around the route with higher-density development closest.
- Creation of a high-quality sustainable community within Eastern Quarry as a whole, with higher-order facilities such as a secondary school being shared by the three sites. These are likely to be located in the market center.
- Integration with adjoining uses at Bluewater, Ebbsfleet, Northfleet West substation, and communities at Swanscombe and Knockhall through linked public transport and green grid routes and sharing of facilities.
- Monitoring of car usage and agreed actions to address this if traffic generation is higher than predicted, as set out in a Travel Plan (ibid., p. 19).

It was envisaged that this element of the Ebbsfleet Valley would be built out over fifteen to twenty-five years. So, here in the Ebbsfleet Valley, we are dealing with two major development sites (excluding the Swanscombe Peninsular to the north). The applications at Eastern Quarry were submitted by Land Securities and came eight years after RPG9a. Hall and Ward (2014, p. 196) note that it took another eight years—until 2012—to reach agreement on key elements of the plan. The legal agreements attached to the 2007 permission included, crucially, key infrastructure and transport investments —including major modifications to the A2 Ebbsfleet and Bean Junctions at Dartford (Dartford Borough Council, 2010, p. 21; Hall & Ward, 2014, p. 196). Paying for and delivering these improvements became critical to the progress of the development, as noted below.

Overall, the Ebbsfleet and Eastern Quarry sites (plus other parts of the Ebbsfleet Valley) were destined to provide 22,600 homes and as many as 60,000 jobs. But they came to be described as the "greatest stuck site in South East England" (Hall & Ward, 2014, p. 191). Following the 2007 permission, Land Securities spent £30 million on site preparation (leveling hills and draining the old chalk pits) and estimated that it would need to spend another £50 million to complete the job (ibid., p. 196). The scale of the site clean-up was itself a cause of significant delay. This came on the back of ten years of negotiations around the detail of development and the cost and delivery of other infrastructure, including schools, open spaces, and community facilities. The involvement of Land Securities, however, gave impetus to the development as major investment began in the preparation of the sites. But the cost associated with infrastructure upgrading was again a major obstacle. The 2007 permission for 6,250 homes at Eastern Quarry 2 required a £40 million highways and infrastructure investment; these investments were set among the key "development triggers" (Dartford Borough Council, 2010, p. 21) and the scheme could not be built out without

Figure 5.9 Castle Hill (Eastern Quarry), Looking toward Swanscombe
Source: Courtesy of Land Securities

them. Eventual agreement on paying for the upgrades happened on the eve of the 2008 financial crisis and, as with the M20A junction upgrade at Ashford, the cost suddenly looked much too high. The contribution, based on the 2007 Section 106 agreement, was negotiated down to just over half of its original amount—to be paid on completion. There was now no upfront investment from potential developers in the enabling road upgrades, and without them the development could not proceed.

Slow progress at Ebbsfleet, and the Eastern Quarry, can of course be attributed to the sheer scale of the scheme, set within an ex-industrial landscape (though also impinged upon, at Eastern Quarry, by the Metropolitan Green Belt, with that impediment being removed in the Dartford Local Plan Review in 2004) that needed a great deal of preparatory work. That preparation raised market confidence, and the prospects for Ebbsfleet looked excellent just before the 2008 crash. The crash ended that confidence and the scheme seemed destined to go nowhere, blocked by the critical question of who would now pay for the infrastructure. For Hall and Ward (2014, p. 199), the failure—during a long period of economic boom prior to the financial crisis—to "reach agreement with developers on a formula that would provide the basic infrastructure and share the value uplift from the resulting developments" proved critical. Looking at the Thames Gateway as a whole, the clarity of the "linear" vision for the forty-mile corridor was never matched by a similar clarity in delivery arrangements: The London Thames Gateway Development Corporation (2004 to 2014) shared its powers with a "bewildering mosaic of nearly thirty other agencies" (ibid., p. 199). There was never a single agency that could assemble, acquire, prepare, and dispose of land, capturing value and reinvesting that value in prerequisite infrastructure. This led to a "glacial rate of progress" (ibid., p. 198): Land Securities announced in 2013 that it would develop 150 residential plots on less than 1 percent of the Eastern Quarry site, adding to the 300 already built at Springhead Park, the land subject to the 1997 Development Brief.

It was in this context that Lord Adonis, in a study produced by the Centre for London, called for the creation of a Development Corporation to oversee the major sites at Ebbsfleet, extending up the Swanscombe Peninsular.

A UDC for Ebbsfleet

It was announced in the 2014 Budget (on March 16) that 15,000 homes would be delivered on the Ebbsfleet site, that an Urban Development Corporation (UDC) would be formed to oversee that development—the first in England for ten years—, and that a £200 million government infrastructure fund would be created to support (and catalyze) the scheme. Ebbsfleet, it was further announced, would become a "garden city" (see HM Treasury, 2014). Government, it seemed, had at long last decided to step in and save its flagship development. The new Development Corporation would cover an area of 674 hectares, comprising the land around the station (i.e. Ebbsfleet proper), the Eastern Quarry (extending westward to the Western Quarry, previously developed as the Bluewater Shopping Centre), and extending up the Swanscombe Peninsular to the north. Two further, non-contiguous, parcels were also to be brought under the jurisdiction of the Development Corporation, on the Thames just above Northfleet.

The major residential development—now a garden city—would remain at Ebbsfleet and the Eastern Quarry. In May 2014, plans were outlined to create an entertainment resource on the Swanscombe Peninsular. This would be designated a "nationally significant infrastructure project" allowing the project to bypass normal planning rules. The aim is to build a leisure complex employing 27,000 workers by 2019.

There was clearly pressure, ahead of the 2015 General Election, to give new impetus to the Ebbsfleet Development. Because of prior planning history, there are 11,200 outstanding dwelling consents in the proposed UDC area. At the time of writing (March 2015), the UDC is in the process of being established. A consultation on its setup was completed in January. The model for the Corporation is a standard one: it will be a statutory body at arm's length from the Department for Communities and Local Government (DCLG), answerable directly to the Secretary of State. A chairman and board members will be appointed by government. It will take over planning, building control, and compulsory purchase powers from local

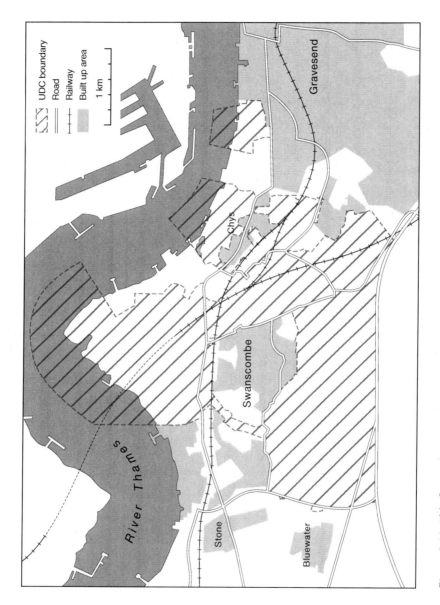

Figure 5.10 Ebbsfleet Urban Development Corporation

authorities. DCLG is currently preparing the legislation required to make the UDC a reality.

It was noted earlier that Land Securities has played a significant role in preparing the Ebbsfleet Valley for development. Its role is now shifting and it is coordinating its activities with the embryonic Development Corporation. Working alongside Arup and Partners, Land Securities has begun working on the principles of a master plan for the Eastern Quarry and Ebbsfleet sites, envisaging green fingers transecting the site north to south, creating the types of green space that one might associate with a "garden city." The team on the ground view Ebbsfleet as a "place for testing innovation," offering a vision of a "green city" embedded in a landscape rich in heritage (Wyman & Davis, 2015).

The Impediments

But there are three nagging doubts over the Ebbsfleet project, now rebranded Ebbsfleet Garden City. These are, in part, political but also reference significant impediments. Ebbsfleet does not feel, to many commentators, like a garden city. There are clearly opportunities to connect urban development to substantial landscape heritage, to bring about a merger between town and country, in line with Howard's original vision. But that vision was also about delivering a model of development that would capture land value uplift by assembling land at close to agricultural use value, hence providing the financial means to engage in extensive place making. The UDC, like the local authorities, has compulsory purchase powers. But land values have already risen, driven upward by the siting of the international railway station and the efforts of Land Securities to improve the site for residential use. It is the private landowners—previously Blue Circle Properties and National Grid, and now joined by Lafarge (which acquired Blue Circle in 2001) and Land Securities—who stand to benefit most from rising land values at Ebbsfleet. Insufficient value was captured for enabling infrastructure. That was clear when the original Section 106 agreement needed to be renegotiated after the financial crash and also now the government has needed to step in with additional cash support.

Out of the seven potential impediments to major development, two have been particularly significant at Ebbsfleet: challenges around capturing value uplift and delivering infrastructure, and the impact of market shift on long-run, slow-burn schemes. Ebbsfleet was hindered by the first challenge from the outset and then became a high-profile victim of the latter. But, in relation to value capture, Ebbsfleet is very unlike England's historic garden cities. This was never to be a greenfield development on a freestanding site with little or no prior development history. Value was lost to the private sector as soon as plans for a new rail link to a new Channel Tunnel were drawn up, and once Ebbsfleet became the site for an international passenger station the "hope value" attached to land at Ebbsfleet soared.

Ebbsfleet has none of the hallmarks of a garden city. Land is in private ownership, consents have been given, and value uplift will not be captured. This has made it easy for critics to argue that what is now emerging at Ebbsfleet is a rebranding of a stalled scheme, rather than a twenty-first-century reimagining of the garden city concept. This was also the case at Chilmington Green. It is undoubtedly true that the vague notion of new garden cities in England is more appealing to government than a process of delivery that predates the modern planning system and the age of private land development and volume house building. Regular state intervention in land assembly and development—often through the New Town model—has been consigned to history and there appears to be little appetite for a return to the past. Indeed, even the revival of the UDC model has been viewed by some as an unnecessary step backward: The Development Corporation at Ebbsfleet has received its share of bad press (Kent Online, 2014), being seen as undemocratic and out of sync with government's localism agenda (government said it would return power to town halls, not take it away). Yet, far from being a retreat from neoliberalism, the UDCs—or, indeed, the special delivery vehicles in other Growth Areas—can be seen as an attempt to shift the regulatory culture within target areas, taking power from traditional local authorities and handing it to agencies whose ethos is more aligned with that of the private development sector.

A Future for Major Sites in England?

The case studies illustrated seven key barriers to effective planning and delivery of major housing sites. How might these be resolved? A variety of proposals has been put forward in recent years, focusing on different approaches to value capture and infrastructure delivery, local democracy and neighborhood control, policy clarity and flexibility, and alignment with market and functional realities. Here, we use a range of recent literature and inquiry outcomes to chart the general direction of current thinking.

1. Value Capture, Infrastructure, and Planning Gain

There is currently renewed interest in England in the use of "compulsory purchase" powers for assembling sites for major residential development at closer to existing use value, thereby capturing more of the costs of infrastructure provision. The Lyons Housing Review (2014) highlights problems with existing compulsory purchase powers: they are controversial (running contrary to evolved orthodoxies around property rights), many local authorities have little experience of their effective use, and they are rooted in antiquated legislation dating back to the mid-nineteenth century (ibid., p. 69). Moreover, although the Land Compensation Act 1961 required that the "hope value attributable to the prospect of development . . . be disregarded, allowing for land to be acquired at close to current use value, in many cases agricultural value" (ibid., p. 70), subsequent case law and precedent has led to the conclusion that planning permission, or likely planning permission, should be taken into account for the purpose of compulsory purchase valuation. Therefore, local authorities are more likely to pay *intended* rather than *current* use value for land acquired under these powers, nullifying its potential place-making benefits and removing the mechanism that delivered garden cities and garden suburbs at the beginning of the twentieth century. This has led to the conclusion that a new Land Compensation Act should be introduced, fixing a compensation premium to current use value in instances where land is designated for a garden city or growth area. Drawing on Wei Yang & Partners and Freeman (2014), the Lyons Housing Review argues that "CPO powers should be based upon current use value plus a generous premium rather than the future use value once development is complete" (Lyons, 2014, p. 71). Yang and Freeman suggest "tapered" premiums, with landowners receiving 300 to 400 percent of current use value. This is significantly less than the 10,000 percent uplift estimated at Ashford. It would allow public bodies to acquire and dispose of sites for development, capturing the value needed to pay for enabling infrastructure.

But more regular use of compulsory purchase at close to current use value is a silver bullet that would, however, be difficult, politically, to administer. A big cultural shift would be needed: to rebalance expectations of social benefit and private profit. In the meantime, and for schemes where compulsory purchase would be inappropriate, there is a need to look at how current mechanisms for infrastructure and development gain are operating. For some large schemes, local authorities and developers have been entering into "strategic land and infrastructure contracts" that offer (through Section 106) agreed timescales for infrastructure delivery. But these approaches remain vulnerable to market shift. A greater proportion of value needs to be captured up front and, as in the cases set out above, central funding is sometimes needed to underwrite essential development.

2. Top–Down Planning and Local Opposition/Democracy

Returning to points made in this chapter and the previous, one of the continuing criticisms of planning in England, especially in more rural locations expected to host urban extensions, is that decision making is not locally rooted. Rather, it is an imposition that is insensitive to local impacts and capacities. There have, of course, been decades of effort to turn planning into a more participative activity, responding to those who have derided its "centrist" tendencies or even its "fatal conceit" (Moroni & Andersson, 2014, p. 5). Critiques of centralized planning often focus on its economic shortcomings (Cheshire, 2011), but it is the "disconnect" with local democracy that has prompted periodic turns to greater "local choice" (in the 1990s), New Localism (in the 2000s), and the effort to "rescale" planning (in the 2010s). But, despite these rhetorical turns (sometimes coupled with structural change), successive governments seem to have retained a belief in directing development and regeneration activity from above. Labour acted through its ramped-up regional planning in the 1990s and 2000s and the coalition government (2010–2015) seemed no less intent on delivering big housing projects (at places like Ashford and Ebbsfleet) than its predecessor. Some communities have been shocked by the apparent mismatch between the rhetoric of localism and the continuation of projects conceived through regional planning. In some instances, localism gave communities greater say in the shaping of development schemes, reducing the "democratic deficit" in decision making. But the scale of some schemes (and the needs that drive them) make them impervious to localized concern. For some communities at least, localism failed to close the democratic deficit and simply widened the gap between expectation of local veto and the reality of a national housing crisis.

3. Overloading of Existing Infrastructure—Public Concern

A key point from the Lyons Housing Review is that providing "... infrastructure and wider benefits to the community is critical to winning public support for new homes" (Lyons, 2014, p. 72). Dear (1992) has shown how spontaneous reactions to development proposals can quickly mature into more sophisticated counterarguments, often centering on the unresolved pressures that development will create. The failure to plan ahead and demonstrate early on that pressures are anticipated and, crucially, that enough value will be captured and retained in order to pay for road upgrades, new schools, and community facilities, seems to be commonplace in large-scale speculative development in England. There are countless examples of big schemes, brought forward by large numbers of separate developers in the 1970s and 1980s, which were without new shops for a decade after completion or which generated demand for new school places that was not met, the result being that children moving into an area needed to be dispersed and ferried to other schools each morning until the infrastructure caught up with the rate of housing growth. The expectation of the market being unresponsive to these externalities, combined with a history of failure to adequately capture community gain from land development (see the last chapter), can create a hostile environment for large-scale housing developments. Kate Barker (2004) drew attention to the lack of incentive to accept new housing a decade ago and since then there have been attempts to tie local authority finance to house building rates and to direct some revenues from development to communities. New mechanisms have also been created that try to levy fixed contributions from the developers of residential and commercial projects, linked to projected infrastructure and externality costs. This has taken the form of the "Community Infrastructure Levy" in England: infrastructure contribution payments linked to the number of homes built or the square-meter volume of development. And, yet, compromises are often reached with private enterprise, reducing the scope of necessary infrastructure investment or, for example, the amount of affordable housing that will be levied from a scheme. These compromises tend to be responses to uncertain market conditions, with the "regulation" (or "public tests") used to seek developer contributions presented as a brake on growth that needs to be released. But, from a public perspective, compromises are seen as broken promises: deals which skew the benefits of development further in favor of landowners and private companies.

4. Policy Shift and "Regulatory Risk"

In a parliamentary democracy, in which local government has the discretion to formulate plans and interpret policy guidance in different ways, there are bound to be 1) periodic national shifts and 2) spatial variabilities in planning for housing. This has resulted in developers building stronger or weaker relationships with different local authorities (Carmona et al., 2001, 2003), favoring particular local working practices aligned to political orientations ranging from the liberal and the laissez-faire to less-flexible and more-pervasive public planning. The national shifts witnessed over the last quarter-century have been perhaps less fundamental than those occurring in the inter-war or immediate post-war period, yet edicts focused on the use of greenfield sites or the status of regional strategies will have a fundamental impact on the credibility of local plans and therefore on the certainty that those plans provide to the development industry. The drivers of policy shift are variable, being in part ideological and in part pragmatic. On the eve of all recent General Elections, debate has focused on whether additional policy change or "stability" will deliver more homes, infrastructure, and investment in England. In the run-up to the 2015 General Election, the RTPI called for a "pause" on the introduction of further legislation, with its Head of Policy and Practice arguing that recent changes have "disrupted investment in homes and jobs, damaged community wellbeing and confused members of the public" (Blyth, 2015, p. 111). Others had indirectly likened the Institute to a "dead parrot," fearful of necessary change. Inevitably, change is disruptive and change in planning introduces regulatory risk. The possibility of change therefore presents a choice between making the best of what's already in place (and allowing it to "bed in") and deciding that an alternative policy could deliver a better outcome. However, the willingness to embrace change in England has been undermined by past experience of incrementalism and incoherency in overall vision.

5. Market Cycles and Viability

In an ideal world, the development of land would follow a linear path, largely uninterrupted by regulation and responding quickly to market signals. The option (treaty agreement) to purchase land would be signed early on, at a time of growing interest in an area but well before the market's "sweet point." Progression from outline to full planning permission would be rapid (and locally uncontested) and there would be quick agreement over developer contributions toward infrastructure, which would be modest. The development would be viable with minimal infrastructure upgrades. Houses would be built quickly in simple development cells, hanging off a dendritic road pattern comprising cul-de-sacs, and they would all be sold off-plan in a single batch, giving the developer an immediate return on investment. Such an ideal might be possible for a relatively small scheme, perhaps bolted onto a new extension of a small to medium-sized town. But really big schemes, in politically or economically challenging locations, which require major infrastructure investment and which will be built out over several decades, may need to negotiate the difficulties of multiple market cycles. According to Salway (2014, p. 73), ideal development opportunities are those where there is: established demand from occupiers; a lack of competing schemes; quick "in and out" potential (e.g. smaller sites or separately permissioned parcels of a larger site), to maximize returns on capital; and the likelihood of a scheme being completed within a single market cycle. Being able to complete in the current cycle reduces the risk of "being caught with a half-completed project during an economic downturn" and also allows developers to invest in an area, to create additional value, and to "reposition a location higher up the price curve" (ibid.). Against these criteria, big development opportunities can score very badly. At regeneration schemes such as Ebbsfleet, huge effort is needed to turn ex-industrial land into a place of market interest, individual projects find themselves competing with others in the wider Thames Gateway, and there is zero likelihood of getting in and out quickly in a single cycle. Success often hinges on necessary up-front infrastructure investment; if that doesn't materialize or if developers are "unable to overcome the initial hurdle of high up-front costs on large sites" (ibid., p. 76), then projects can become stuck. These issues are often amplified in difficult political situations: the fifty-two years spent musing over development at Stevenage West serves as a warning to developers that they should pick their opportunities carefully, pursuing those that have a good level of local support as well as score well against other key criteria. The current arrangements for development seem to offer no magic formula for more rapid progression of major schemes, though, time and again, infrastructure investment figures as a significant risk to the viability of projects.

6. Flexible Planning?

Certainly the planning system, and the way it is operated locally, need to be attuned—as far as possible—to current market realities and future prospects. Although the Planning and Infrastructure Act 2013 gave developers the right to have planning agreements reviewed in light of changing economic circumstances, in many cases they were already reaching compromises with local authorities on the scale, timing, and nature of Section 106 contributions. The Community Infrastructure Levy is arguably less flexible than Section 106 (Lyons, 2014), being tied to a charging schedule adopted in a local plan, with any changes to that schedule requiring a plan review and a retesting of the soundness of any CIL revisions. However, the planning system in England has a general disposition toward flexibility; although it is "plan-led" (adopted local plans are the primary consideration in development control decisions), it is not "compliance-based" and there is considerable scope, within planning committees, to weigh local policies against other material considerations. In this way, approaches and agreements affecting major housing sites have been reviewed and modified by local authorities, though across England the propensity to be flexible has depended on local relationships and the different ways in which policy has been implemented. Flexibility—making necessary adjustments during the life of a local plan, for example by bringing additional land forward for development or revisiting planning agreements—is perhaps less important, however, than the predictability of decision making. Salway (2014, p. 79) argues that, in relation to major sites, "planning is only an issue if it is slow and unpredictable in outcome."

7. Major Sites and Cross-Border Working

In the months and years after the dismantling of the regional planning apparatus—and the revocation of regional spatial strategies—a number of organizations have stepped up to assert the value of strategic planning. Long-term, cross-border cooperation is viewed by many as crucial to the future growth prospects and wellbeing of cities (in particular), enabling them to cope with change. Now the dust has settled on the RSS revocation, there is greater circumspection as to the merits and shortcomings of the old system. It seemed to provide a stable strategic framework for local development planning, but lacked deeper political buy-in. Its procedural focus, and lack of accountability to local electorates, meant that it was unable to navigate or resolve local tensions—as illustrated in the case of Stevenage—but often made these worse, requiring unwilling partners to forge ahead with unwanted projects. The answer, according to the RTPI (2015), is to invest time in building long-term, locally focused, voluntary arrangements that are politically led and accountable. These arrangements will work best where the rationale for cooperation is clear and well-articulated. However, the RTPI (2015, p. 21) adds that evidence from England has "demonstrated the value of allowing areas to make their own choices regarding who to associate with." Such "association" is the logical choice where broad, mutual benefit is acknowledged. In the case of housing development, there are certainly instances where major sites that straddle a shared boundary are the obvious candidates for development, and there is mutual benefit for neighboring authorities bringing these forward in a coordinated way. But, in other instances, the benefits are clearly skewed; under-bounded towns and cities being the case in hand. In the aftermath of the revocation of the East of England plan, Stevenage Borough and North Hertfordshire have a "duty to co-operate" (under the Localism Act 2011). They must find a way to accommodate the subregion's projected housing demand. The government's Planning Inspectorate will reject local plans that do not demonstrate "cooperation." Yet, the problem seems intractable: the expansion of Stevenage onto the North Hertfordshire greenbelt is politically toxic and it is difficult, at this stage, to see how alternative processes of strategic planning might deliver a solution. Moreover, the under-bounding of growing towns and cities should perhaps not be seen as a strategic planning issue at all (unresolvable owing to the imbalance of potential benefits from cooperation), but rather as a question of administrative boundary logic. If Stevenage, and other towns facing similar situations, had their own expansion space (looser borders) then the prospects for their future growth would not be determined by political debate in a neighboring authority. There have been calls for a new Boundary Commission to take a comprehensive look at this issue.

Closing Remarks

In two chapters, we have shone a light on the nature and scope of planning in England and how the local operation of the planning system has impacted, specifically, on the delivery of new homes on major development sites. The narrative of the previous chapter was that the power of planning to *deliver* direct outcomes (by framing and facilitating public sector projects, including post-war urban renewal and new towns) gave way to a *regulatory* power during the second half of the twentieth century. In essence, the system stands back from the development process, having been directed to respect private property rights, and plays only a regulatory part in the delivery of new homes. This is problematic when there is a failure to capture value uplift from the granting of planning permission, and therefore either the financial benefit of development flows disproportionately to landowners or the lack of resource for infrastructure causes development to stall. Some recent analyses of development viability (e.g. RICS, 2012) show how post hoc attempts to draw "planning gain" from housing schemes, through Section 106 agreements, jeopardize their economic viability. The same analyses also reveal that land costs were a significant component of total development cost, meaning that prices were high and value was lost. Arguably, viability was undermined not by post hoc planning agreements but by the failure to capture value uplift much earlier on. In relation to the seven impediments to housing development on major sites identified in this chapter, value capture and infrastructure investment are the most fundamental, linking as they do to public concern over development, potential infrastructure stresses, and the stalling of slow-burn, long-run development during the market cycle.

However, while the focus of this chapter and the last has been on the planning system and its interaction with residential development, another important point has been made: that the localized and general problems of that development, and linked issues of housing supply, are only a small part of the overall housing crisis in England. Even a much higher annual rate of house building, stemming from greater success and regularity in the delivery of large schemes, would have a small impact on the housing market and housing affordability when set against the wider demand for housing, driven by the tax treatment of residential property and leading to concentrated domestic and international investment in housing. These big schemes will ease access pressures in particular locations, if enough non-market housing can be reserved for key workers and less-affluent households, but the wider crisis has much deeper roots.

References

Allmendinger, P. (2011). *New Labour and Planning: from New Right to New Left*. London: Routledge.
Amec Environment and Infrastructure UK Ltd. (2013). *Review of the Green Belt around Stevenage: Part 1—Survey against Green Belt Purposes* (Final Report). Leamington Spa, UK: Amec.
Ashford Borough Council. (2008). *Local Development Framework: Adopted Core Strategy*. Ashford, UK: ABC.
Baker, M., & Wong, C. (2013). The delusion of strategic spatial planning: what's left after the Labour government's English Regional Experiment? *Planning Practice & Research*, 28(1), 83–103.
Barker, K. (2004). *Review of Housing Supply*. London: HM Treasury.
Barker, K. (2014). *Housing: Where's the Plan?* London: London Publishing Partnership.
Blyth, R. (2015). Proposals for planning in the next Parliament. *Town and Country Planning*, 84(3), 11.
Breheny, M. (Ed.) (1996). *The People: Where Will They Go? National Report of TCPA Regional Inquiry into Housing Need and Provision in England*. London: Town and Country Planning Association.
Carmona, M., Carmona, S., & Gallent, N. (2001). *Working Together: A Guide for Planners and Housing Providers*. London: Thomas Telford.
Carmona, M., Carmona, S., & Gallent, N. (2003). *Delivering New Homes Planning, Processes and Providers*. London: Routledge.
Cheshire, P. (2011). *Some unintended productivity consequences of good intentions: the British land use planning system*. London: Spatial Economics Research Centre, LSE.
Colin Buchanan and Partners. (1967). *Ashford Study: Consultants' Proposals for Designation*. London: HMSO.
The Construction Index. (2012, August 24). *Plans submitted for 5,750-home Ashford suburb*.

Cope, H. (1999). *Housing Associations*. Basingstoke, UK: Macmillan.
Dartford Borough Council. (2010). *Ebbsfleet Valley Strategic Site: Background Paper*. Dartford, UK: Dartford Borough Council.
Dartford Borough Council, Gravesham Borough Council & Kent County Council. (1996). *Ebbsfleet Development and Environment Framework*, Dartford, UK: Dartford Borough Council, Gravesham Borough Council, & Kent County Council.
Dear, M. (1992). Understanding and overcoming the NIMBY syndrome. *Journal of the American Planning Association, 58*(3), 288–300.
Department for Communities and Local Government. (2011a) *National Planning Policy Framework*. London: DCLG.
Department for Communities and Local Government. (2011b). *Laying the Foundations: A Housing Strategy for England*. London: DCLG.
Department for Communities and Local Government. (2011c). *Draft National Planning Policy Framework*. London: DCLG.
Department of the Environment. (1991). *Circular 7/91: Planning and Affordable Housing*. London: HMSO.
Department of the Environment. (1992). *Planning Policy Guidance Note 3: Housing*. London: HMSO.
Department of the Environment/Thames Gateway Taskforce. (1995). *The Thames Gateway Planning Framework—RPG9a*. London DoE.
Dorling, D. (2014). *All That Is Solid: How the Great Housing Disaster Defines Our Times, and What We Can Do About It*. London: Penguin.
Edwards, M. (2015). *Prospects for Land, Rent and Housing in UK Cities*. London: Government Office for Science.
The Express. (2011, March 26). *A Very Rural Revolution*.
Gallent, N. (2008a). Planning and Development in the Countryside. In M. Woods (Ed.), *New Labour's Countryside: Rural Policy in Britain Since 1997*. Bristol, UK: Policy Press.
Gallent, N. (2008b). Strategic-local tensions and the spatial planning approach in England. *Planning Theory & Practice, 9*(3), 307–323.
Gallent, N., Hamiduddin, I., & Madeddu, M. (2013). Localism, down-scaling and the strategic dilemmas confronting planning in England. *Town Planning Review, 84*(5), 563–582.
Gallent, N. & Robinson, S. (2012). *Neighbourhood Planning: Communities, Networks and Governance*. Bristol, UK: Policy Press.
Government Office for the South East. (2009). *The South East Plan (South East Regional Spatial Strategy)*. Guildford, UK: GOSE.
Gravesham Borough Council. (1997). *Development Brief: Land West of Springhead Road*. Northfleet, UK: Gravesham Borough Council.
Halcrow/Ashford Borough Council. (2002). *Ashford's Future: Ashford's Capacity—A Handbook for Change*. Ashford, UK: ABC.
Hall, P. (2014). Why are the Great "Stuck Sites" Stuck? In A. Adonis, B. Rogers, & S. Sims (Eds.), *Go East: Unlocking the Potential of the Thames Estuary*. London: Centre for London, pp. 60–71.
Hall, P. & Ward, C. (2014). *Sociable Cities: The 21st Century Reinvention of the Garden City* (2nd ed.). London: Routledge.
Hamiduddin, I. & Gallent, N. (2012). Limits to growth: The challenge of housing delivery in England's "under-bounded" districts. *Planning Practice & Research, 27*(5), 513–530.

HM Government. (1987). *Housing White Paper*. London: HMSO.
HM Treasury. (2014). *National Infrastructure Plan 2014*. London: TSO.
Kent Online. (2010, September 7). *Chilmington Green protests against town plan*.
Kent Online. (2014b, July 15). *Councillors say urban development corporation set up to oversee 15,000 home garden city in Ebbsfleet could be undemocratic and ignore local residents*.
Kent Thames-side Partnership. (1995). *Looking to the Future*. Blue Circle Properties Ltd, Kent County Council, Dartford Borough Council, Gravesham Borough Council & the University of Greenwich.
Lock, D. (2000). Housing and Transport. In B. Edwards & D. Turrent (Eds.), *Sustainable Housing: Principles and Practice*. London: E&FN Spon, pp. 36–43.
Lyons Housing Review. (2014). *Mobilising Across the Nation to Build the Homes our Children Need*. London: Lyons Housing Review.
Moroni, S. & Andersson, D. E. (2014). Introduction: Private Enterprise and the Future of Urban Planning. In D. E. Andersson & S. Moroni (Eds.), *Cities and Private Planning*. Cheltenham, UK: Edward Elgar, pp. 1–16.
National Housing Federation. (2009). *Home Truths 2009: How the Recession has Increased Housing Need—South East*. Bristol, UK: NHF.
Office for National Statistics. (2008). *Regional Gross Value Added (GVA)* Available at: www.statistics.gov.uk/downloads/theme_economy/NUTS1-2-3.pdf, accessed on September 7, 2009.
Office of the Deputy Prime Minister. (2003). *Sustainable Communities: Building for the Future*. London: ODPM.
Planning. (2014, April 24). *How we Did it: Shaping a Community Along Garden City Lines*.
RICS. (2012). *Financial Viability in Planning—RICS Guidance Note*. London: RICS.
RTPI. (2015). *Strategic Planning: Effective Cooperation for Planning Across Boundaries*. London: Royal Town Planning Institute.
Salway, F. (2014). A Developer's Perspective. In A. Adonis, B. Rogers, and S. Sims (Eds.), *Go East: Unlocking the Potential of the Thames Estuary*. London: Centre for London, pp. 72–79.
South East England Development Agency. (2006). *Regional Economic Strategy*. Guildford, UK: SEEDA.
Sturzaker, J. (2011). Can community empowerment reduce opposition to housing? Evidence from rural England. *Planning Practice & Research*, 26(5), 555–570.
Swain, C., Marshall, T., & Baden, T. (Eds.). (2013). *English Regional Planning 2000–2010: Lessons for the Future*. London: Routledge.
Urban Initiatives with DTZ Pieda Consulting, Alan Baxter and Associates, Turner and Townsend, & Studio Engleback. (2005). *Greater Ashford Development Framework, Final Masterplan Report April 2005*. London: Urban Initiatives.
Wei Yang & Partners, & Freeman, P. (2014). *New Garden Cities: Visionary, Economically Viable and Popular: Entry for Wolfson Economics Prize*. London: Wei Yang & Partners.
Wellings, F. (2006). *British House-builders: History and Analysis*. London: John Wiley & Sons.
Wyman, L. & Davies, M. (2015). *Paper presented to the RTPI/Bartlett School of Planning Seminar, January 21, 2015*.

6 Power and Decision Making in Hong Kong's Planning System

Introduction

Although human activities in Hong Kong have a very long history—dating back around 5,000 to 6,000 years—its development as a human settlement commenced around the year AD 973. The early period of development proved foundational for the later economic development of this small but strategic development node in Southern China, notably its manufacturing and port functions. By the fourteenth century, Hong Kong had become an outpost for coastal defense in southern China, accommodating only a small population. Before the British took possession of Hong Kong Island in 1841, it had become a fishing port of 7,450 people, supported by a smattering of other economic activities, including farming, salt production, pearl production, incense making, and sea trading (Liu, 2009). However, after British colonization in 1842, Hong Kong's trading port function was greatly enhanced. Just over a hundred years later, Hong Kong's processing industries were flourishing due to the international division of labor in the industrial production process, laying the foundation for its development into a modern city. Owing to its British colonial history, Hong Kong's planning system shares an origin similar to those of England and Australia. Furthermore, not only has its colonial history left irremovable footprints on the land system, its housing policy and housing management practices have also been under strong British influence. Significant divergence has arisen, however, owing to a plethora of factors. Thus, the discourse on Hong Kong's planning governance modes over the past years and their impact on land and new housing supply in this and the next chapter has to be preceded by an understanding of the key distinctiveness of Hong Kong's government and urban system vis-à-vis those of England and Australia.

Either as a colony of Britain or as a special administrative region of the People's Republic of China, Hong Kong is a city endowed with a political border and a high level of autonomy by its sovereign state to run its internal affairs. Its government structure is thus much simpler than those of England and Australia: it has only a single-tiered government, which has full control of planning and land supply issues. Further, as a city with its own political border, the impact of uncontrolled internal migration on the housing market is a much smaller issue than that of English and Australian prime cities. For instance, the abolition of the "touch base policy" on October 24, 1980 in Hong Kong required immediate repatriation of illegal immigrants from mainland China from that date onward.

Politically, as a colonial government that only introduced a preliminary form of representative government in the run-up to the handover of Hong Kong's sovereignty to China in 1997, the influence of political parties on planning approaches was minimal until the 1990s, unlike in England. There had been, of course, changes in planning approaches over the years, but they were mostly prompted by pragmatic reasons, as discussed later. Party politics has been growing since 1997. However, the recent community fight for the 2017 election of the Chief Executive by universal suffrage was unsuccessful. The government's proposal of an election plan with wider representation than the last exercise was voted down by the Legislative Council on June 28, 2015. Thus, evolution to parliamentary democracy is unlikely to take place in Hong Kong in the foreseeable future. Accordingly, planning paradigm shifts owing to oscillations of the ruling party, as in the case of England, will not happen for some years to come.

Another unique characteristic of Hong Kong's urban system is the state ownership of land, declared upon the official designation of Hong Kong as a British colony in 1842. It turned all freehold land held by incumbent landowners and new land to be developed for future use into leasehold, except for one small church site. This has important ramifications for the supply of land for new homes, especially public housing, as the government does not have to rely solely on the release of land from existing land lessees and home owners for housing (re)development. Further, the property development rights of home owners and developers are also circumscribed in the land leases, in addition to, and sometimes preceding or differing from, those prescribed in land-use zoning documents. Thus, the importance of planning tools in circumscribing development rights and intensity is less significant than in English and Australian cases. The Hong Kong government thus legally possesses both the ownership and development rights, though the exercise of the former to deny land lease renewal has seldom been invoked. The state ownership of land also enables the Hong Kong government to directly provide affordable housing through the public rental housing program and the subsidized owner-occupier housing programs to half of its population.

A further departure of Hong Kong's urban system from those of both England and Australia, or their cities, is its composite urban form, characterized by a main urban core and multiple decentralized development nodes with very high concentrations of people, mostly accommodated in super high rises. Thus, not only does the definition of population targets in strategic plans have implications for housing land requirements, the determination of development intensity in land-use zoning plans at the district level is also an important planning tool in creating development space to meet housing needs. In addition, the high population density in the development nodes, that is, the main urban area and the nine new towns, demands grave attention be given to the qualitative aspects of land development, especially in residential areas.

Residential development in Hong Kong is often organized into high-rise housing estates comprising from three or four to tens of blocks. These estates are generally equipped with a varied range of community facilities and public space depending on the scale of development. The livability and the connectivity of these densely populated estates thus heavily depends on neighborhood and infrastructure planning and development. The origin of estate planning can be traced back to the early 1970s, when the development of new towns was rejuvenated to provide better livability for the general masses under the Ten Year Housing Program, Hong Kong's first longer-term public housing program. Therefore, when examining the politics involved in the planning of, and the land supply for, new homes and housing outcomes, the qualitative aspect, including community facilities for meeting daily needs, public space, neighborliness, circulation, human comfort, and the like, cannot be overlooked.

Apart from an emphasis on the qualitative aspect, in providing an account of the changes in the planning paradigm of Hong Kong in this chapter, the societal context, particularly the political, economic, and social conditions (instead of changes in the elected government) will form the backdrop, due to the absence of a fully elected government in Hong Kong as mentioned above. In particular, the quest for land for housing development will be used as a major backbone of understanding the changes in the planning governance system for three reasons. First, the general changes in the mode of planning governance have been well documented in Bristow (1984), Wan (2005), Ng (2008), and Wan & Chiu (2008). Second, as housing is the major user of land, understanding the evolution of planning in association with housing development will yield a deeper understanding of the enforcement process than what the extant literature referred to above can reveal. Third, as argued later, changes in the governance and power of urban planning have mainly been housing-induced, though for different reasons in different time periods. While harbor reclamation was a key factor for the recent sharp turn to a participatory planning mode, this only occurred between 1997 and 2005, and its influence has already been well mooted in Wan (2005), Ng (2006, 2008, 2011), and Wan & Chiu (2008).

Thus, within the contexts outlined above, the next section discusses the scope of and the power within planning by initially looking into the land tenure system, then the emergence and development of the planning system and the ways that they define the power of the major stakeholders and their relationships. This is followed by a close examination of decision-making processes, and the governance and objectives of urban planning in relation to housing development in different time periods. The last section of the chapter summarizes and explains the changing role and influence of the planning regulatory tools, state ownership of land, the community and the market in Hong Kong's effort to source land for satisfying the housing needs and demands of an expanding population in a transforming political economy.

Scope of and Power within Urban Planning

The gist of urban planning concerns decisions on spatial development and on the means and institutions to deliver the intended spatial development objectives. The ways that urban planning decisions are made and delivered define and reflect the power of planning and the power structure within the planning system, which is embedded in the wider political, social, and economic systems. The planning decisions and the way that the decisions are made in turn influence the beneficiaries of the land resource. In reality, however, land development can precede the formulation of a spatial planning mechanism, as was the case of Hong Kong in its early colonial days. There has only been one true landowner in Hong Kong since August 29, 1842: the state, which referred to Britain prior to July 1997, and to the People's Republic of China since July 1997. Ownership was exercised through and administered by the local government of Hong Kong both before and after the handover of sovereignty in 1997. By the Hong Kong Reunification Ordinance (the Hong Kong legislation that confirms the continuation of the pre-1997 legal, judicial, and public service systems, transfer of property ownership and rights after the handover of the government on July 1, 1997), China has transferred all properties that belonged to the British Crown before the handover to the Hong Kong Self Administrative Government, which has been the true landowner of Hong Kong since July 1, 1997 (Merry, 2003; Nissim, 2011).

As argued by Bristow (1984), the Hong Kong government had discharged from the outset "a town planning responsibility in terms of determining the principal laying-out and use of land in the Colony" (p. 57). Land was one of the earliest concerns of the new colony owing to its rapid development, as acknowledged in the first gazette of Hong Kong (Collins (1952), quoted in Bristow (1984, p. 22)). There was a great need for the central arrangement of land to accommodate housing and offices and to regularize the disposal of land among the merchants who speculated on Hong Kong becoming a British colony (Bristow, 1984). But, before we look into Hong Kong's scope of planning and power relations in the planning system, we need to understand its landownership system and land disposal mechanisms, as they are fundamental to land development control in Hong Kong.

Landownership and Disposal System

As recounted by Liu (2009) and Nissim (2011), Britain took possession of Hong Kong Island on January 26, 1841, and declared it a free port in March

1842. The island was formally ceded to Britain permanently at the ratification of the Nanking Treaty on August 29, 1842. The cession of the Kowloon Peninsula took place in 1860 and the leasing of the New Territories for ninety-nine years began in 1898. Land sites were occupied informally and built upon immediately following British possession in 1841, as merchants were speculating on Hong Kong becoming a British territory. The very first government attempts to lease land for building use were by auction on the annual rent to be paid. When proven to have caused overbidding, private treaty (application in person for land use with terms specified by government) was adopted. Auction had nonetheless developed to become the dominant method of land disposal, only losing its dominance between November 2002 and 2009, due to depressed market conditions; it returned to its position in 2010, but has again lost its supremacy to tendering since 2011/12 (Lands Department, 2015). It has nonetheless always been accused of having caused Hong Kong's "high land price" phenomenon.

At the outset, land was not to be sold outright, but leased for a maximum term of seventy-five years upon the payment of a premium, with a renewal possibility at the government's discretion (Nissim, 2011). The lease period and possibility and conditions of renewal varied over time. As delineated by Merry (2003) and Nissim (2011), in 1849 the government made a bold decision to allow all crown leases made for a term of seventy-five years to be extended for a further term of 924 years—that is, to become a lease term of 999 years in total—in effect rendering perpetual leases. However, this lease policy was retracted after forty-nine years as the government came to realize that leasehold land of 999 years was equivalent to freehold land, thus depriving government of its control over land in the colony and sharing land value increase over time. Thus, the land lease period reverted to seventy-five, or, at the most, ninety-nine years in 1898, with the possibility of one renewal only.

At the same time, the British government also instructed that at the expiry of the leaseholds the government should not confiscate all land value, as tenants' good efforts in developing and managing the land would have contributed to the increase in value. This view, as argued by Nissim (2011), has had a long-lasting effect on the treatment of land value at lease expiry. Indeed, when many of these leases expired in 1973, the Government Leases Ordinance enacted at the time to deal with the renewal issues stipulated that land leases with the right for renewal were to be renewed without a premium (that is, no payment for granting another term of use), but an annual rent calculated at 3 percent of ratable value was to be paid. Leases without renewal rights were to become renewable, subject to the payment of a full premium based on prevalent land value. Not only is this ordinance still enforced today, but, under the Sino-British Joint Declaration signed between the Chinese government and the British government in 1984, at the handover of Hong Kong to China all non-renewable leases would become renewable and no longer need to pay market-value premiums at renewal, but lessees would be liable to pay an additional annual rent calculated at 3 percent of ratable value.

Thus, leasehold land in Hong Kong is equivalent in practical terms to freehold land—that is, lessees have the continued exclusive use of the land and the right to transfer this right to another party at a price, subject to the annual payment of an insignificant rent to the government. While the government possesses the legal right to take back or "resume" land leased for public purposes under the Land Resumption Ordinance (Merry, 2003), this right has been prudently and rarely exercised. However, owing to the common high-rise structure of most residential buildings in Hong Kong that incurs multiple ownership, the quasi-freehold property right is constrained, in a way similar to the strata system of Australia. The land on which multi-owned buildings are constructed is divided by the developers into shares and the home purchasers acquire the shares according to the size of the unit they purchase. The shares are undivided, however, meaning that no purchaser can claim specific ownership of a particular part of the land (Merry, 2003). The exclusive use of the units purchased by individuals and the right to transfer ownership, and the governance and the operation of the common areas in the building or estate within which groups of buildings of the same development project are situated, are stipulated in a legal document called the Deed of Mutual Covenant, which is binding on all purchasers and their tenants. The multiple ownership of a housing site has significant implications for the supply of housing through redevelopment, as under the current regulation the consent of 80 percent of the unit owners has to be obtained to invoke the court order for compulsory sale. Thus, England's affordable housing provision through planning application controls on redevelopment would not be feasible in Hong Kong.

Apart from the location of the site to be sold, which may or may not be directed by a spatial plan depending on the time period when the site was designated, an important mechanism affecting the use of the site on leasehold land is the conditions specified in the land lease, or in its preparatory document, known as the "Conditions of Grant" (Merry, 2003). The grant or the land lease is a contract between the government, as the landowner, and the developer, as the lessee, stipulating the conditions under which the land is to be used. In the main, they include the lease period, site area, the use of structures built on the site, the time period within which the development should take place, and specific site conditions, such as building height restrictions, and other obligations, such as the provision of community facilities. The land lease may or may not take into account the requirements or stipulations of district land use plans, as the leases may be granted before the publication of these plans. Thus, there might be inconsistencies, which can only be addressed during redevelopment. However, at the time of drafting, land leases or Conditions of Grant would usually be formulated on the basis of the district plans, especially the statutory outline zoning plans.

So, if the leasehold land system in Hong Kong is almost equivalent to a freehold system, does it make any difference to the government's role in facilitating land supply for housing development, especially subsidized housing, compared with governments in freehold systems such as England and Australia? The answer is yes. First, although Hong Kong's history can be traced back four thousand years, at the time when Hong Kong was declared a British possession in 1841 it was only a small port with fishing and small-scale trading as its major activities. Thus, declaring all land to be Crown land gave the government plenty of land resources to maneuver as the colony developed spatially alongside the growth of, initially, trading activities and, subsequently, industrial activities. Second, although because of political sensitivity the colonial government avoided developing the village areas and in fact had maintained the right of the indigenous villagers to build houses for their offspring, the sale of land in unoccupied areas had become a major source of land supply for housing for the rapidly growing population and for guaranteeing government revenue through land sales.

Third, as coined by Merry (2003), the government of Hong Kong is not only the biggest landowner but also the biggest tenant in the city, as its Hong Kong Housing Authority operates a massive public housing program accommodating half of the population (as outlined in Chapter 1). Such provision was possible because of the continuous availability of new urban fringe areas due to the incessant and rapid city development in the 1970s and 1980s. Though building new towns in the urban fringe incurred resumption of farmland from indigenous residents, state ownership of land provides the legal basis and "public purposes" provide the legitimate basis for doing so. Similarly, state ownership of land makes it possible for the government to create new land at its disposal through sea reclamation. As of today, 25.5 percent of the land developed in Hong Kong is sourced from sea reclamation (Civil Engineering and Development Department, 2015). Nonetheless, the above two methods of creating land for housing development became difficult after 1997 because of increasing environmental consciousness, intensifying local politics, a more democratized populace, and a stronger consciousness to protect the value of one's property, thus leading to a rejection of the construction of public housing by the community in proximity to their homes, as discussed in the next chapter.

Thus, by being the sole supplier of new land, the Hong Kong government has control in steering the urban form of the city both vertically and horizontally, as well as supplying land for new housing development and other activities. Though market initiatives and responses have also been important, the government does not need to rely on the use of planning tools or the willingness of developers or home owners to be able to provide affordable housing to lower income families. State landownership and the land lease system alone are nonetheless insufficient land factors to enable Hong Kong to meet housing needs and demand quantitatively and qualitatively, nor are they adequate to enable the city to evolve into a global city.

A land use planning system was needed as early as when Hong Kong was founded as a colony, and over the years a comprehensive spatial planning system has been developed.

The Planning System and its Scope

Bristow (1984) ascertained that the first layout to guide the development of Hong Kong was drafted as early as 1843, but the first major attempt to adopt urban planning principles came much later, in the 1920s, under the 1922 Town Planning Scheme. The former was found premature for implementation, while the latter had a head start but was not fully realized because of the economic depression of the 1930s. Nonetheless, because of the pressing sanitary and overcrowding problems endured by large influxes of refugees from China fleeing from Japanese occupation, the inefficient and congested traffic system, and haphazard developments in the urban areas causing severe sanitary and health issues, the government enacted the Town Planning Ordinance in 1939, whereby a Town Planning Board was set up to redress the problems. The Board was tasked to draft statutory plans for the future layout of existing and potential new urban areas and the types of buildings thereon for the approval of the governor and his executive council. Thus, while in 1922 an overall development plan was pioneered and implemented in subsequent years as far as circumstances allowed, in 1939 an important step was taken to prepare for the drafting of statutory land use zoning plans at district level. Hence, a preliminary planning hierarchy had been formulated by 1939, but its implementation had to wait until the Second World War was over in 1945.

In 1947, three town planning architect posts and a Town Planning Office were created in Hong Kong to help rehabilitate the city through planning efforts. In addition, Patrick Abercrombie, a renowned planner in Britain, was invited to come to Hong Kong to formulate an overall plan and major recommendations for the colony's post-war development. The Planning Office had actually conducted a comprehensive land utilization survey, drafted detailed zoning plans for the whole colony, and completed industrial layouts in areas that later became the new industrial satellite towns. Based on these foundations, Abercrombie's report of 1948 made comprehensive and farsighted proposals, including a cross-harbor tunnel, reclamation, railway relocation to a location that was at the time less central, removal of military establishments, the opening up of new industrial and residential areas, and new towns in the New Territories (Town Planning Office, 1988). These plans, however, did not formalize, and the Office was dissolved in 1951. Abercrombie's major recommendation of developing the urban areas around the harbor to improve their overcrowded living conditions was not taken up as it was considered too slow and expensive.

Rather, new towns were listed on the policy agenda by mid-1952, concurrent with the formation of the Hong Kong Housing Authority, which was established to build public housing (Chief Building Surveyor to the Director of Public Works, cited in Bristow, 1989). Major urban expansion schemes were first launched in east Kowloon and east Hong Kong Island to provide resettlement sites for squatters who were mostly refugees from China, and to provide factory sites (Report of Interdepartmental Committee, 1954, cited in Bristow, 1989). It was in 1956 that the government firmly committed to building new towns to provide housing space to cope with housing demands for population expansion due to natural increase, immigration, and refugee influx from mainland China, and to provide more decent homes for the inadequately housed (Special Committee on Housing, 1956). In the 1950s and 1960s, the planning effort concentrated on exploring the possibility of building five new towns. Eventually, the first outline development plans were produced for three new towns (Tsuen Wan, Sha Tin, and Tuen Mun) in 1962, 1964, and 1965, respectively, later known as the "first-generation new towns." Altogether, the government aimed to construct 2.19 million resettlement and low-cost housing units in these new towns to solve the grave housing shortage at the time (Bristow, 1984; Town Planning Office, 1988; Public Works Department, 1965, cited in Bristow, 1989).

At the same time, the 1922 Town Planning Scheme also evolved to become the 1969 Colony Outline Plan (which was slightly amended to become the Hong Kong Outline Plan in 1974), comprising a planning manual and a summary of major large-scale development plans providing broad-brush planning directions (Bristow, 1984, p. 132; Hong Kong SAR Government, 2007). The Ten-Year Housing Program announced in October 1972 necessitated a reassessment of public housing sites obtainable from the new towns, leading to the decision to build three "second-generation new towns" (Yuen Long, Sheung Shui/Fanling, and Taipo) under the Outline Plan (Planning Division, 1969). In 1978, after a reassessment of the housing program in relation to the government's long-term aim of providing permanent, self-contained, unshared, reasonably spacious, and affordable dwellings for all households, two more new towns, in Northeast Lantau and Junk Bay, were proposed (Figure 6.1). Thus, urban planning from the 1950s to the 1970s was dominated by new town planning in order to meet the housing needs of the rapidly growing population and the government's intention of providing a better living environment. As remarked by Murray MacLehose in his 1972 Policy Speech, the impetus for this shift was growing recognition of "the poor housing conditions [that] constitute a constant source of conflict between the government and the populace" (Hong Kong Governor, 1972).

Under the broad spatial development strategy were outline land use zoning plans, formulated according to the statutory requirements and procedures of the Town Planning Ordinance, though not all developed areas were covered then. In parallel, the departmental development and layout plans were drafted to provide administrative guidance to government departments in the implementation of the plans. Beyond these tiers were the Buildings Ordinances, notably the Buildings (Planning) Regulations, which

168 Hong Kong: Planning, Power, and Decisions

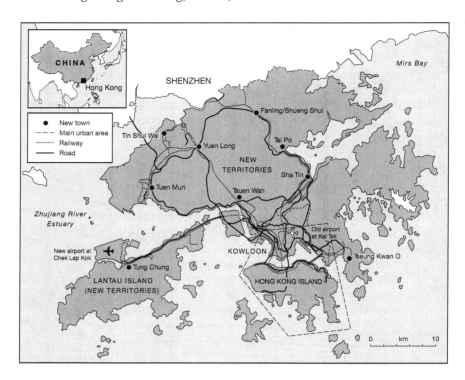

Figure 6.1 Spatial Development of Hong Kong
Source: Author

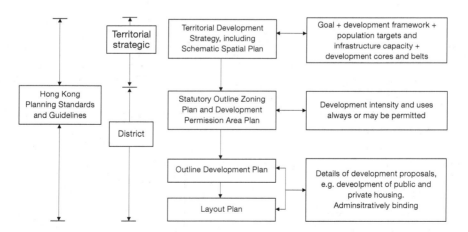

Figure 6.2 Hierarchy of Plans in Hong Kong
Source: Based on Planning Department (2005)

empowered the building authority to enforce the statutory land-use zoning plans through the building plan approval process (Bristow, 1984; Town Planning Office, 1988). Thus, by the early 1970s the main components of Hong Kong's planning system that we know today were in place. Figure 6.2 illustrates Hong Kong's current planning hierarchy. In a similar way to the English system, it comprises two levels: strategic planning at the territorial level and land use planning at the district level. A subregional planning level was in place before the mid-2000s but since then has been subsumed under strategic planning, and the subregional plans continue to provide reference for the drafting of district plans. We need to look at the strategic and district levels of the plan more closely.

Territorial Development Plans

A territorial strategic plan provides a long-term planning framework and development goals and principles for the city through directing the lower level of plans, and integrating government policies on land use, transport infrastructure development, and environmental matters. Although new town planning received paramount attention from the 1950s to the 1970s as the major means of providing sites to accommodate the rapidly growing population and manufacturing activities, a return to the main urban areas was deemed necessary in 1980 as the next phase of land development arose. There were three major reasons for this. First, the anticipated saturation of the new towns in being able to provide housing by the mid-1990s; second, the completion of major transport infrastructure in the main urban area (Island Eastern Harbour Corridor and the first underground railway line running through Kowloon and Hong Kong Island), enhancing development potential and reducing commuting time; and, third, the preference of the public to live in the main urban area (Town Planning Office, 1988). In addition, there was an urgency to redevelop the existing urban area owing to the annual cap of 50 hectares of land sale imposed on the colonial government by the Sino-British Declaration.

Consequently, the first longer-term territorial development strategy of Hong Kong was based on more comprehensive projections of territorial economic and social needs and better integration with transport planning, and focusing on the main urban areas and reclamation along the two sides of the harbor was conceived in 1982 (Bristow, 1984, pp. 118–119; Town Planning Office, 1988; Hong Kong SAR Government, 2007). It was eventually approved by the government in 1984, the year in which the Sino-British Declaration was signed to confirm the return of Hong Kong to China after 1997. Subsequently, the 1984 strategy was reviewed in 1986 owing to the rapidly growing population and the repositioning of Hong Kong in relation to China's burgeoning economic development (Planning Department, 1995, p. ii). Consequently, the Port and Airport Development Strategy, relocating the airport from the city center to the far-west outlying island, and a subregional plan, the Metroplan, were formulated in 1989 and 1991 respectively to realize the tenet of "returning to the main urban area" of Hong Kong's first longer term territorial development strategy of 1984. A major goal of the Metroplan was to improve the heavily populated areas around the harbor where it was "heavily congested, with dilapidated living conditions and a lack of essential amenities" (Lands and Works Branch, 1988, p. 4). Thus, this plan finally called for efforts to deal with the quality issues in the main urban area that were pointed out in the Abercrombie Report four decades previously.

In view of the impact of China's rapid economic development on Hong Kong, causing shrinkages in manufacturing but expansion in entrepôt activities, a review of the 1984 Territorial Development Strategy was found to be necessary in 1990. Eventually, in 1998, the Territorial Development Strategy Review (TDSR) produced Hong Kong's new longer-term development strategy, which took into account development trends in south China (especially in the Pearl River Delta), projected rapid population growth, and the need to substantially increase land supply to quench the housing affordability problem, which was partially due to the 50-hectare cap on annual land sales. (Planning Department, 1995, p. ii; Planning, Environment and Lands Bureau, 1998). The priority of land development was to ensure adequate housing provision to satisfy housing needs and to improve housing conditions and affordability, thus setting up an unprecedented annual housing production target of more than 85,000 housing units from redevelopment or new town development. In addition, it introduced strategic environmental assessment under a land use–transport–environmental framework. Finally, a more visionary strategy responding not only to economic causes but also to greater environmental and community concerns was made in 2007—the Hong Kong 2030 Planning Vision and Strategy. While it takes up the vision of the Commission on Strategic Development established in 1998 to develop Hong Kong as Asia's World City, it also upholds the principles of sustainable development and public engagement (Hong Kong SAR Government, 2007). Figure 6.3 shows the broad schematic spatial plan of Hong Kong under the 2030 strategic plan, outlining the broad direction of spatial development, regional transport corridors, and conservation areas (Hong Kong SAR Government, 2007). In 2015, the government started to formulate a territorial strategy transcending 2030. Thus, since the mid-1990s, territorial planning in Hong Kong has incrementally emphasized a regional dimension, especially its connections with southern China.

District Plans

District plans in the Hong Kong context are detailed land use plans that translate and implement broad planning objectives and principles stipulated at the territorial and subregional level to the local level. Before the enactment of the Town Planning Ordinance in 1939, the Building Ordinance provided

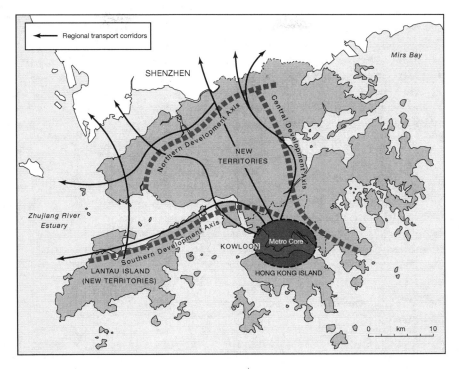

Figure 6.3 Spatial Plan Under the 2030 Planning Vision and Strategy, 2007
Source: Adapted from Hong Kong SAR Government (2007)

statutory planning controls at district level (Bristow, 1984, pp. 52–53). Following the enactment of the Town Planning Ordinance, statutory outline zoning plans have been made to steer district development in urban areas. The Ordinance was amended in 1991 to allow the promulgation of development permission area plans to control development in non-urban areas. The former have no time limit, while the latter, which are interim plans pending the making of zoning plans, are only valid for three years, though they can be extended by up to one year upon the Chief Executive's approval. Both types of plans stipulate land-use zones, development intensity and parameters, and major road systems, and are therefore closely connected with housing quality and quantity. The other district plans are the non-statutory department plans comprising outline development plans and layout plans, which are administratively binding and show greater development details.

Development-Related Tools

The Hong Kong Planning Standards and Guidelines is also non-statutory. It is a policy document currently comprising eleven chapters setting out the provision standards, locational factors (such as density zones), assessment methods, and site requirements of various land uses. It also provides guidelines for preparing planning briefs or proposals for development projects or comprehensive development areas. The Buildings Ordinance is the statute that mandates the building authority to enforce the statutory land-use zoning plans at the development stage, and its Building (Planning) Regulations provide the legal basis for the interpretation of the development parameters of the land-use plans when building plans are submitted to the building authority for approval. In other words, statutory land-use zoning plans are enforced and interpreted by the building authority under the building laws, not by the planning authority. Thus, there could be discrepancy between the planning intentions formulated by the planning authority and the interpretation of these intentions by the building authority. Finally, as discussed before, land leases specify the use and the capacity of development sites according to statutory land-use zoning plans, if they exist. As the government is the only true landowner, land leases become a powerful tool in enforcing land use plans.

Plan-Making and Enforcement Processes: Power Relations and Politics

Power and politics in urban planning are constituent with the power relations and politics of the community in which they are embedded. More specifically, the mode of urban planning as a strand of public administration also reflects a government's approach in managing the community's public resources and public affairs, especially so if land is state-owned and if income generated from land represents a significant source of public revenue, such as is the case with Hong Kong and mainland China. Power relations within the planning system are always in a state of flux, evolving with or transforming the general urban governance structure or public administration approaches (Wan, 2005; Wan & Chiu, 2008; Bryson et al., 2014). The power relations in Hong Kong's plan-making and enforcement processes are no exception.

Despite the administrative restructuring within the government to facilitate urban planning and land supply, as detailed in Bristow (1984), changes in planning governance, involving the government, the private sector and civic society, were slow until the future of Hong Kong after 1997 was mooted between the British and the Chinese governments in the early 1980s. The governance approach basically maintained a government and professional-led mode or a traditional public administration framework aiming to achieve efficiency and economic growth. It was only in 1982, the year when Britain and China started to negotiate on the future of Hong Kong, that the democratization process was set off, with the introduction of one-third of the members of the District Boards being elected. After the signing of the Sino-British Declaration in 1984 to confirm the handover of

Hong Kong to China in 1997, measures were incrementally implemented to nurture the formation of a representative government in Hong Kong. These included, in the main, the introduction of indirect and, subsequently, direct election into the Legislative Council (which enacts laws, approves government budgets, and monitors the work of the government), and the introduction of new functional constituency seats in the Council (Liu & Yue, 1996). A participatory mode quickly emerged upon the change of government in 1997, triggered by the impending implementation of a large-scale harbor reclamation project under the 1991 Metroplan. The harbor protection movement eventually led to the current networked, multi-sectored participatory planning approach. This process of transformation and the underlying forces driving the changes deserve more attention. We shall begin with the making of territorial and subregional plans.

The Making of Territorial and Subregional Plans: Incremental Public Participation since 1990

As discussed above, territorial plan making in Hong Kong began for pragmatic reasons: the need to make central arrangements for land supply to meet rapidly emerging economic activities. Due to the nature of a colonial government emphasizing economic efficiency and the constantly high demand for land for the growing economy and population, territorial plans made before the 1990s were directed by the government, namely the bureaucrats and the technocrats. There was no mention of public consultation in the making of the 1922 Town Planning Scheme, the informal master plan of 1947 of Patrick Abercrombie, the new town plans in the 1950s and the 1960s, the Colony Outline Plan/Hong Kong Outline Plan in the late 1960s and 1970s, or even in the first longer-term territorial plan of 1984. However, to quench the increasing discontent against the general authoritarian governing approach, the government had gradually set up specific offices (such as the Strategic Planning Unit), internal committees (such as the Land Development Policy Committee advising the governor on land development proposals), and advisory committees comprised of official and non-official members, to enhance the administration of various public affairs. The government was nonetheless reluctant to open up the administrative structure to public consultation, let alone public participation, giving the reason that most people preferred efficiency and simplicity to consultation and complexity (Financial Secretary's speech of March 28, 1968, quoted in Bristow, 1984, p. 110). The Legislative Council, which monitored government work and approved budgetary proposals, was the institution that scrutinized planning and land matters, among its other duties. However, before 1985, the council members were either government officials or elites (businessmen and senior professionals) directly appointed by the government. Indirect election to the Council and partial direct election (eighteen out of eighty members) were only introduced in 1985 and 1991 respectively, when Hong Kong entered into a transitional period after the signing of the Sino-British Declaration in 1984.

Finally, public consultation was introduced in the making of a subregional plan, the Metroplan of 1991, subsequent to the announcement of the first territorial development strategy of 1984, for three possible major reasons. First, as discussed, after the signing of the Sino-British Declaration in 1984, Hong Kong officially entered into the transitional period and the colonial government introduced a representative government mode to prepare Hong Kong for becoming a highly autonomous self-administrative region in China after 1997. Thus, there was a change from the authoritarian governing mode to one that was more consultative. Second, unlike the previous territorial plans, this subregional plan was a true longer-term plan drafted to meet projected and forecasted needs and demands, inevitably resulting in more than one development option as different scenarios of future growth were estimated. Seeking the views of the public, rhetoric though it might be, would give legitimacy for the final choice, as well as lessening the pressure on the government if the scenarios based on which development option was chosen did not materialize. Third, as stated in the introduction of the Metroplan Selected Strategy, the realization of the Metroplan's objectives required the investment of both the public and private sector (Government Information Services, 1991, p. 2), and the participation or acceptance of the property owners. Thus, unlike the new town development, which heavily relied on public-sector investment, as discussed later, public consultation was necessary in the case of Metroplan to solicit the views of the community and to rally their support.

However, it has to be noted that the Port and Airport Development Strategy (PADS), announced in 1989, which just preceded the Metroplan, did not go through a public consultation exercise. It was probably because, as detailed and argued in Ng (1993), relocating the airport had already been mooted as early as 1946, and Chak Lap Kok, which was eventually chosen as the relocation site, had been first recommended in 1974 and studied in detail by professionals in 1982 and 1983. Thus, when the proposal was reactivated in 1988 after its suspension in 1984 due to political and economic uncertainty, the government was quite determined to pick Chak Lap Kok, although two alternative sites were also proposed. There could have been, however, an important time factor for not taking this golden opportunity to start nurturing a participatory community, despite the scale and significant long-term impact of this massive infrastructure project. The colonial government may have felt it necessary to get the project off the ground as soon as possible because its remaining ruling period in the city was less than ten years. The urgency to launch and hence to complete the project before 1997 may have been due to the financial benefits that the project could bring to British construction and related companies in this grandiose project, or the desire to be remembered as a benevolent government symbolized by this mammoth infrastructure project, or because of the government's genuine intention to ensure the completion of the massive project before its departure to bring long-term benefit to the people of Hong Kong.

The Metroplan proposal, initially issued in April 1988 and confirmed in 1991, was thus the first government attempt to formally involve the grassroots level and community groups in strategic plan making. Documents on the aims, foundations, and planning frameworks and plan proposals were issued, and briefing and discussion meetings were held with various social and professional groups (Government Information Services, 1991). As a new endeavor, the public consultation exercises were inevitably rudimentary and maybe even tokenistic. The public was consulted on development proposals resulting from technical work undertaken by government officials and professional consultants, initially on the proposed goals and objectives, then on the constraints and opportunities for new development (including housing) in the main urban area, and the final planning options for future development (Lands and Works Branch,1988). The treatment of collected public views was nonetheless not made known publicly. What needs to be noted was the proposal for large-scale reclamation projects at the heart of Victoria Harbour after the removal of the airport, practically turning the harbor into a big channel. The conundrum here, however, was the absence of strong objections to this proposal at the time but the eruption of community opposition on environmental and heritage preservation grounds when planning for the use of the reclaimed sites was to start in 1994. The social actions were led by the Society for the Protection of the Harbour, established in 1995.

The civic movement eventually led to the passing of the Protection of the Harbour Bill at the last sitting of the Legislative Council of the Colonial Government. As detailed by Wan (2005), Ng (2006, 2008), and Wan & Chiu (2008), after a series of subsequent social and legal actions, and rounds of planning amendments in the late 1990s and early 2000s, not only has the scale of the reclamation projects flanking the two sides of the central harbor since been significantly reduced, but the land-use planning of the reclaimed sites has also been heavily influenced by public consultation. Eventually a widely represented Harbourfront Enhancement Committee was set up by the government to systematically feed public views for the future planning and the use of the harborfront area. Since the beginning of the new millennium, as discussed in detail in the next chapter, a "planning with the people" approach has been in the making in Hong Kong.

Concurrently, public participation in the preparation process of the 1998 Territorial Development Strategy Review was incrementally stepped up. The making of this strategy spanned eight years (1990—1998) because of the need to lengthen the plan-making process so that the strategy had the input and endorsement of the new government established after the handover of Hong Kong to China in 1997. Two public consultation exercises were organized, in 1993 and 1996 respectively, with the latter particularly extensive, lasting six months and covering a wide scope of stakeholders—individuals, community groups, professionals, and academics. Substantial views were collected on the proposed goal, objectives and strategic development options for Hong Kong in the medium term (1998—2006) and longer term (1998—2011), as well as on other issues of concern. Comprehensive reports, including government responses, were produced, distributed to commentators, and made known to the general public (Planning Department, 1995; Planning, Environment and Lands Bureau, 1998). Thus, while still basically taking a "planning for the people approach," the government became more accountable to the people for its final choices. Hence, in the 1990s, a fundamental shift in the planning culture began to emerge in Hong Kong.

Nonetheless, the consultation exercises of the Territorial Development Strategy were not without difficulties and problems. To the government, the major problems in consulting the public on a long-term development plan were the vagueness of long-term development for the members of the public and their lack of immediate concern for a distant development. The wide scope of issues to be included involving underlying working assumptions and the uncertainties of long-term projections made the management of public consultation difficult (Hong Kong SAR Government, 2007, p. 16). In the formulation process of the latest long-term planning strategy in 2007, the Hong Kong 2030: Planning Vision and Strategy, apart from devising technical solutions to these problems, such as providing extra guidance in public consultation exercises to enhance meaningful responses, an important strategy was taken to turn the planning approach from "planning for the people" to "planning with the people," further involving the public in planning the environment in which they live.

The measures adopted for the public consultation exercises conducted at each of the three major planning stages included agenda setting and baseline review, identification of key planning issues and formulation of an evaluation framework, and formulation of scenarios and development options (Hong Kong SAR Government, 2007, p. 16). In addition to this strategic move, public consultation techniques in public forums had also become more mature, as observed by the author, moving away from mere presentations by government officials and expression of views by invited or preregistered commentators leaving little time for interactive discussion and allowing dominance by opinion leaders or interest groups. The use of websites to disseminate information, the hire of independent and professional moderators to chair consultation forums, the collection of questions/views from attendees and the random drawing of questions, the holding of small group workshops to work out development scenarios, and the appointment of expert panels to provide professional views all helped public consultation exercises to be more effective. Needless to say, professional groups or developers, the key players in the market, are better organized and prepared in their written submissions to the government and therefore had greater influence in the final outcome. However, as the government undertook to explain the responses and choices in the final planning reports available to the public, the chosen development and planning options have to be accountable to the public. This shift in the planning paradigm is more explicit in district planning.

The Making of District Plans: from Elitist to Mass Participation since 2005

As discussed, there are two types of district plans in Hong Kong: the administrative departmental plans and the statutory outline zoning plans stipulating the uses of all sites covered by the plans. The former are technical action plans prepared by the government behind closed doors in parallel with the latter. The discussion in this section focuses on the latter, as their formulation directly involves all the major stakeholders in a planning system: the government, the market, and civic society. Nonetheless, it has to be noted that the former have implications for housing supply types, as government departments involved in land sales, subsidized housing provision, and public finance negotiate to determine the allocation of specific housing sites for respective public- or private-sector development, and the land sale program for private housing development.

Unlike in the Territorial Development Strategy, decisions on the outline zoning plans have immediate and legal effects on the interests of and benefits for—and the value of the properties owned by—members of the public. The plans determine the use of land resources and shape the urban landscape and affect the sustainability of Hong Kong's spatial system. Given the powerfulness of these plans, the openness and the transparency of the operation of the Town Planning Board have been of concern to the public, especially after 1997, when the populace became increasingly aware of their civil rights (e.g. freedom of expression and freedom of assembly) under an indigenous government, as argued in Wan (2005), Ng (2008), and Wan & Chiu (2008). As shown in Figure 6.4, these plans are formulated according to the provisions in the Town Planning Ordinance that prescribes the decision making process, the composition of the decision making panel, i.e. the Town Planning Board, and mandates public engagement (in the form of raising objections to proposed plan amendment or new plans) at different stages of the plan-making and plan application-considering processes. As recaptured by Ng (2014), amendments to the Ordinance originally enacted in 1939 were slow due to the opposing interests of the stakeholders. As reflected in the views collected from the first comprehensive review of the Ordinance in 1991 and the subsequent 1996 White Bill on the Ordinance, on the one hand, the public, interest groups and property owners (often represented by politicians) pushed for greater transparency and greater public involvement in the planning processes, including the appointment of Town Planning Board members and compensation for the negative effect of new plans on property value; on the other hand, the government, the business sector, property developers and real estate professionals asked for higher efficiency

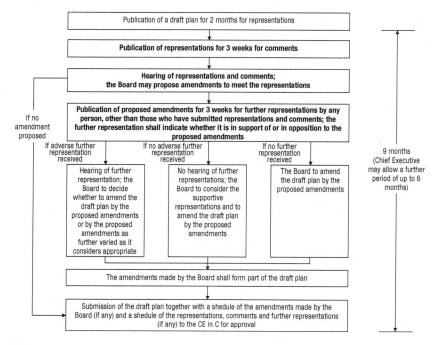

Figure 6.4 Plan-Making Process, Hong Kong
Source: Based on Town Planning Board (2005)

in the planning process and greater certainty of development rights, possibly through a stricter land use zoning system (Chiu & Lau, 1991; Ng, 1993, p.308). Eventually, only an interim amendment of restricting the objection processing time to nine months was passed by the Legislative Council in 1998 to expedite the planning process.

In view of the formidable hurdles in reconciling opposing views involved in a comprehensive redrafting of the Ordinance, in 2003 the government and the Town Planning Board changed their tactic and decided to amend the Ordinance by phases, dealing first with less-controversial issues. Consequently, the amended Ordinance enacted in 2005 endowed the public with greater power and involvement in the plan-making process (highlighted in Figure 6.4), legitimizing plan-amendment proposals made by the public, and seeking public views on the proposals and public comments on these views before the proposals are considered by the Town Planning Board. The process was also made more transparent by opening up the Town Planning Board meetings for public viewing in response to the long-term criticism that the Board had been operating in a black box. The deliberation on decisions is nonetheless done behind closed doors to enable free discussion from the board members. Meeting minutes summarizing the deliberations

Hong Kong: Planning, Power, and Decisions 179

are nevertheless available to the public. Further, all proponents (developers, property owners, and anyone in the community) of plan amendments and planning applications must obtain the consent of, or notify, the landowner of the application sites, as far as practicable, before they are processed by the Planning Department and considered by the Town Planning Board (Figure 6.5).

Apart from the change from a colonial government to an indigenous government, this civic awakening and readiness of the government to incrementally empower the public in the planning process may also have been due to the growing global trends of, for example, increasing concerns about the quality of the living environment and preservation of natural and cultural heritage, and rising awareness of the environmental impact of human activities. Further, the adoption of an accountability system by the second government of HKSAR in 2002 and the unprecedented long spell of decline in the economy and in the real estate sector engendered by the 1998 Asian Financial Crisis had given impetus and room for enabling a more civic-minded planning approach.

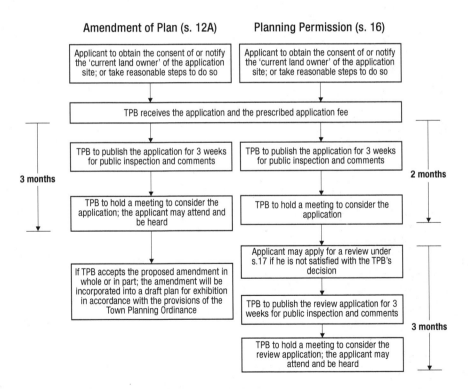

Figure 6.5 Planning Application Process, Hong Kong
Source: Planning Department (2004)

The revival of the harbor reclamation plans shortly before and after the change of government in 1997 encapsulated these trends and induced the drastic transformation of the pro-growth and elitist mode of governance before 1997 to that of a more participatory mode as detailed in Wan (2005), Ng (2008, 2011), and Wan & Chiu (2008), and in the next chapter. The transformations are apparent in both the making of the Territorial Development Strategy and the District Plans in the 2000s, as discussed above. The institutional change, the greater civic-rights awareness, and the fight for full universal suffrage in the past two years have turned Hong Kong into a highly politicized community. Public affairs, especially the acquisition and planning of land for new housing supply, have often been politicized in the sense that, apart from protecting and fighting for the legitimate interests of the direct stakeholders, they have been used by politicians and other groups to make political gains and to rally support for enhancing democracy, as discussed in the next chapter. The acquisition of land and the turning of the acquired land into usable sites for new housing development, be it for social, public finance, or economic reasons, has often been mediated through planning. Thus, the changes in planning governance, which are closely associated with the political environment, also affect the quantitative and qualitative supply of housing, especially in a dense and high-rise built environment.

Conclusion: Planning, Governance, and Housing Supply

With only a land area of 1,104 square kilometers, which is largely comprised of hilly terrain, and a population which grew from 7,450 people in 1841 to 7.2 million in 2015, planning has played an important role in Hong Kong's housing development to enable the city to win a reputation for its efficiency and good urban management. The enactment of the Town Planning Ordinance in 1939 represented an earlier attempt of the colonial government to use planning regulatory tools to resolve the gravely aggravating livability problems, to build a better-organized city, and to provide certainty in property development to enhance economic growth. Abercrombie's 1947 blueprint went beyond the regulatory tools and delved into strategic planning, advocating the redevelopment of the overcrowded urban area, the opening up of new industrial and residential areas, and the construction of new towns. The eventual government attempt to plan for the construction of six new towns in the 1950s and mid-1960s implemented these ideas, which was further boosted by the Ten-Year Housing Program launched in 1972.

The 1970s and 1980s were the heydays in Hong Kong's land development history: a de facto closed-door planning system and a land use zoning system providing a high degree of development certainty, and no community concern about reclaiming land from the sea, enabling the government to create land effectively and to exercise fully its property rights as the sole landowner. Constructing most of the new towns in the coastal areas to enable land reclamation from the sea reduced the need to resume land from the indigenous residents through a legal process. Under these circumstances, while public housing estates were to be equipped with a wide range of community facilities, no public consultation was needed in the planning process for the housing estates and new towns, except for public inspection (raising objections) of proposed outline zoning plans under the Town Planning Ordinance. By not implementing an affordable housing policy that relies on the private owners' and developers' collaboration, as in the case of the United Kingdom, community endorsement becomes a much less important issue under a colonial and authoritarian government.

The Metroplan announced in 1989 marked a different era. Having to involve property owners and developers in redeveloping the main urban areas, public consultation had to be introduced, ushering in the greater role of the market and the populace, though this new endeavor seemed rather tokenistic. The eruption of opposition in the formulation of development plans of the harbor reclamation sites in the run-up to the return of Hong Kong to China could have resulted from global trends of increasing awareness of environmental protection and conservation of natural heritage. It also reflects the rapid social change that took place in Hong Kong at a politically transitional stage, necessitating governments' better understanding of social ethos and preferences. An inactive property market also allowed the slowing down of the planning process to nurture a change in the planning approach.

The participatory mode in the formulation of the 1998 TDSR and the Hong Kong 2030 Planning Vision and Strategy, plus the revision of the Town Planning Ordinance in 2005, responded incrementally to this call. However, with a populace itchy to establish full democracy, and a political system not yet allowing political parties to form governments, as they could in England and Australia, planning issues may have been politicized beyond the aim of prompt provision of quality and affordable housing. Since 2011, increasing planning and land development controversies arose partly because of the intensifying tension in the political system. It was also partly due to the government's view that a severe land supply shortage was the fundamental problem, causing acute housing affordability problems, and hence relentless effort was made to search and develop new land for housing development. A planning and land supply system that took pride in its efficiency and certainty—a statutory land-use zoning system and government control of new land supply—has thus been under severe challenge.

The increasingly participatory mode of planning between 1998 and 2004 was in fact partially enabled by market conditions. The plummeting of housing prices by 60 percent and transactions by 50 percent gave room and time for considering quality issues at the planning stage, such as the lowering of development intensity in the redevelopment of the old airport site to enhance visibility and air quality. The weak market conditions also allow time for more meticulous public consultation, best illustrated by the revision of the harbor reclamation plans. Given the weak housing demand and the large potential supply from committed projects, developers actually supported these moves in order to reduce future land supply. The lengthening of planning processes and the suspension of further land searches in the mid-2000s in fact engendered the short land supply situation of today.

Currently, strong external and local demands for residential properties against a short land supply situation have caused housing prices to reach new heights and unaffordability, fostering a price-to-income ratio of 16:1. This has become one of the biggest social issues in Hong Kong today. The contentious nature of new land development, be it reclamation projects or land resumption from existing users in greenfield sites, has quickly made the planning process a political battlefield. The government has very recently begun to openly question the legitimacy of the lengthy public consultation processes in developing new areas under a severe land shortage situation (Hong Kong SAR Government, 2015). It is to be seen whether the enhanced participatory mode of planning made possible by the downward property cycle discussed above and detailed in the next chapter will be reversed by the current upward cycle, underscoring the hidden power of the market in planning governance. The role of the market will be discussed in greater detail in the next chapter.

References

Bristow, M. R. (1984). *Land-use Planning in Hong Kong: History, Policies and Procedures*. Hong Kong: Oxford University Press.

Bristow, M. R. (1989). *Hong Kong's New Towns: A Selective Review*. New York: Oxford University Press.

Bryson, J. M., Crosby, B. C., & Bloomberg, L. (2014). Public value governance: Moving beyond traditional public administration and the new public management. *Public Administration Review*, 74(4), 445–456.

Chiu, R. L. H. & Lau, A. (Eds.) (1991). *Proceedings of A Conference on the Comprehensive Review of the Town Planning Ordinance*. Conference jointly organized by the Department of Extra Mural Studies, The University of Hong Kong, and the Hong Kong Institute of Planners, Hong Kong, November 9, 1991.

Civil Engineering and Development Department. (2015). *The Geology of Hong Kong (Interactive On-line): 11 Onshore Superficial Deposits and Fills*. Available at: www.cedd.gov.hk/eng/about/organisation/s.html, accessed on December 12, 2015.

Government Information Services. (1991). *Metroplan: The Selected Strategy: An Overview*. Hong Kong: Government Printer.

Hong Kong Governor. (1972). *The Full Text of the Speech Given to the Legislative Council on October 18th 1972 by H. E. the Governor, Sir Murray MacLehose*. Hong Kong: Government Printer.

Hong Kong SAR Government. (2007). *Hong Kong 2030: Planning Vision and Strategy*. Hong Kong: The Development Bureau and the Planning Department.

Hong Kong SAR Government. (2015). *The 2015 Policy Address*. Hong Kong: The Information Services Department.

Lands and Works Branch. (1988). *Metroplan: The Aims*. Hong Kong: Government Printer.

Lands Department. (2015). Land Sale Records. Available at: www.landsd.gov.hk/en/landsale/records.htm, accessed December 12, 2015.

Liu, E. & Yue, S. Y. (1996). *Political Development in Hong Kong since the 1980s*. Hong Kong: Research and Library Services Division, Legislative Council Secretariat.

Liu, S. (2009). *A Brief History of Hong Kong* (in Chinese). Hong Kong: Joint Publishing.

Merry, M. (2003). *Hong Kong Tenancy Law: An Introduction to the Law of Landlord and Tenant*. Hong Kong: LexisNexis Butterworths.

Ng, M. K. (1993). Strategic planning in Hong Kong: lessons from TDS (Territorial Development Strategy) and PADS (Port and Development Strategy). *Town Planning Review*, 64(3), 287–311.

Ng, M. K. (2006). World-city formation under an executive-led government: The politics of harbour reclamation in Hong Kong. *Town Planning Review*, 77(3), 311–337.

Ng, M. K. (2008). From government to governance? Politics of planning in the first decade of the Hong Kong Special Administrative Region. *Planning Theory & Practice*, 9(2), 165–185.

Ng, M. K. (2011). Power and rationality: The politics of harbour reclamation in Hong Kong. *Environment and Planning—Part C*, 29(4), 677–692.

Ng, M. K. (2014). The state of planning rights in Hong Kong: A case study of "wall-like building," *Town Planning Review*, 85(4), 489–511.

Nissim, R. (2011). *Land Administration and Practice in Hong Kong*. Hong Kong: Hong Kong University Press.

Planning Department. (1995). *A New Development Framework for Hong Kong—a Response to Change and Challenges*. Hong Kong: Planning Department.

Planning Department. (2004). *Town Planning (Amendment) Ordinance 2004*. Available at: www.pland.gov.hk/pland_en/tech_doc/tp_bill/pamphlet2004/figure 2_e.jpg, accessed on December 1, 2015.

Planning Department. (2005). *Hierarchy of Plans*. Available at: www.pland.gov.hk/pland_en/press/publication/ar_10/english/about.html, accessed on November 15, 2015.

Planning Division. (1969). *Planning Memorandum No. 5: The Application of Population Density Control to Outline Zoning and Outline Development Plans and Related to Building Heights and Coverage*. Hong Kong: Crown Lands and Survey Office.

Planning, Environment and Lands Bureau. (1998). *Territorial Development Strategy Review: A Response to Change and Challenges*. Hong Kong: Hong Kong SAR Government.

Special Committee on Housing. (1956). *First Interim Report*. Hong Kong: Government Printer.

Town Planning Board. (2005). *Planning-making process*. Available at: www.info.gov.hk/tpb/en/plan_making/participate.html#mkp, accessed on November 20, 2015.

Town Planning Office. (1988). *Town Planning in Hong Kong*. Hong Kong: Buildings and Lands Department.

Wan, Y. K. P. (2005). *Governance of Residential Land Use Planning in Hong Kong*. Doctoral thesis submitted to the University of Hong Kong.

Wan, Y. K. P. & Chiu, L. H. R. (2008). Transforming the governance of plan-making in Hong Kong. *Journal of Place Management and Development*, 1(3), 256–271.

7 Land Supply and New Housing Provision in Hong Kong

Introduction

Hong Kong has a dualistic housing system comprising an equal-sized public and private housing sector, despite its general laissez-faire economic system. Outside of the public housing sector, the government takes a liberal approach by which it provides a superstructure for the healthy functioning of the market and allows market players to make their own decisions, and only introduces temporary and expedient measures when problems such as significant affordability decline arise. This market-oriented approach can also be seen in the government's supply of new development sites to the market as the sole owner of land, that is, the government adopts the market principle in exercising its landownership right. As such, the market has a major influence in the governance of planning and development, alongside political and social changes. The pro-growth and elitist-led planning approach before 1997 is often justified by, and commended for, achieving high market efficiency, a cornerstone of Hong Kong's economic success. Although it is valid to argue that land development and planning in Hong Kong is driven by the "exchange value" of land and by the desire to achieve high rates of economic development (Ng, 1999, 2008), it needs to be noted that land also has to be developed to meet housing needs and to combat housing affordability problems. This was especially the case in 1997, when the housing price reached a historically high level owing to the robust economy and the annual land sale cap of 50 hectares, instituted in the Sino-British Declaration of 1984 (see Chapter 6). Though this quota had been relaxed after 1994, it nonetheless restrained the government from using significant increase in land supply as a major price-cooling strategy (Chiu, 2007).

This chapter continues to explore the influence of planning and planning governance on the supply of new housing in Hong Kong but focuses on the post-1997 period. It gives greater attention than that in Chapter 6 to the impact of housing market conditions on land use planning and land supply, as explained in the Chapter 6 conclusion. By reviewing market trends and analyzing major development projects since 1997, this chapter investigates how market conditions and changes in planning governance within the wider political context have incurred the frenetic search of land by the post-1997

SAR government leaders and the barriers counteracting these efforts. Initially it reviews the property cycles and discerns the influence of planning governance in relation to other factors in land supply, deliberating and arguing that it is only in the post-1997 era that planning and its governance mode have had a more significant impact on land supply than state ownership of land. It then examines a large-scale redevelopment case in the 1990s that has had a long-lasting impact on Hong Kong's planning governance. Subsequently, it reviews the major new development projects since 2011, focusing on how the more participatory planning approach has influenced the quantity and quality of housing supply. It finally discusses whether the shift to a more pluralistic planning paradigm constitutes barriers to effective production of a more amenable residential environment and whether it undermines development certainty and development rights.

The Market Situation and the Land Search Efforts

As pointed out in the last chapter, with the intention of establishing Hong Kong as a trading port in Britain's international trade route the land market was active in the colony's very early days. However, the housing market only really started to grow in the mid-1970s, when the world economic recession following the 1973 Oil Crisis ended, and also when the middle class emerged as a result of the continuous and rapid economic growth grounded in the export production manufacturing industry that took off in the early 1960s. Since then, Hong Kong's housing market has gone through four cycles. The first price peak emerged in 1981–1982, and crashed in 1982 when the future of Hong Kong after 1997 was brought to the table (Figure 7.1). The second price peak occurred in 1991–1992, when new land supply, restricted by the 50-hectare annual quota of the 1984 Sino-British Declaration (Chapter 6), was unable to meet the surging demand triggered by Deng Xiaoping's visit to Southern China in 1991 to reaffirm China's open-door policy in the wake of the 1989 June Fourth Incident. Despite China's agreement to relax the annual land lease quota and the government's subsequent price-cooling measures, the buoyant economy and the post-war baby boomers reaching household expansion stage only allowed a mild price reduction of 20 percent. Thus, other social and economic factors were at work influencing housing affordability.

The third price peak, which topped all past price hikes, occurred in 1997 as a result of rocketing housing demand but diminishing supply. The strong demand was engendered by an economic boom following the election of the most popular candidate for the position of first Chief Executive of the new government in 1996, who promised stability and good economic prospects. However, housing supply was found to be declining, a corollary of the price-cooling measures of the early 1990s, which turned away new investment in large-sized apartment projects. Confronted by acute housing affordability problems (Figure 7.2), the new government then announced an aggressive

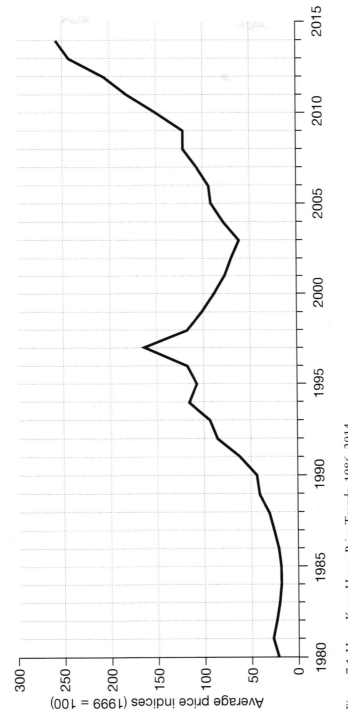

Figure 7.1 Hong Kong House Price Trends, 1986–2014
Source: Rating and Valuation Department (2014)

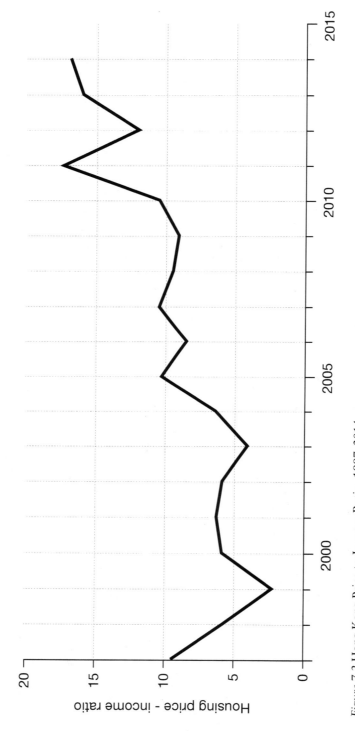

Figure 7.2 Hong Kong Price-to-Income Ratio, 1997–2014
Source: Based on Centadata (2014) and Census and Statistics Department (2014)

land development plan, producing 133 hectares of land annually, made possible by the lifting of the land sale quota after the handover of the government on July 1, 1997. It pledged to build 85,000 housing units annually to meet the projected housing demand over the following ten years (Chiu, 1998).

Nonetheless, housing prices had quickly plummeted since 1998 and the low price lasted for an unexpectedly prolonged period because of the Asian Financial Crisis and the Severe Acute Respiratory Syndrome outbreak of 2003. Apart from the poor economic conditions, the significant increase in housing supply in a weak market due to the post-1997 aggressive land development plan was also an important cause of the 60 percent fall in housing prices between 1997 and 2003. Housing prices began to restore incrementally after 2003 as the economy gradually came out of the trough. As shown in Figure 7.1, the subsequent Global Financial Crisis only had a short-term negative impact on housing prices, which resurged in the second half of 2009. By 2010, the fourth housing price peak, which continues until the present, had formed, reaching a new historic level and creating unprecedented affordability problems. Land shortage was put forth by the government as the root cause of the price hike, attributable to the suspension of new land searches during the post-1997 economic depression.

It should be noted that, except for the first property cycle, which was triggered by economic growth, land supply in the other three property cycles has been either a direct or an underlying cause of market upturns and downturns. Land shortage and excess had been politics- and policy-induced in the second (1991/1992–1996) and the third (1997–2009) property cycles respectively. The impact of the changing governance in planning since 1998 on residential land supply and housing supply was only felt in the fourth property cycle, which started in 2010 and lasts until today. Another notable development was that, amid the property cycles, the provision of public rental housing has continued and reached a peak of 55,492 units in 2000/2001 due to the new government's decision to expand production in the new town areas in 1998 and the shift of subsidized owner-occupier housing to rental purposes following the suspension of the home ownership scheme in 2002 in response to market decline. State ownership of land was the major factor guaranteeing the continued supply of affordable housing regardless of the ups and downs in the property market.

We need to investigate more deeply the relationships between the current price hike, land supply and the urban planning process. As shown in Figure 7.2, the price-to-income ratio in the private housing sector had been on the rise after the decline in 1998, reaching a new height initially in 2007 and then rising sharply in 2011. Figure 7.3 explains the supply-side factors of the affordability outcome: new construction projects remaining at low levels even after the economic revival in 2005, and the impact from the Global Financial Crisis of 2008 and 2009. In fact, private housing production only hit 13,400 units in 2010, 9,500 in 2011, 10,100 in 2012, and 8,300 in 2013. These productivity levels fell far short of the supply target that was finally formulated and announced in the Long Term Housing Strategy of 2014: 480,000 housing units for the ten years between 2015/2016 and 2024/2025, averaging 48,000 per year, with 40 percent (19,200 units) as private housing and 60 percent (28,800 units) as public housing (Transport and Housing Bureau, 2014). Though productivity may pick up in the latter part of the ten-year period as more land is sought and formed to produce housing sites, the short supply has already engendered price surges (Figure 7.1) and the breathtaking price-to-income ratios of 12–17:1 (Figure 7.3).

An important factor that compounds housing price inflation and fluctuation is the openness of the Hong Kong economy to foreign investment generally and to property investors specifically. It is only since February 2013 that discriminative tax measures have been levied on foreign property buyers. The aftermath of the Global Financial Crisis has resulted in hot money from the West flowing into Hong Kong's housing market, fueling price hikes. Although the government identified that between 2011 and 2012 an average of 85 percent of residential property buyers were local people, in the primary housing market—which is regarded as the price setter—an average of 15 percent were non-local buyers, and another 17 percent were local and non-local company buyers (Financial Services and the Treasury Bureau, 2013). Thus, the influence of external investors on Hong Kong's property prices is not insignificant, especially in the high-priced segment, luring speculators and churners.

While supply-side solutions take a long time span to materialize, demand-side controls can be implemented instantaneously. Price-cooling measures implemented since 2010 included progressively increasing stamp duties on higher-priced properties, doubling the stamp duty of second-home buyers, instigating early and additional payment of stamp duties by non-local property investors, applying a special stamp duty for those who resell properties within three years (the highest rate being 20 percent of the sale price), and restricting selling to external purchasers in some development projects. The implementation of these measures did not encounter much opposition as affordability problems haunted the community. While these measures had some dampening effects, they quickly lost their magic a year later. In fact, they calmed down only transactions, and not price levels, as can be seen from Figure 7.1. What then accounts for the sustained price level and therefore affordability problems faced by the people of Hong Kong? Apart from the demand-suppression methods, what solutions from the supply side has the government offered? In particular, what planning tools have been used?

At the dawn of the market's revival from the Global Financial Crisis in 2010, as the sole supplier of new land and the largest land supplier the government took stock of the land reserve and reviewed the sources of new

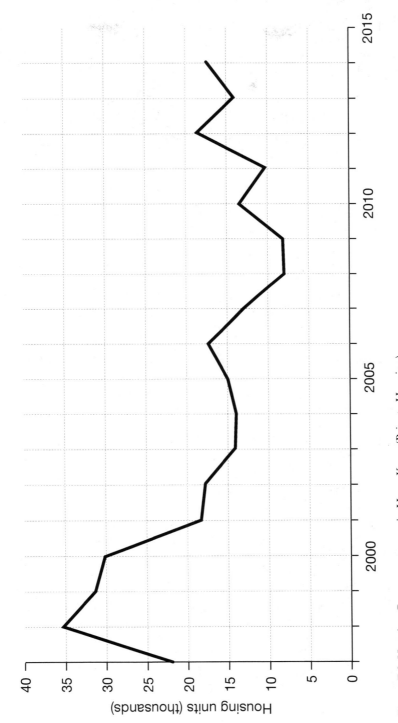

Figure 7.3 Housing Commencements in Hong Kong (Private Housing)
Source: Transport and Housing Bureau (2015)

land supply, identifying that reclamation from the sea had been the most effective, comprising 25.5 percent of total developed land (Civil Engineering and Development Department, 2015). For the actual increase in new land supply, the government merely announced the rezoning of 30 hectares of obsolete industrial land for residential use and changed the land sale method from an application list system[1] back to public auction and tendering methods, which allowed the government to actively put out land for sale, taking a lead to respond to market demand more promptly. It was in August 2012 that the new Chief Executive announced ten measures to redress the acute market imbalance, but only two pertained to land and housing supply—expediting the processing of presale applications to facilitate early provision in the market, and the rezoning of thirty-six government–institutional–community sites to residential use to produce 11,900 housing units, which was about 25 percent of the annual production target announced under the Long Term Housing Strategy of 2014.

The subsequent two annual policy speeches of the Chief Executive took on a more comprehensive and aggressive approach, pledging not only to create enough land for housing construction, but to set up an unprecedented land bank able to provide land to support development needs any time. Among the various sources of residential land listed in Table 7.1, rezoning of statutory land uses, opening up new development areas in the rural areas, and harbor reclamation are the major sources. Nonetheless, under the current planning regime, which advocates and allows a high level of public participation, as deliberated in the last chapter, all these methods inevitably involved consultation with the general public, the district councils and the affected residents. The opening up of new development areas further invokes the lengthy and formidable land resumption or expropriation process from property owners.[2] Rezoning has also aroused strong local objections, as the interests of residents are directly affected. Albeit less directly infringing onto property rights, the progress of reclamation outside of Victoria Harbour has been the slowest and on a smaller scale. This could be due to the very high costs of large-scale reclamation and the potential for strong objection from the community generally and from green groups specifically. The politicization of public affairs in recent years in association with the community's fight for universal suffrage in the election of the Chief Executive have fueled the debates and aggravated the barriers in the above land-acquisition processes. The increasingly open planning processes, involving both land use zoning and the land application mechanism, have become a major battlefield. The next section reviews how, since 1998, major new development projects associated with housing supply have been affected by the more participatory mode of planning governance, the most significant being the South East Kowloon Development Scheme.

Table 7.1 Sources of Residential Land, 2014–2015

Time Period	Land Acquisition Approaches (2013–2015)	Housing Units (Estimate, 2013)

Short and Medium Term	Rezoning:
	    Obsolete GIC sites for residential development
	    Obsolete greenbelts for residential use
	    Rezone industrial and deserted land for residential use
		55,300

	Redevelopment:
	    Redevelopment of public housing estates
	    Revitalization of industrial buildings for residential use
	    Redevelopment of former squatter areas and former quarry
		19,700

	Mass Transit Stations: Development of the mass transportation and property	8,700
	Large Scale Development: New Development Areas	Data not yet available

	Relaxation of Outdated Restrictions/Streamlining Procedures:
	    Streamlining agreement on land premium or land exchange application for residential development
	    Increase the maximum domestic plot ratio
	    Relaxation of development intensity control
		45,000

Long Term	Rezoning: Rezoning industrial and deserted land for residential use rezoning brownfield sites in the New Territories	53,800
	Reclamation: Reclamation near Lantau waters	Data not yet available
	Redevelopment: Development projects of the Urban Renewal Authority	Data not yet available
	Large-Scale Development: New Development Areas	Data not yet available

Source: Hong Kong SAR Government (2014, 2015)

Planning Governance and Housing Supply since 1998

South East Kowloon Development Scheme: Transforming Governance

As highlighted in Chapter 6, the South East Kowloon Development Scheme (SEKDS) triggered off a drastic shift from a government-led to community-led planning approach in the late 1990s. As this transformation process has already been discussed in detail in Wan (2005), Ng (2006), Wan and Chiu (2008), and Ng (2011), this section focuses on how the transformation process has impacted on housing supply, both quantitatively and qualitatively. Subsequent to the announcement of the scheme under the Metroplan in 1989, the first Outline Master Development Plan was published in 1993. It involved a redevelopment area of 376 hectares in the airport area and 300 hectares of land reclaimed from the sea to build a "city within a city" of 676 hectares, accommodating 285,000 people on 146 hectares of residential land and providing 110,900 jobs (Table 7.2). Housing provided would be mainly public rental housing and subsidized owner-occupier housing affordable to the low-income and lower middle-income families respectively. However, the public was only briefly consulted on this plan in 1994 (Planning Department, 1993; Wan, 2005).

Subsequently, following the planning and development practice prevalent at the time, the government went ahead with the engineering feasibility study and completed it in 1998. The master plan was revised accordingly, covering a total new land area of 579 hectares and increasing the population target to 320,000, requiring about 100,000 homes to be built (Table 7.2), but maintaining the same employment target (Planning Department, 1998). This plan would thus provide sites to help accomplish the annual housing production target of 85,000 units set by the new government under the 1998 Territorial Development Strategy Review and the Long Term Housing Strategy of 1998. Meanwhile, as discussed in Chapter 6, there was rising community concern with regard to the proposed large-scale reclamation of the central harbor in 1994, epitomized by the formation of the Society for the Protection of the Harbour in 1995, and the eventual passing of the Protection of the Harbour Bill in 1997 at the last sitting of the Legislative Council under the colonial government. The two subsequent Outline Zoning Plans derived from the feasibility study and the revised master plan in September 1998 received strong objections during the two-month public inspection period, amounting to a total of 845 objection submissions to the Town Planning Board (Wan, 2005). There were criticisms from both the developers and concerned groups that important information was missing, such as the rationale for the planning of a large metropolitan park and the environmental impacts of the proposed reclamation and heavy road traffic (Wan, 2005).

Consequently, the government and the Town Planning Board took on a full consultative planning approach. First, it instituted a new concept plan

Table 7.2 Planning Revisions of South East Kowloon Development Scheme, 1992–2012

Plans	Year	Total area (ha)	Reclaimed area (ha)	Target population	Residential land (ha) (% of total site area)
Outline master plan (OMP)	1993	676	300	285,000	146 (23%)
Updated OMP (after feasibility study)	1998	579	299	319,431	114 (20%)
Draft Kai Tak OZP	1998	579	299	320,000	175 (30%)
Outline concept plan	1999	451	123	240,000	104 (23%)
New Outline Master Development Plan	2001	460.8	133	260,000	96.8 (21%)
Draft Kai Tak OZP	2002	457	133	258,700	66 (14%)
Revised preliminary outline development plan	2006	328	0	86,000	37 (11%)
Kai Tak OZP	2007	323	0	86,000	36 (11%)
Kai Tak OZP	2012	323	0	89,800	34 (11%)

Source: Based on Planning Department (1993, 1998, 2002, 2006, 2007, 2012), Territorial Development Department (1998, 2001), and Wan (2005)

stage, and consulted the public on the concept plan to get them involved at an early planning stage. Second, it further consulted the public at the outline zoning plan preparation stage, rather than only after a draft plan was completed and gazetted under the statutory procedure. Third, the consultation methods were also improved so that more informative materials were provided; all relevant professional institutes and organizations and local organizations were systematically consulted, and more interactive public forums were organized. As a result of the lengthy process of consultation and under the restriction of the Protection of the Harbour Ordinance, the revised outline zoning plan announced four years later substantially reduced the total area of the scheme by 21 percent (122 hectares), the harbor reclamation area by 56 percent (166 hectares), the residential area by 62 percent (109 hectares), and the population by 19 percent (61,300 people) (Table 7.2). Objections to this draft plan plummeted to forty, and the plan was finally approved by the Chief Executive in Executive Council in 2002 (Planning Department, 2002; Wan, 2005).

However, further revision was necessitated. In 2004, the court ruled in favor of a judicial review sought by the Society of the Protection of the

Harbour against the Town Planning Board's proposal to reclaim the typhoon shelter for a small harbor park connected to the north shore of Hong Kong Island. The government and the Town Planning Board thus felt the need to seek the Court of Final Appeal's elaboration of "presumption against reclamation" under the Protection of the Harbour Ordinance in order to avoid future challenges to development projects involving harbor reclamation. The court clarified that reclamation was only allowed if there were overriding public needs, that is, a compelling and present need with no reasonable alternative to reclamation. It nonetheless did not specify or give examples of "overriding need." Recognizing that it was hard for housing and related auxiliary facilities to meet the overriding public need test, the Town Planning Board revised and republished the outline development plan and, accordingly, the outline zoning plan of SEKDS again, based on a zero-reclamation scenario. Eventually the plans were approved in 2006 and 2007 respectively, based on a zero-reclamation scenario (Planning Department, 2004). As a result, the total area of the scheme, the harbor reclamation area, the residential area and the population were further reduced significantly by 29 percent (134 hectares), 100 percent (133 hectares), 45 percent (30 hectares), and 66 percent (172,700 people) respectively (Table 7.2, Figure 7.4). In a similar way to other approved plans, this plan receives applications for further revision as time goes by. In 2012, a minor revision was approved in response to local objections to a proposed town center development on the ground of visual impact (Planning Department, 2012).

Thus, conceived at a time when Hong Kong was going through a politically transitional and "opening-up" stage, coupled with the community's rising concern with environmental and heritage preservation, the planning of SEKDS took fifteen years (1992–2007) to complete. While the shift from a "planning for the people" to "planning with the people" approach has materialized, the successful institution of participatory governance mode came with a price: a total reduction of 109.78 hectares of residential land and depriving 199,000 people of the opportunity to live in the heart of the city within easy reach of the major city activities. Furthermore, the reduction in residential areas zoned as Residential (Group A) to enable a less-congested living environment also implied lower production of public housing, which is usually located in areas with the highest development intensity in order to maximize economies of scale. In contrast, where development intensity is lower, developers will capitalize on the less-compact environment and build higher-priced residential properties targeting higher-income groups rather than average families.

The repeated revision of the development plan also delayed the availability of the area for housing construction. This delay coincidentally occurred after the outbreak of the Asian Financial Crisis, a time when housing demand was unprecedentedly low. Looked at from another perspective, the market depression provided the opportunity for a shift in the planning paradigm as there was no urgency to redevelop this vast site. Some of the objections, in fact, were related to livability issues, such as the proposal to locate the

Hong Kong: Land Supply and New Housing 197

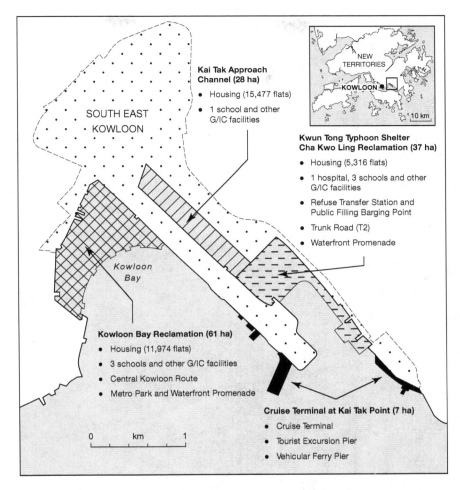

Figure 7.4 Planned Developments in Proposed Reclamation Areas of South East Kowloon Development, 2004

Source: Adapted from Planning Department (2004)

metropolitan park to the shore area to be connected with the waterfront promenade and the lowering of building heights in the waterfront areas to enhance better ventilation and the urban landscape. Hence, overall, the trade-offs lie in the reduction of housing supply, especially for lower-income families, versus a living environment of better quality and a more sustainable approach in urban development. In the subsequent years after the completion of the SEKDS plan, as highlighted in the last section, the housing market conditions turned around and the Hong Kong community became more politicized in the fight for universal suffrage for the election of the Chief Executive in 2017. Thus, the government's proactive search for land for

198 Hong Kong: Land Supply and New Housing

housing production met with more obstacles. Unlike the SEKDS case, where there were no local residents, most of these land search exercises affected local residents or residents in the vicinity, rendering the planning process even more challenging.

Land Search in a Buoyant Market: Quantity Versus Quality

As highlighted in the previous section, since 2012 the Hong Kong government under its new Chief Executive has launched an extensive and comprehensive land search throughout Hong Kong to identify sites for possible development, and has subsequently undertaken planning actions on possible sites. Among these efforts are land use rezoning (usually from industrial and government land uses to residential use), redevelopment projects, small-scale new development projects and three large-scale new development projects (Figure 7.5 and Table 7.3). All these projects have met with different levels of local objections on issues ranging from requests for local facilities, through traffic and environmental issues, to compensation for land resumption.

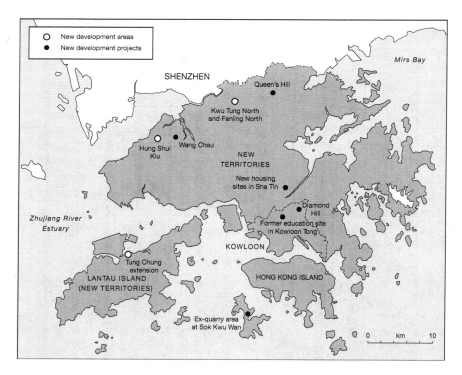

Figure 7.5 Major and Controversial Land Development Projects, 2011–2014, Hong Kong

Source: Authors

Table 7.3 Major Land Development Projects, 2008–2014

Project	Proposal	Original Housing Target	Community Response	Government Action
Rezoning Cases				
Queen's Hill in Fanling, N. T.	GIC (Education) R(A)	11,000 units of subsidized rental and owner-occupier housing	District Council: Inadequate infrastructure and community facilities	Pending
Former education site in Kowloon Tong, Kowloon	GIC ‡ R(B)	495 units of high-priced private housing	Local university: Strong opposition, proposed to keep for university expansion	Retained as GIC (special education). Housing units reduced by **495**
Wang Chau in Yuen Long, N. T.	Greenbelt and Open Storage CDA	17,000 units of subsidized rental housing	Rural committee: Objected to resuming open storage areas for residential development	Rezoned the greenbelt only. Housing units reduced by **13,000**
Small New Development Projects				
Diamond Hill, Kowloon	CDA (housing development)	4,200 units of subsidized rental and owner-occupier housing	District Council: Ventilation problem	Added a ventilation corridor. Reduced community building height. Increased retail facilities. Added a culture shopping street. Enhanced connectivity. Housing units reduced by **150**

continued . . .

Table 7.3 Continued

Project	Proposal	Original housing target	Community response	Government action
Small New Development Projects... Continued				
New housing site in Sha Tin, N. T.	Housing development	740 units of subsidized owner-occupier housing	Local residents: R(A) ǂ greenbelt	Rejected by Town Planning Board. 740 HOS units retained
Ex-quarry area at Sok Kwu Wan, Lamma Island, N. T.	Two options: Housing development-cum-tourism and housing development	1,000–2,800 subsidized and private housing units	Local community: Supported the tourism-cum-housing option. Preservation of local character. Provision of affordable housing. Improvement of transport. Protection of the natural shoreline and ecology	Proposed the tourism-cum-housing development option with a housing target of 1,900 units awaiting financial approval from Legislative Council
Large New Development Projects				
North West New Territories	Hung Shui Kiu New Development Area. Mixed development	60,100 units (215,000 population)	Public concerns: Compensatory village (including agricultural use). No means test for admission to public rental housing. In-situ relocation. More favorable compensation deal	Pending

North East New Territories	Kwu Tung North and Fanling North New Development Areas. Mixed development	60,700 units (174,900 population)	District Council and local residents: In-situ relocation. Reprovision of villages. No means test for admission to public rental housing. Increase in cash compensation from HK$0.6 million to HK$2 million. Interest groups: No relocation, no demolition. Greater housing supply, especially subsidized housing. Provision of public facilities	Legislative Council approved funding for the further works. A slight increase of 6,100 units
Tung Chung New Town Extension	Mixed development	138,000–153,000 population	Residents and interest groups: Supported the mixed development proposed. Balanced housing mix. Improvement of external connectivity. More and fairer distribution of community and recreational facilities. Minimized impacts on ecology and preserve cultural heritage	Proposal for extension (2014): 48,000 housing units for 140,000 population. Pending Legislative Council's approval

Notes:
N. T.—New Territories
R(A)—Residential (Group A) (Maximum plot ratio: 6:1)
R(B)—Residential (Group B) (Maximum plot ratio: 4.5:1)
CDA—Comprehensive Development Area
GIC—Government, Institution, or Community

Sources: Civil Engineering and Development Department & Planning Department (2012a, 2012b, 2013a, 2013b, 2014a, 2014b, 2015); Development Bureau (2015); *Mingpao* (2013); Various Documents of Legislative Council Panel on Development (2015); Various News Reports, *Sing Tao Daily* (various years).

Small-Scale Development Projects

As for the rezoning cases, as exemplified by the cases of Queen's Hill, the former Hong Kong Institute of Vocational Education site, and the Wang Chau Public Housing projects, as widely reported in the mass media, involved changing obsolete government, institution, and community sites, non-vegetated greenbelts, and vacant open storage sites to residential sites for either public or private housing. The community responses included requests for more infrastructure and community facilities, retaining the site for education as it was adjacent to a university (from which the opponents came), and land resumption objections/bargaining from existing owners/users. While the Queen's Hill case is still pending, the original zoning of the education site was retained but allocated for special educational use, and the public housing project went ahead but on a much-reduced scale. In these three cases, the revision of plans responding to local views resulted in a total loss of at least 13,495 housing units (Table 7.3).

A new housing project pertains to redeveloping an ex-quarry site in the outlying island of Lamma for residential development. Two options were proposed for development, and after two rounds of public consultation that raised concerns about the amenity of the living environment and protecting the natural ecology, the tourism-cum-housing option was chosen by the planning authority. A total of 1,695 housing units were deleted from the final plan. Another two small-scale new housing projects were both subsidized housing projects. Local concerns regarding the Diamond Hill project pertained to ventilation and community facilities, to which the government made a very positive response involving a reduction of 150 units. The other project in Shatin involved a land use rezoning application, with local residents attempting to change the site into a greenbelt. The Town Planning Board, however, turned down the application.

The most significant are three large-scale new development projects: the reactivation of two New Development Areas (NDAs) in the rural areas of the New Territories that were shelved in the early 2000s owing to the low demand for land at the time, and the extension of the Tung Chung New Town, which is adjacent to the Hong Kong International Airport and planned to provide support to the new airport. These three projects, if all eventually approved by the Legislative Council, will become the largest sources of housing supply in the next decade.

Large-Scale New Development Projects

New Development Areas

Two new development areas are planned: Hung Shui Kiu New Development Area in the North West New Territories and Kwu Tung North and Fanling North New Development Areas in the North East New Territories. Apart from supplying residential land for 215,000 people and other types of land supply in the medium to long term, being strategically located in the North West New Territories and well connected, Hung Shui Kiu will also serve as a "regional economic and civic hub" (Civil Engineering and Development Department & Planning Department, 2015). Because this new development area is close to Shenzhen and efficiently linked with the Greater Pearl River Delta region, new strategic highway infrastructure connecting the new development areas with the urban area will also be planned to address the long-term development needs of the North West New Territories. With a public–private housing mix of 51:49, the new development area will help redress the imbalance in the housing mix of the Tin Shui Wai New Town (Civil Engineering and Development Department & Planning Department, 2015), which has a high proportion of public housing (78 percent).

The Kwu Tung North and Fanling North New Development Areas are the extension to the Fanling/Sheung Shui New Town, which will have a total population of about 460,000 upon full development (Civil Engineering and Development Department & Planning Department, 2013b). The extended new town will meet medium- to long-term housing demand, and will be an integrated community providing a wide range of employment opportunities, as well as commercial, community, recreation, leisure, and cultural facilities supporting the larger population. Emphasis has also been given to the formulation of an urban design framework to provide a good quality urban environment, optimizing the natural ridgelines and watercourses to provide an interesting townscape, vibrant activity areas, connected open spaces, and a green network for residents' enjoyment (Civil Engineering and Development Department & Planning Department, 2013b).

Between the two New Development Area projects, the Hung Shui Ku project has just completed the third round of public consultation and no draft land use outline zoning plan has yet been made. In contrast, Kwu Tung North and Fanling North were reactivated earlier in 2008, and went through three rounds of public consultation and the engineering feasibility study by the end of 2012 and July 2013 respectively. Eventually, a draft outline land use zoning plan was gazetted for public inspection in December 2012, and finally approved by the Chief Executive and the Executive Council on June 19, 2015. As the project involves large-scale land resumption from the rural population, the planning process has aroused great concern from the stakeholders.

Nineteen interest groups, social concern groups, and local organizations such as rural committees reacted strongly to the planning proposals, including taking drastic action such as blocking previously open private roads. The issues brought up by the stakeholders included doubts on the urgency for large-scale new development, better compensation deals, earmarking a larger proportion of the new land for subsidized housing, raising the development intensity to enhance future housing supply, and mixed views on the provision or extension of public facilities, such as sewage treatment works, road expansion, and the provision of recreation facilities (Legislative Council paper CB(1)61/12–13(05)). These concerns might be related to personal interests, notably rehousing and compensation for land resumption, or genuine concern for community development. However, what emerged in the latest public consultation exercise in 2012 was the suspicion that the development of this border area was to pave the way for the integration of Hong Kong with the neighboring city of Shenzhen across the border in order to enhance the free movement of the mainlanders to Hong Kong. Some even argued that the development project was an act of the Hong Kong government in selling out Hong Kong to mainland China, undermining the principle of "One Country, Two Systems" (Legislative Council paper CB(1)61/12–13(05), paragraph 11).

Thus, among the concern groups petitioning against the development were the Defend Hong Kong Campaign and Action Group Against Hong Kong Being Planned by the Mainland. Their emergence and actions reflected the politicization of planning issues at a time when the future election method of the Chief Executive was being hotly debated, and when anti-mainlander sentiment was bloated due to the rampant cross-border purchase of daily and luxurious goods by mainlanders. As a result of the opposition and community pressure, and also because of the low development intensity because of the hilly terrain and the premature infrastructure planning, the scope of the plan was scaled down, excising the border area in Ping Che. The residential area was accordingly halved, reduced from 168 hectares to 83 hectares (Table 7.3). However, since the proposed development intensity of most of the excised areas was low (a plot ratio of 2:1) and with the increase of development intensity in other residential sites, potential housing supply actually increased slightly from 53,800 to 59,900 (Table 7.3). The project expanding the Tung Chung New Town near the new airport trod a different path.

Tung Chung New Town Extension

The Tung Chung New Town was planned in 1992 to support the new airport, due to open in 1998, as well as to provide a gateway to Hong Kong via the airport. With an area of 916 hectares, its population target was originally set at 260,000, but increased to 320,000 in 1996. Located in a sparsely populated area and served by a mass transit system, Tung Chung is also expected to provide facilities serving the population in the southwestern region of the New Territories. The major land uses are housing, community facilities, and service industries. By 2011, it had completed three phases of development, accommodating a population of nearly 80,000 people. In 2012, the government started to plan for the fourth phase of development. After an initial round of consultation with the general public in 2012, the government proposed, in 2013, a new extension area of more than 200 hectares, 134 hectares of which would be reclaimed land, accommodating a population of 153,000 in 53,000 public and private housing units. Responding to the much-criticized socio-spatial disparity problems between the eastern and western areas, the government proposed to extend the underground railway line to the western area and to provide more community facilities (Civil Engineering and Development Department & Planning Department, 2013a).

However, in the second round of consultation, held in May 2013, attended by the local residents, to which this author was invited to serve as a member of the Expert Panel to assist in the exercise, many local problems were brought up again. These included inadequate external and internal transport, inadequate community facilities (especially shopping facilities for daily needs in the western area), and the disparity of these provisions between the east and the west. Other issues were insufficient local employment, the urge to fully preserve a natural river in the western area, the need to strike a better balance between development and preservation of the natural landscape (including objection to sea reclamation), concerns about the visual impact of the proposed building heights, and objections to the relocation of a temple claimed to have been offering counselling services to the local residents. Apart from the livability and environmental protection issues, many also expressed their vision of Tung Chung's further development and how it could be made to become a vibrant and amenable place to live.

The plan was subsequently revised in 2014, scaling down the reclaimed area to 120 hectares, the population size to 140,000, and housing units to 48,000. A proposed small reclamation project (14 square kilometers) in the western area was scrapped to preserve better the natural ecology of the area, while the building height profile was also revised to be more in line with the natural topography. This revised proposal was generally well received by the residents in the third public consultation exercise (Figure 7.6). Currently, the plan is being finalized by the government and is going through the environmental impact assessment process.

The socio-spatial inequity problem in Tung Chung was generated by its planning and development approaches and processes. Four private housing estates, one subsidized owner-occupier housing estate, and one public housing estate were constructed in the eastern part of the new town, where an underground railway station was constructed (Figure 7.6). As a result of the housing types, the population was mostly middle- to lower middle-income families with higher disposable incomes than low-income families. The larger population and the presence of a railway station in the eastern part provide good accessibility for residents and transient tourists from the airport, making it financially viable to provide more and higher orders of recreation, retail, and entertainment facilities and goods, resulting in a more vibrant community.

In contrast, in the western part, where only a very large public rental housing estate and some village low rises were established, where there is no connection with the mass transit system, and where there are minimal

206 Hong Kong: Land Supply and New Housing

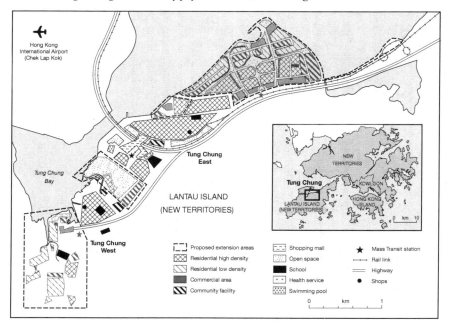

Figure 7.6 Tung Chung Extension
Source: Based on Civil Engineering and Development Department & Planning Department (2014b)

Figure 7.7 Village Housing in Tung Chung West
Source: Rebecca L. H. Chiu

Figure 7.8 Public Rental Housing in Tung Chung West
Source: Rebecca L. H. Chiu

community and retail facilities, there has been a concentration of low-income earners (Figure 7.6). Due to the remoteness of the new town from the main urban area, requiring a total commuting time of three hours every day and more for this western area, only the poorest of the poor live here, that is, those who have no concern about commuting time and costs because they do not intend to seek employment, with the intention of living on government subsidies. Thus, in contrast to the eastern part, this section of the new town has a depressing and deserted ambience. During the consultation exercise, the local people expressed bitter concern about not being directly accessible to the transit system, the lack of higher-order facilities and the poor intra-town transport. As a result, the extension plan proposes to add a railway station, private housing and subsidized owner-occupier housing to enhance accessibility and community mix. No doubt the proposals promise a more socio-spatially balanced, accessible, vibrant, and self-contained living environment for the local residents, and thus are generally accepted by the local community. Also, as the extension plan does not incur any land resumption from existing landowners, the planning process has been smoother than that of the New Development Areas in North East New Territories.

Conclusion

This chapter has discussed how the political and economic environments of Hong Kong have precipitated property cycles, and, in turn, how these cycles have, on the one hand, influenced the supply of residential land and housing and, on the other, accentuated the ups and downs of the cycles. Being the sole supplier of new land, unlike in the English and Australian cases, the government is an active and direct player in the market. In its multiple capacity as the rule setter, the custodian of public wellbeing and a direct market player, the government may not play each of these roles to its maximum, as it has to compromise the interests of these different dimensions. But it would be difficult to argue that the government's multifaceted capacity poses a barrier to timely and sufficient supply of land for housing construction, as it could be argued the other way, that is, that its multiple roles provide a wider perspective for making more balanced decisions.

Equally, most of the responses from the community are legitimate concerns, at least *prima facie*, and should not be considered as barriers, including the protection of the value of their fixed assets. They reflect the public value on livability generally held by the community, and the underlying political contexts and issues prevalent at the time. Nonetheless, what we need to note and resolve is the reduction in residential land and therefore the diminution of housing supply as a corollary to the pursuit for a more livable environment and a more democratic society. These reductions pose planning losses for low-income families waiting for public rental housing, and for lower middle-income families, especially younger families, struggling to purchase their own homes in the market but failing due to continuously rising housing prices as a result of the short housing supply. The apparent trade-offs are a more participatory planning process and a more empowered civil society versus less land and housing supply and therefore higher housing prices, and better livability versus a slower pace in improving the housing quality of disadvantaged groups and less certainty for housing market players. The ensuing questions are: whose interests should have priority; who shapes public value, for whom and for what; are the disadvantaged groups heard sufficiently even under a more democratized system; and in a highly politicized planning system how much is democracy, how much is politics, and how much is abuse?

It is very easy to say that the government, and, in this case, the planning authorities, should play a balancing act. However, in an increasingly democratizing and politicizing society such as that of Hong Kong, the present residents usually have louder voices than the yet-to-emerge future residents of the new development areas. It seems absurd to argue that in a democratizing community the government should stand firmer to protect the interests of the general community against local interests. Such an undertaking would no doubt require stronger political stamina and a commitment of the government to act as conflict manager. However, as discussed above, the most recent attempts of the government to acquire new land for housing development have provided mixed results. It may become the case that, as elsewhere, if housing problems continue to accentuate and loom large as a social issue, it may give the government the mandate to wind back public participation, or, alternatively, to exercise its landownership rights more forcefully in opening up greenfield sites, including reclamation and excising country parks, to make land available for housing development. The evolution of planning politics will continue to unfold, and hopefully for a better housing future.

Notes

1. A system whereby a developer applies for a site to be sold from the government's list of sites available for purchase, offering a premium for the purchase. Should the government find the premium acceptable, then the site will be triggered for sale in a public auction. Should no bidder offer a price higher than that offered by the original applicant, the applicant is obliged to buy the land at the price that is offered. The government regarded this method as a market-led approach in land sales and suitable in an inactive market (Budget Speech, 2008).
2. As explained in Chapter 6, although land is state-owned in Hong Kong, once leased to developers in a land sale exercise it becomes de facto private land, which can be resumed before land lease expiry only for public purposes. Automatic renewal is also normally expected.

References

Centadata. (2014). *City One Shatin*. Available at: http://hk.centadata.com/ptest.aspx?type=3&code=XSHNIHSXHT&ref=CD2_Main, accessed on November 16, 2015.

Census and Statistics Department. (2014). *Table E031: Domestic Households by Household Size and Monthly Household Income (Table 9.4 in Quarterly Report on General Household Survey)*. Available at:www.censtatd.gov.hk/fd.jsp?file=D5250035E2015QQ02E.xls&product_id=D5250035&lang=1, accessed on November 16, 2015. Hong Kong: Census and Statistics Department.

Census and Statistics Department. (2015). *Hong Kong Annual Digest of Statistics (2015 Edition): Table 17.13 Land Usage Distribution (as at end-2014)*. Available at: www.statistics.gov.hk/pub/B10100032015AN15B0100.pdf, accessed December 17, 2015.

Chiu, L. H. R. (1998). The home ownership drive of HKSAR. *Planning and Development*, 14(1), 12–20.

Chiu, L. H. R. (2007). Planning, land and affordable housing in Hong Kong. *Housing Studies*, 22(1), 63–81.

Civil Engineering and Development Department. (2015). *The Geology of Hong Kong (Interactive On-line): 11 Onshore Superficial Deposits and Fills*. Available at: www.cedd.gov.hk/eng/about/organisation/s.html, accessed on December 12, 2015.

Civil Engineering and Development Department & Planning Department. (2012a). *North East New Territories New Development Areas Planning and Engineering Study—Stage Three Public Engagement Digest*. Hong Kong: Civil Engineering and Development Department & Planning Department.

Civil Engineering and Development Department & Planning Department. (2012b). *Planning and Engineering Study on Future Land Use at Ex-Lamma Quarry Area at Sok Kwu Wan, Lamma Island—Feasibility Study Stage One Community Engagement Digest*. Hong Kong: Civil Engineering and Development Department & Planning Department.

Civil Engineering and Development Department & Planning Department. (2013a). *Tung Chung New Town Extension Study—Stage Two Public Engagement Digest*. Hong Kong: Civil Engineering and Development Department & Planning Department.

Civil Engineering and Development Department & Planning Department. (2013b). *North East New Territories New Development Areas Planning and Engineering Study—Information Digest*. Hong Kong: Civil Engineering and Development Department & Planning Department.

Civil Engineering and Development Department & Planning Department. (2014a). *Planning and Engineering Study on Future Land Use at Ex-Lamma Quarry Area at Sok Kwu Wan, Lamma Island—Feasibility Study Stage Two Community Engagement Digest*. Hong Kong: Civil Engineering and Development Department & Planning Department.

Civil Engineering and Development Department & Planning Department. (2014b). *Tung Chung New Town Extension Study—Stage Three Public Engagement Digest*. Hong Kong: Civil Engineering and Development Department & Planning Department.

Civil Engineering and Development Department & Planning Department. (2015). *Hung Shui Kiu New Development Area Planning and Engineering Study Stage Three—Community Engagement Digest*. Hong Kong: Civil Engineering and Development Department & Planning Department.

Development Bureau. (2015). *Kwu Tung North/Fanling North New Development Areas – Official Website*. Development Bureau, The Government of Hong Kong SAR. Available at: http://ktnfln-ndas.gov.hk/en/index.php, accessed on November 4, 2015.

Financial Services and the Treasury Bureau. (2013). *The Administration's Responses to Matters Arising from the Meeting of the Bills Committee on Stamp Duty (Amendment) Bill 2013 held on 22 November 2013*. Available at: www.legco.gov.hk/yr12-13/english/bc/bc05/papers/bc051213cb1-491-2-e.pdf, accessed on April 20, 2015.

Financial Secretary. (2008). *The 2008–09 Budget: Speech by the Financial Secretary, the Hon. John C. Tsang moving the Second Reading of the Appropriation Bill 2008*, February 27, 2008, Hong Kong.

Hong Kong SAR Government. (2007). *Hong Kong 2030: Planning Vision and Strategy*. Hong Kong: The Development Bureau and the Planning Department.

Mingpao. (2013, May 22). *65% of the 25,000 objections to the rezoning of the Lee Wai Li site to residential use came from Hong Kong Baptist University.*
Hong Kong SAR Government. (2014). *Policy Address 2014.* Available at: www.policyaddress.gov.hk/2014/eng/index.html, accessed on December 3, 2015.
Hong Kong SAR Government. (2015). *Policy Address 2015.* Available at: www.policyaddress.gov.hk/2015/eng/index.html, accessed on December 3, 2015.
Legislative Council Panel on Development. (2015). *Submission on Hung Shui Kiu New Development Area Planning and Engineering Study, LegCo Paper No.:CB(1) 1273/14–15(04), LegCo Paper No.:CB(1)1273/14–15(05), LegCo Paper No.: CB(1)1273/14–15(07), LegCo Paper No.:CB(1)1273/14–15(08), LegCo Paper No.:CB(1)1273/14–15(10).* Hong Kong: Legislative Council.
Ng, M. K. (1999). Political economy and urban planning: A comparative study of Hong Kong, Singapore and Taiwan. *Progress in Planning, 51*(1), 1–90.
Ng, M. K. (2006). World-city formation under an executive-led government: The politics of harbour reclamation in Hong Kong. *Town Planning Review, 77*(3), 311–337.
Ng, M. K. (2008). From government to governance? Politics of planning in the first decade of the Hong Kong Special Administrative Region. *Planning Theory & Practice, 9*(2), 165–185.
Ng, M. K. (2011). Power and rationality: the politics of harbour reclamation in Hong Kong. *Environment and Planning—Part C, 29*(4), 677–692.
Planning Department. (1993). *Southeast Kowloon Development Statement: Executive Summary.* Hong Kong: Planning Department.
Planning Department. (1998). *Outline Zoning Plans of South East Kowloon Development Scheme: S/K19/1 and S/K21/1.* Hong Kong: Planning Department.
Planning Department. (2002). *Outline Zoning Plans of South East Kowloon Development Scheme: S/K19/3 and S/K21/3.* Hong Kong: Planning Department.
Planning Department. (2004). *South East Kowloon Development Comprehensive Planning and Engineering Review.* Hong Kong: Planning Department.
Planning Department. (2006). *Kai Tak Planning Review: Revised preliminary outline development plan.* Hong Kong: Planning Department.
Planning Department. (2007). *Outline Zoning Plans of South East Kowloon Development Scheme: S/K22/2.* Hong Kong: Planning Department.
Planning Department. (2012). *Outline Zoning Plans of South East Kowloon Development Scheme: S/K22/4.* Hong Kong: Planning Department.
Rating and Valuation Department. (2014). *Private Domestic—Price Indices by Class (Territory-wide) (from 1979).* Available at: www.rvd.gov.hk/doc/en/statistics/his_data_4.xls, accessed on November 13, 2015.
Sing Tao Daily. (March 15, 2012; August 2, 2012; September 20, 2012; February 10, 2014; March 13, 2014; March 27, 2014; June 13, 2014; June 20, 2014; June 26, 2014; July 3, 2014; October 26, 2014).
Territorial Development Department. (1998). *Feasibility Study for Southeast Kowloon Development: Executive Summary.* Hong Kong: Territorial Development Department.
Territorial Development Department. (2001). *Comprehensive Feasibility Study for the Revised Scheme of Southeast Kowloon Development: Executive Summary.* Hong Kong: Territorial Development Department.
Transport and Housing Bureau. (2014). *Long Term Housing Strategy.* Hong Kong: Transport and Housing Bureau.

Transport and Housing Bureau. (2015). *Statistics on Private Housing Supply in Primary Market*. Available at: www.thb.gov.hk/eng/psp/publications/housing/private/pshpm/stat201509.pdf, accessed on November 16, 2015.

Wan, Y. K. P. (2005). *Governance of Residential Land Use Planning in Hong Kong*. Doctoral thesis submitted to the University of Hong Kong.

Wan, Y. K. P. & Chiu, L. H. R. (2008). Transforming the governance of plan-making in Hong Kong. *Journal of Place Management and Development, 1*(3), 256–271.

8 Conclusion
Planning, Democracy, and Control in the Delivery of New Homes

The starting point for this book was escalating concern over shortfalls in new housing supply in three very different contexts: Australia, England, and Hong Kong. We used a comparative framework to ask whether optimal conditions for housing delivery might lie in better understanding the very different approaches to planning control and land supply, which define our three case study locations. In this concluding chapter, we draw together the national/territorial experiences and local illustrations to provide a broader view of the politics (and questions of democracy and power) that are central to the exercise of development control through the planning system. We consider, in particular, two core issues: the ownership of land and development rights, and the influence of representative democracy on housing outcomes, tracing these two themes through the comparative markers outlined in Chapter 1. A number of key issues are drawn out, relating to the ways in which governments support housing production and investment, the roles of the private sector, not-for-profit bodies, and individual households in providing new homes, and the balance of power and control across urban governance and planning arrangements.

Landownership and Development Rights

From the vantage point of Australia—with its vast continent but limited geography of urban settlement, land-hungry patterns of housing development, and powerful private land developers—government retention of landownership, as in Hong Kong, or the capacity to procure affordable housing as part of new development, as in England, seems highly appealing. Beyond the planning system, Australian governments have retained very few levers by which to control the pace and nature of land and housing development. It was not always so. As noted in Chapter 2, in the early 1970s a scheme to encourage state land commissions resulted in significant moderation of the housing market (producing around 10 to 15 percent of new building lots) up until the 1990s (Milligan, 2003; Troy, 2012). Yet, even when government does have a higher level of control over key development sites—as with the two case study examples highlighted in Chapter 3—very little affordable housing has been achieved. Instead, the superior design, accessibility, and environmental outcomes delivered through significant public expertise and investment have been capitalized into prices and rents, reinforcing spatial sorting by wealth across Sydney's greater metropolitan region. A similar record is apparent across major renewal areas in other Australian cities (Greive et al., 1999; Shaw, 2013).

But the endemic "stuck site" phenomenon afflicting England (Hall, 2014) and, perhaps to a lesser degree, Hong Kong does not seem to have a parallel in Australia, despite regular industry complaints about slow decision timeframes (Steele, 2012) and the costs of infrastructure provision (Ruming et al., 2011). Such complaints have been heard and responded to in the form of ongoing planning system reform efforts across all of the Australian jurisdictions, as well as modest Commonwealth and state infrastructure grants (Gurran & Phibbs, 2013b; Ruming et al., 2014). Indeed, a national-level upswing in housing completions between 2012 and 2015 suggests that Australia's housing market is relatively responsive to shifts in demand, and is not demonstrably "constrained" by planning-system barriers when the market is rising.

Of course, complete dependence on the private market, with its inevitable fluctuations, means that new housing supply is often out of step with demographic drivers of housing need, including population growth and household formation. There will also be a widening gap between overall provision of new homes and the availability of dwellings that are adequate and affordable for lower-income groups (which are not economic for the private sector to provide without subsidy in the form of government land, capital support, or deep rental aid). Before its dismissal by the (conservative) Liberal government on its election in 2013, Australia's National Housing Supply Council estimated this deficit of affordable homes to be more than 500,000 dwellings, or around six percent of the total housing stock, and rising (National Housing Supply Council, 2013).

Allocation of Development Rights

One of the keys to understanding why so few mechanisms for securing affordable housing outcomes exist in the Australian system relates to the ways in which development rights are allocated via the land use planning system. In Chapter 1 we summarized approaches to land use planning with reference to a spectrum from discretionary through to rule-bound (fixed development rights) forms of development control. Australia falls into an intermediate category whereby control of the nature and location of new housing occurs in the context of detailed, legally binding land use plans that assign development rights and obligations. This system offers a degree of certainty for the private sector, providing information about the types of uses that will be permitted on a particular site, as well as for the surrounding locality. However, the capacity to secure wider community benefits through the development process is divested once the plan is made, since it is at this point that development "rights" are inferred—and land values are defined. Technically, the Australian planning system also incorporates discretionary decision-making approaches through merit criteria that must be satisfied before most types of significant development can be permitted. But it is increasingly the practice that legally enforceable land use plans allocate baseline development "rights," while discretion is used to permit proposals that seek to vary the existing standards. One outcome of this system—which offers both certainty *and* flexibility for developers (but, arguably, neither for concerned neighbors)—is high rates of planning approval. Around 90 percent of development proposals are approved in Australia (Productivity Commission, 2011), a figure which rises to 95 percent in Sydney (Gurran & Phibbs, 2013a).

This broad-brush description of the Australian planning context summarizes arrangements across eight distinct jurisdictions and thus is necessarily simplistic. As discussed in Chapters 2 and 3, and further below, a number of political interests and processes overlay this basic framework, and there are certainly some jurisdictions—such as the state of Victoria—where discretionary and contestable decision-making processes constrain efforts to diversify new housing supply in affluent suburbs (Taylor, 2013). But the important point here is that when development rights are conferred—overtly or by implication through the designation of particular housing zones—land values are immediately affected. The owner of the land—either a private individual or the public sector—enjoys the full value uplift arising from the strategic planning process, minus the costs of meeting any attached obligations for providing local infrastructure or other community benefits. A similar benefit is conferred following planned or actual public investment in infrastructure or services benefitting the locality.

As outlined in Chapters 2 and 3, the political climate in Australia has always worked against the possibility of wider public benefits being secured through the private development process. Most recently, property interests have mounted effective arguments that even existing development obligations—in the form of design standards and local infrastructure provision—are too onerous and must be wound back through planning "reform." Similar debates have been heard in England, as discussed in Chapter 4. But, in contrast to the English case, where local powers to decide on the amount and location of new homes have been seemingly reinforced by recent changes to the planning system, in Australia a different situation has occurred. Rather, there seems to have been a strengthening of developer "rights" as discretionary refusal powers are wound back, but expanded discretionary planning powers—particularly those resumed by the state—to approve proposals that appear far beyond the parameters of legal plans (Steele & Ruming, 2012).

Thus, constraints affecting new housing supply in Australia appear somewhat different to the case of England, as outlined in Chapters 4 and 5.

Like Australia, the state retains only limited land holdings and instead relies heavily on the private sector to bring sites forward for development. But, unlike Australia, the nationalization of development rights in 1947 (under legislation—the Town and Country Planning Act—that created a comprehensive planning system) changed the status quo. While the new Act required the drawing up of local land use plans to inform planning control, these schemes did not confer a right to develop. Rather, development rights are assigned through the discretionary issue of a planning permit. As explained in Chapter 4, it is this control, exercised through the discretionary process of plan permitting, which enables local authorities to secure significant wider public benefits through the private development process, such as affordable housing. Yet this discretion to grant or refuse permission—and to facilitate or block development—undermines certainty in the English system and thus has been implicated as a key constraint to new housing supply. Planning is seen to generate "regulatory risk" during the processes of policy design (and change), plan making, and decision taking. This risk may reduce private-sector commitment to developments, particularly larger ones, and may cause some strategic housing schemes to stall and ultimately fail (see Chapter 5).

In contrast, the statutory land use zoning mechanism that exists in Hong Kong ensures certainty of development rights, as planning permits are not needed for developments complying with the zoned uses. Planning applications are only mandated for secondary uses (such as a tourism or retail activity within a residential zone), as specified in the zoning plan. Nonetheless, residential zoning does not specify private or public housing uses. Rather, the tenure and development mode of residential projects are only determined by government departments and bureaus when compulsory plans for particular sites are prepared. This remains an administrative, non-statutory process that is not subject to public input.

Thus, as landowner—able to sell land and/or construct housing to generate public revenue—and as landlord to the tenants of public housing, the government of Hong Kong retains significant proactive planning powers. Overall, the government assumes broad socioeconomic responsibilities and seeks to deliver benefits to different community sectors to the extent that prevailing economic conditions allow. However, these functions have been increasingly subject to community pressure in line with the government's shift toward a more pluralistic governance mode after 1997.

Overall, our comparative case studies suggest that the English planning system seems to impose greater constraints and uncertainty on new housing development than that generated by the planning systems in Australia and Hong Kong. But it would be very one-eyed to conclude that Australia's model is superior; while housing output might be more buoyant in the Australian case (when the market is rising), this new production is not demonstrably addressing the shortage of affordable homes for lower-income groups. By contrast, the English model by definition ensures that new housing development incorporates affordable homes, funded in part by the value uplift generated by the planning process. The national retention of development rights thus operates as an inbuilt defense against planning-induced land value appreciation, securing space for not-for-profit housing provision within a wider private market context. While many of the apartments approved for the banks of the Thames in London over the past decade may serve as "safe deposit boxes" for international investors (Rees, 2014), their construction was also instrumental in generating significant contributions toward affordable housing and for local infrastructure. Even if local planners had been able to insist on more modest apartments geared toward middle-income earners, the rising force of demand in a world city such as London, inflamed by domestic demand-side pressures (such as tax incentives for property development and consumption: see Gallent, 2015) and the increasingly international nature of housing investment (Valentine, 2015), would inevitably result in price inflation. Thus the power to secure affordable homes—financed by, but quarantined from, the profit-driven market—remains critical in the English context.

An addendum, however, to this positive note is that the UK government has in recent years become increasingly concerned with the "crisis in home ownership" that seems to have accompanied rising investment in housing. The buy-to-let market has grown rapidly since the mid-1990s and the purchase of homes by non-resident foreign investors now accounts for 15 percent of the market across London. This has generated significant house-price pressure and created the "generation rent" phenomenon, with many aspiring home owners effectively locked out of that tenure. With its majority in Parliament, the Conservative Government that came to power in May 2015 is once again touting home ownership as the remedy to broader housing woes. It seems to have turned against buy-to-let, reducing the rate at which interest relief can be claimed on mortgages (from 2017) and increasing stamp duty (land tax) on buy-to-let purchases (from 2016). But, most significantly, in relation to securing affordable homes through the planning system, it has prioritized the delivery of discounted starter homes over social renting or intermediate tenures. It seems likely that there will be a shift, in the years ahead, from developer involvement in providing genuinely "affordable" housing (linked to local wage levels) to delivering starter homes for sale with a 20 percent discount and a £450,000 cap in London. That cap, which will likely be the normal sale price wherever such homes are available in many parts of the city, will mean that this new dominant form of affordable housing will only be accessible to households with substantial incomes (in excess of £100,000 per annum) and large deposits.

And these recent threats seem set to join other difficulties that have undermined the supply of affordable housing in recent years. The case studies examined in Chapter 5, for example, show that the procurement of affordable housing through planning agreements is under pressure as large potential housing sites in private ownership struggle to get off the ground, owing to the demise of publicly-led New Town projects, blockages in the provision of infrastructure, and local political pressures. Further, as highlighted in Chapter 5 with particular reference to "stuck sites" in Ashford, the timing of value-capture arrangements (levied on developers at the point of development rather than on landholders when permitted land is sold) leave agreed infrastructure and affordable housing commitments vulnerable to subsequent market shifts.

Landownership and Proactive Planning

Both the English and Australian cases highlight the ways in which gradual divestment of "proactive" planning powers over the latter half of the twentieth century increased the significance of regulatory development control as the sole instrument for guiding housing outcomes. Seeking greater powers of intervention without disrupting the overall parameters of the market-driven approach to housing delivery, in both countries special purpose urban development corporations have been formed by government to oversee outcomes on major sites. These special purpose development vehicles bypass local authorities and typically combine powers to acquire land and to assign development rights. But, rather than a shift back toward proactive planning powers within government, the urban development corporation models of England and Australia appear designed to liberate private developers from remnant regulatory constraints and obligations imposed by standard permitting processes.

By contrast, in Hong Kong the state retains landownership and thus the power to proactively plan for new housing supply. It also controls development rights as legal owner of the land and through its planning powers. This state ownership of land has rendered the role of planning in circumscribing development rights and securing social benefits less significant than in the case of England and Australia. Critically, the state ownership of land has enabled the Hong Kong government to directly provide affordable housing through rental and subsidized ownership schemes. Of course, as discussed further below, this high level of public involvement in affordable housing provision reflects ongoing state commitment and a political context in which such commitment aims to ensure social stability. But, as highlighted in Chapters 6 and 7, unfortunately these expansive powers through landownership and the control of development rights have not been sufficient to overcome increasing impediments to new housing production, particularly when it comes to delivering public rental housing and catering for low-income groups.

While on the one hand Australia's more liberal planning system appears to offer a bonanza for the property sector, in fact it has become a catch-22. With development rights increasingly implied by planning decisions, land values skyrocket when land is rezoned or even in anticipation of rezoning. This is because land values are determined by residual valuation, which subtracts development costs from potential profit (estimated with reference to existing house sales). If price expectations are not met, landowners can easily withhold their land from sale—or development—until the market rises. Thus, in assigning development rights through rezoning, the government has relinquished control of the development process, while at the same time contributing to escalating price appreciation. This itself becomes a demand-side constraint to new supply, at least until the next property boom. Exacerbating these effects is that speculation is limited to the process of land development rather than housing construction (which primarily occurs on a contracted basis). Thus, while there may be surplus sites during periods of low demand, speculative overbuilding is almost non-existent.

To add insult to injury, government-owned land is almost always involved in Australia's major development projects—as in the case studies of Green Square and Rouse Hill—but even public landownership has failed to deliver affordable housing outcomes at scale. Ironically, the government's land development agencies are often required to mimic the private sector in extracting maximum profit from its land development projects—with rising land and housing values over the life of a development scheme regarded to be an important indicator of success.

Representative Democracy and Power in the Planning Process

As outlined in Chapter 1, there are structural differences in the ways in which central and local levels of government, and other actors (such as developers, home owners, and civil society) are able to exercise power through the planning process. In England, local planning authorities lead the allocation of land and sites for housing development, although this process is indicative rather than binding. The local level is also the primary scale for determining planning decisions. This contrasts with the Australian case, where the state government ratifies strategic planning and rezoning processes and drives significant infrastructure decisions (although much of the detailed work may be undertaken at the local level). There is only a single tier of government in Hong Kong, but the widespread consultation surrounding strategic planning processes implies that representative democracy is an important force in contemporary plan making.

Arguably, more attention to local-level views would appear warranted in the closely settled context of Hong Kong and in many parts of England. In these highly settled locations, undeveloped land surely assumes a much higher symbolic value than might be expected in lower-density settings such as Australia (although this is not necessarily so, as discussed below). In any case, engaging with and accommodating local views about new development has become a very significant part of the planning process in Hong Kong since the mid-1990s and has always been a definitive characteristic of the English system (albeit with persistent concerns over levels of engagement and the degree to which communities can influence planning decisions: Gallent & Robinson, 2012). As discussed in Chapter 6, in the case of Hong Kong, civil society itself was instrumental in unleashing a traditionally closed planning and land supply process, and in fostering attention to quality rather than solely efficiency or quantity. From the 1990s onward, public consultation became an important consideration in the allocation and production (through reclamation) of public land (which was increasingly opposed).

Representative Democracy and Reform

Similarly, although local democracy and the balance between central and local government have fluctuated in England, the current phase appears firmly tilted toward the local level. The revocation of regional housing targets from 2011 has reinvigorated the power of local authorities and has been accompanied by the formalization of "neighbourhood" planning at the community scale (Parker et al., 2015). So, in England, and increasingly in Hong Kong, the views of local communities seem to hold more weight in the planning process than is the case in Australia. This is not to say that local residents—particularly home owners—are not an important factor in understanding the ways in which Australia's urban settlement patterns have evolved. On the contrary, the emphasis on greenfield sites for housing development, which persists across most of Australia, reflects the fact that planning and housing production in undeveloped contexts without the need to accommodate existing residents is a far easier proposition. As outlined in Chapter 3, where very high density development is occurring, the tendency has been to focus on special sites; again, where there is a lower risk of confronting resident opposition.

Successive planning system reforms—many of which have proceeded under the banner of housing supply and affordability—have sought to further reduce local political involvement in the development control process by implementing standardized local planning instruments, state-wide codes for expanding the range of development types that can be automatically approved, and the appointment of special regional and state level panels (Ruming et al., 2014). But, while cast as "depoliticization," in fact such changes reflect the relative power of producer groups and their interests, which have gained particular traction at state and national scales. The relatively weak position of local government under Australia's federal system, whereby the states and territories maintain strong control over local councils and their planning and development control responsibilities, has also tended to help maintain the status quo.

Politics

Thus, home owners in all of our three countries are an important political force, at local and at national levels. But they are not the only political players who steer the planning system to deliver particular housing outcomes. In particular, producer groups have proven adept at defining the policy debate such that self-serving, self-evident claims are reinforced. As outlined in Chapter 4, in England the Home Builders Federation and other private sector organizations have had an important "corporate" influence on policy discourse and in the design of planning policy and targets for housing delivery. In Australia it can be difficult to determine the difference between policy arguments advanced by the public and private sectors. Professional lobbyists, ideological "think tanks," and industry "peak" groups have all played a major and increasing role in defining Australia's urban and housing policy agendas, particularly at the national and state levels. This is also true in England, where key government ministers have strong links with right-leaning think-tanks and many of their policy ideas are inspired by a close circle of political advisors who exhibit strong anti-planning and anti-regulation tendencies. In Hong Kong, similar groups also play a role but are often concealed behind different community groups or government advisory committees. Due to the large scale development associated with high rises, especially high-rise housing estates incurring substantial financial outlays, the housing market is dominated by large developers. Although their influence on government's spatial development and land-supply policy is rarely acknowledged, especially within the current highly sensitive political environment, property interests are undoubtedly mediated through various business links at different levels and in multiple areas.

Arguably, corporate interests and ideological perspectives advanced through these channels may undermine democratic policy processes. But, in the case of Australia, cleavages between producer interests and the assumed position of the vast majority of voters in home ownership appear only at the local scale. At national and even state levels there is considerable alignment between the interests of existing home owners and those expressed by the property development industry (i.e. to preserve generous demand-side incentives for property investment, and to enable ongoing greenfield development beyond established residential suburbs). While elements of the property lobby also call for a wholesale deregulation of prevailing planning controls in service of unlimited density around urban centers and public transport, when actioned these proposals deliver windfall gains to sitting property owners. Therefore, contests between home owners and developers play out most dramatically when proposals appear to threaten the social milieu, for instance through the development of affordable rental accommodation for lower-income groups. This situation also arises in England, where there is concern not only for the social milieu but also the impact on house prices and "exclusivity" associated with on-site delivery of affordable housing. This concern leads to a number of outcomes: the spatial separation of affordable from market housing on larger, lower-density housing sites comprising single-family homes (working contrary to the pepper-potting and tenure-mixing objectives of planning agreements);

the separation of owners and renters in higher-density schemes by ensuring that access corridors are not shared and that renters enter apartment buildings via "poor doors"; and developers being permitted to make cash contributions in lieu of affordable housing on site in some instances.

With increasing concern over the capacity of younger generations to enter home ownership, there has been much public hand-wringing by Australia's politicians at national and state levels, but little serious action is likely while the electoral balance remains firmly tipped in the other direction. Meanwhile, the national-level Commonwealth government can blame state and local planning processes for inadequate land and housing supply, pleasing the powerful property lobby without increasing the call on public funds to support the social sector. As noted in Chapter 2, the position was summed up by former federal Treasurer Joe Hockey who infamously suggested that aspiring home owners "get a better job" if they wanted to buy a house (ABC, 2015). By contrast, his successor Scott Morrison retreated to the more politically palatable exhortation of blaming state and local governments for affordability pressures and calling for planning system reform to release new supply.

The discourse in England is very similar. Ministers have been lambasted for telling unhappy renters—worried that they will never own a home of their own—that they would be better off moving out of London. Likewise, it is considered bad form to blame existing home owners entering the amateur rental market (through buy-to-let) for adding to house price inflation or to suggest that such inflation might be lessened by new property taxes, which might take some of the fire out of the market and shift investment pressure to commodities other than housing. But it is considered fair game to engage in planner baiting, accusing local authorities of not doing enough to bring forward land for additional housing or to facilitate development through faster and more efficient local planning. The planning system and its local implementation provides government with a useful lightning rod for frustrations that are really about the way housing is distributed through a global market and consumed, often as nothing more than a lucrative investment.

Still, questions of new housing supply remain important in England, and contests over the location and extent of that supply appear balanced between local and central levels of government. An ongoing process of planning system reform in the English context—designed initially to lessen local constraints to development and subsequently, it seems, to restore decision powers to the local level—appears to have played some part in erecting additional barriers to the delivery of new homes, epitomized by the phenomenon of "stuck sites." With the majority of voters still in home ownership (although the level is dropping, hence the arrival of the new support measures noted above), approval for the existing demand- and supply-side settings seems set to endure. Practically, there is little chance of reducing the costs of home ownership in order to calm the market and emphasis will remain with supply solutions, ineffective as they may be in the face of surging demand-side pressures (Valentine, 2015). The Conservative government is adept at forwarding political solutions to a narrowly defined "crisis in home ownership," but, as yet, no big answers to the wider "crisis of housing access" have emerged. Similarly, with increased dependence on the private sector to deliver new housing, adjustments to policy and planning provisions are expected to favor producer interests: supply- rather than demand-side solutions are easier to sell to voters and, of course, house builders. Associated with the supply side is the dismantling of Section 106 requirements for affordable housing contributions through renegotiation of previously agreed amounts (now under the Planning and Infrastructure Act 2013), or the threatened roll-back of the entire system (in favor of discounted starter homes). But, as shown in the case of Australia, there is no guarantee that such measures will trigger the desired supply response, or that general supply will increase the availability of affordable homes for lower-income groups. It remains to be seen whether the not-for-profit housing sector—far more significant than its counterpart in Australia—will exert sufficient political pressure to offset these challenges and maintain the important provisions for affordable housing inclusion through England's local planning and development processes. Such pressure is increasingly important because, as demonstrated across the Australian and English cases, it is lower-income renters whose interests appear neglected in the political processes surrounding planning for new housing development.

Many of these considerations appear irrelevant to the Hong Kong case. There is no need to use the planning system to secure affordable housing outcomes through the planning process; rather, government land and control of development rights provides the basis for widespread affordable rental and subsidized home ownership programs. Similarly, government land-ownership has also ensured that public and affordable housing development is not beholden to local community sentiment. Thus, around 50 percent of households in Hong Kong reside in public or subsidized housing, implying an important constituency for the government's affordable housing schemes. However, as public involvement becomes an ever more important feature of urban decision making in Hong Kong, new constraints delimiting the exercise of these government powers are emerging. In stark contrast to the cases of Australia and England, the politics of land supply, and the power to define the policy agenda, appears to be shifting toward, rather than away from, an emboldened civil society. Yet, in common with Australia and England, the lower-income younger generations seeking an affordable home may find their interests poorly represented in Hong Kong's new urban housing debates and in a housing market that, as with the examples of Sydney and London, is frequently overwhelmed by external investors.

Lessons

In the final analysis, what can be learned from this three-case study comparison? Policy and planning reform efforts in all three countries have long sought, in different ways and with different degrees of success, to import "quick fixes" from international settings in order to address domestic concerns. This practice seems at no risk of abating. If anything, the forces of globalization have facilitated a form of internet policy shopping that has greatly accelerated the appetite for foreign panaceas. But, while the problems (sluggish housing production and rising affordability pressures) may be shared and even the remedies generalizable (greater government support for new housing production, tied to affordable outcomes), replicating success from elsewhere is generally far more difficult. Rather than firm conclusions or lessons, the value of comparison is often to expose unfounded policy claims and misguided solutions, while highlighting opportunities for more sustained and effective forms of intervention.

Indeed, our comparison of attempts to promote housing supply across Australia, England, and Hong Kong has exposed a series of common policy modes, which warrant ongoing scrutiny. These modes include the preoccupation with reducing "red tape"—by slashing and standardizing local planning controls—and the impact of such reforms on the quantity, quality, location, and cost of new homes. Related attempts to relieve planning "constraints" by lifting obligations to provide agreement for infrastructure (Australia) or affordable housing (England) mean that inadequate facilities and services will become a new constraint to residential development, while the quantity of affordable homes produced will only decline.

Overall, it is clear that the private sector has failed in all of our three case study countries to step in when the government (through withdrawal of subsidy or direct provision of non-profit housing development) has stepped out. Many commentators too, have blamed the land use planning system and process—three very different systems, in three very different political contexts—for hindering the private market response to housing demand. But our three cases raise questions about such assumptions.

Perhaps most significantly, the differences in each of the cases highlight the dangers in rushing to planning system deregulation as a quick fix for either housing supply or affordability pressures. In the case of Australia, assumed planning constraints appear exaggerated—with supply output closely following shifts in market demand—such that when demand lifted (fueled by falling interest rates) so did housing output. Planning system deregulation then only generated a further transfer of public control over the development process to the private sector, for little obvious community return. Housing production stayed stagnant during sluggish markets, while housing affordability—measured in terms of the capacity of lower-income groups to achieve home purchase, or access stable rental accommodation near employment—only declined during the building boom. Further, the lack of mechanisms to secure affordable homes through periods of rapid development—even on government-owned sites—severely undermines any claims that increased supply improves affordability outcomes for those in greatest need. In fact, successive planning interventions in Australia (particularly those on major sites within the capital cities) have facilitated an immense transfer in wealth from the public sector to existing home owners and property investors, while failing to share the benefits of development and renewal with aspiring home owners and lower-income renters. Yet, in a bid to increase housing output in England, the very mechanisms that maintain affordable housing outcomes through new development processes are under threat. These mechanisms are crucial in England, as they deliver affordable housing access opportunities in a market overwhelmed by investment pressure. The only obvious substitute for bureaucratically allocated affordable housing, delivered through a land or tax subsidy (or on state-owned land, in the case of Hong Kong), is a fully functional housing market that delivers house-price sanity for the many rather than investment opportunities for the few. Since that seems a long way off, it is critical that mechanisms for providing genuinely affordable homes are maintained.

The lessons of the comparative analysis presented here may be to look more carefully at the existing structures and mechanisms already in place in each case as the basis for more considered problem diagnosis and prescription, informed by the mistakes of other places as well as their successes. The English model has, until now, effectively maintained socially mixed communities in the heart of London and across the other high-demand areas of the country in the face of global economic pressures. Furthermore, the system has helped support a strong not-for-profit housing development sector able to operate countercyclically, as demonstrated during the Global Financial Crisis. These features are surely worth celebrating and sustaining even as difficult questions arise about the adjustments needed to address chronic barriers to new housing delivery in the market. If the Australian model represents one extreme—that of a free market enabled rather than restrained by the interventions of the state—the Hong Kong case is surely the other. Both systems seemed to work in their own way until the 1990s, when the legacies of financial deregulation and state divestment in social housing provision began to bite in Australia and when the people of Hong Kong began to demand a voice in urban affairs.

If Australia has been able to deliver high-quality homes through the private sector, more or less at a pace and scale that is in line with market trends, the cracks lie in deepening social divisions arising as a result of uneven housing wealth and corresponding spatial disadvantage. The prescriptions seem fairly obvious and lie in the tying of government land and infrastructure—existing resources already invested in major urban development processes—more closely to the establishment of a viable not-for-profit housing alternative. Again, there has been some success on this last front in England. But rising income and housing inequality in both of these countries point to growing systemic tensions that will ultimately need redress through more radical approaches to the regulation of housing markets and a rebalancing of property rights between people needing a home and investors wanting a profit. Finally, the case of Hong Kong demonstrates how a broad-based target group for subsidized accommodation—and a commitment to high-density and modest building forms—can ensure ongoing viability of public housing without the need for additional government grant (once access to land has been secured).

Are There Optimal Approaches to Planning for Housing Supply?

At the outset of this book we asked whether we could discern optimum approaches to planning for housing development, in terms of setting an appropriate framework for allocating land and regulating development proposals, building consensus across local communities and between different stakeholders, and delivering a steady supply of well-located homes to meet diverse housing needs. The elements of an "optimal" approach are sketched in trace outline across each of the cases examined here—Australia's strategic regulatory framework for housing development through codified rules, combined with significant government support for private development in major renewal and greenfield sites; England's locally driven process for permitting particular developments, while securing community benefits such as affordable housing and other social infrastructure; and the capacity of the Hong Kong government to activate the state ownership of land and the highly regulated planning system to deliver affordable owner-occupied and rental accommodation to a broad cross-section of society. Yet, in many ways the three cases examined in this book also reflect the dominance of entrenched property politics—at central and local scales. In all three systems the politics of land supply, housing provision, and housing consumption have operated to limit the scope of the planning system in responding to the spectrum of housing needs across diverse, mixed-income communities and across different points in the market cycle. The challenge is to ensure that wider community interests, beyond those of property owners seeking to preserve their housing wealth, are also able to be heard. This is a challenge shared by the planning and housing systems of Australia, England, and Hong Kong: to give voice to a broader array of needs, to consider how those needs can be met in a variety of ways and in different settings, and to design approaches to future housing delivery that prioritize the urgent need for *homes* in well-planned places for the many, rather than simply facilitating investment opportunities for the few.

References

ABC. (2015). *Joe Hockey Accused of Insensitivity over Sydney House Prices*. Sydney: Australian Broadcasting Commission.

Chiu, R. (2010). The transferability of Hong Kong's public housing policy. *International Journal of Housing Policy*, 10(3), 301–323.

Hall, P. (2014). Why are the great "stuck sites" stuck? In A. Adonis, B. Rogers, & S. Sims (Eds.), *Go East: Unlocking the Potential of the Thames Estuary*. London: Centre for London, pp. 60–71.

Gallent, N. & Robinson, S. (2012). *Neighbourhood Planning: Communities, Networks and Governance*. Bristol, UK: Policy Press.

Gallent, N. (2015). Investment, global capital and other drivers of England's housing crisis, *Journal of Urban Regeneration and Renewal*, 9(2), 122–138.

Greive, S., Jeffcote, R., & Welch, N. (1999). Governance, regulation and the changing role of central Perth: Is there room for affordable housing? *Urban Policy and Research*, 17(3), 225–233.

Gurran, N. & Phibbs, P. (2013a). Evidence-free zone? Examining claims about planning performance and reform in New South Wales. *Australian Planner*, 51(3), 232–242.

Gurran, N. & Phibbs, P. (2013b). Housing supply and urban planning reform: The recent Australian experience, 2003–2012. *International Journal of Housing Policy*, 13(4), 381–401.

Milligan, V. (2003). How different? Comparing housing policies and housing affordability consequences for low income households in Australia and the Netherlands. *Netherlands Geographical Studies*, 318.

National Housing Supply Council [NHSC]. (2013). *2013 State of Housing Supply Report; Changes in the way we live*. Canberra: Treasury.

Parker, G., Lynn, T., & Wargent, M. (2015). Sticking to the script? The co-production of neighbourhood planning in England. *Town Planning Review*, 86(5), 519–536.

Productivity Commission. (2011). *Performance Benchmarking of Australian Business Regulation: Planning, Zoning and Development Assessments; Productivity Commission Draft Research Report*. Canberra: Australian Government.

Rees, P. W. (2014, May 31). *Londoners "priced out" of housing market*. Interview with the BBC. Available at: www.bbc.co.uk/news/uk-england-london-27628579.

Ruming, K., Gurran, N., & Randolph, B. (2011). Housing affordability and development contributions: New perspectives from industry and local government in New South Wales, Victoria and Queensland. *Urban Policy and Research*, 29(3), 257–274.

Ruming, K. J., Gurran, N., Maginn, P. J., & Goodman, R. (2014). A national planning agenda? Unpacking the influence of federal urban policy on state planning reform. *Australian Planner*, 51(2), 108–121.

Shaw, K. (2013). Docklands dreamings: Illusions of sustainability in the Melbourne docks redevelopment. *Urban Studies*, 0042098013478237.

Steele, W. (2012). Do We Need a "Slow Housing" Movement? *Housing, Theory and Society*, 29(2), 172–189.

Steele, W. & Ruming, K. J. (2012). Flexibility versus certainty: Unsettling the land-use planning shibboleth in Australia. *Planning Practice and Research*, 27(2), 155–176.

Taylor, E. J. (2013). Do house values influence resistance to development?—A spatial analysis of planning objection and appeals in Melbourne. *Urban Policy and Research*, 31(1), 5–26.

Troy, P. (2012). *Accommodating Australians; Commonwealth Government involvement in housing.* Sydney: The Federation Press.

Valentine, D. R. (2015). *Solving the UK Housing Crisis: An analysis of the investment demand behind the UK's housing affordability crisis.* London: Bow Group.

Whitehead, C. M. E. (2007). Planning policies and affordable housing: England as a successful case study? *Housing Studies, 22*(1), 25–44.

Index

Ashford 129–133; context 129–130; impediments 137–138; new housing 132; origin 129–130; urban extensions 130–133

Australia 23, 29–57; centralization of urban opportunities 61–62; changing housing system 60–66; colonial settlement 30–31; composition of dwelling commencements by sector 1984–2015 39; constraints to affordable housing supply 83–84; dwelling completions 30; environmental planning 34–35; financial and taxation settings 52; government involvement in land supply 33–34; government responses to housing affordability problem 38–50; historical evolution of settlement 60; home ownership (importance of) 31–32; housing problems in new millennium 35–38; housing shortage 29, 37; housing supply comstraints 37; implications for addressing housing affordability 53–54; infrastructure backlog 34–35; key stages in land use planning process 45–46; land development 44; legal scope of urban land use planning systems 41–42; Master Builders' Association 32; National Housing Supply Council 52; planning approval 43; planning for affordable housing 47–50; planning process 40–47; planning, role of 60–66; political arguments 50–53; private developers 47; public and private sectors, role of 40; public housing 33–34; regulatory reform 38, 62; rise in house prices 53; role of different actors 48–49; structural changes 36–38; town planning laws 32–33; urban consolidation 34–35, 60–61; urban containment (see urban consolidation); urban planning and housing 29–57; urban planning, scope of 40; urban settlement structure 37; urbanization 32

Cheeseman's Green 133–134
Chilmington Green 135–137
comparative markers for analysis 5–8
comparative planning and housing studies 2–4
comparative research 2–4; approach 4–5; methods 4–5
Cumberland Council 63

delivery of new homes: planning, democracy and control 213–228
development rights, allocation of 214–218

Ebbsfleet 138–148; Castle Hill 144; context 138–140; Eastern Quarry 140–145; Ebbsfleet Valley Development Sites 141; impediments 147–148; origin 138–140; UDC for 145–147
England 23–24; *see also* major development sites in England; English planning system
English planning system 87–113; balance of power 109; balancing act 93–94; community action 100–101; Control Shift 94–95; decision making 92–101; decline in public housing projects 96–97; democratic accountability 91–92; devolution, and 88; distribution of capital funding 105–106; governance of

urban planning 92–101; house prices, and 107–108; key tenets of Labour planning 94; Labour and Conservatives, and 92; land and corporate influences 99–100; land tax 99; local authorities 109; local democracy 85–86; local politicians 104; local state, role of 89; localized governance 108–109; national policy 101–102; nature and scope of development 97–98; Neighbourhood Planning in England 104; New Town Development Corporation 91; New Towns program 97; NPPF 95; planning permission 90; power and democracy 87–113; power and influence in planning and development 108–111; power and scope 88–92; power shifts 88; private development interests 96; reform 87; rescaling of planning 105; responsibility for supplying land 110–111; SHLAA 103–104; sufficiency in land supply 102; Town and Country Planning Act 1947 89–90; town planning schemes 89; urban planning and land supply 101–108; viability of development 103; zoning 90

financing housing production and consumption 10–12

globalization 224
government support 9–13
Great Australian Dream 51
Green Square 66–73; apartments and open space 81; City West Housing Company 70; comparison with Rouse Hill 78–83; completed and projected new dwellings 73; development area and precincts 69; dwelling stock 80; metropolitan context 67; mixed residential and commercial development 72; mortgage and rent payments 81; population growth 71; prices 72–73; South Sydney Local Environmental Plan 68; statistics 70–71; Structural Masterplan 68

Hong Kong 24–26, 159–184, 185–211; development 159; development-related tools 171–172; district plans 170–171; district plans, making of 177–180; dualistic housing system 185; from elitist to mass participation 177–180; hierarchy of plans 168; high-rise housing estates 161; house price trends 1986–2014 187; housing commencements (private housing) 191; incremental public participation since 1990 173–177; land search efforts 186–193; land search in buoyant market 198–208; land supply 185–211; landownership 162–166; large-scale new development projects 202–208; major and controversial land development and market situation 186–193; major land development projects 2008–14 199–201; new development areas 202–203; new housing provision 185–211; plan-making and enforcement processes 172–173; plan-making process 178; planning application process 179; planning application projects 2011–2014 198; planning, governance and housing supply 180–182, 194–198; planning system and scope 166–169; politics 160; power and decision making in planning system 159–184; power relations and politics 172–173; power within urban planning 162–180; price-to-income ratio 1997–2014 188; quantity versus quality 198–208; scope of urban planning 162–180; small-scale development projects 202; small-scale societal context 161; sources of residential land 2014–15 193; South East Kowloon Development Scheme 194–198; spatial development 168; spatial plan under 2030 Planning Vision and Strategy 171; status 159–160; territorial and subregional plans 173–177; territorial development plans 169–170; Tung Chung New Town 204–208; urban system 160–161

housing product diversity 16–20
housing provision by sector Australia, England, Hong Kong 2001–14 16
housing supply: optimal approaches to planning 226; role of planning 3–4
Howard, John: land supply, on 51

Index

intervention, scale of 3

key characteristics, Australia, England and Hong Kong 2014 9

land use planning and development control 13–15
landownership and development rights 213–219
landownership and proactive planning 218–219
literature on comparative urban and housing analysis 5–8

major development sites in England 115–157; barriers to housing supply 117– 118; case study sites 122–124; cross-border working, and 153–154; delivering new homes 115–157; financial drivers of market 116; flexible planning 152–153; future 148–154; house prices and houses built 119; housing affordability 121; housing crisis, and 118–120; infrastructure 148–149; local opposition/democracy 149–150; loss of non-commodity housing, and 116; market cycles 151–152; overloading of existing infrastructure 150–151; planning gain 148–149; policy shift 151; public concern 150–151; regulatory risk 151; strategic planning, and 120–124; top-down planning 149–150; value capture 148–149; viability 151–152

New South Wales: housing shortage 62–66; median sales prices 82; State Planning Authority 63

optimal approaches to planning: housing supply, and 226

planning, democracy and control: delivery of new homes 213–228
planning process: power in 219–223; representative democracy in 219–223
planning system: power and control 20–23
planning system deregulation: dangers of 224

politics 220–223; corporate interests 221; house prices, and 222–223; producer groups 221
politics, planning and housing supply 1–28
power: planning process, in 219–223

representative democracy: planning process, in 219–223; reform, and 220
Rouse Hill 73–78; apartments 79; comparison with Green Square 78–83; diverse housing types 78; dwelling stock 80; fragmented development 74; house under construction 80; metropolitan context 67; mortgage and rent payments 81; regional plan 73–74; regional retail and commercial area 77; scrutiny of plans 76

South East Kowloon Development Scheme 194–198; planned development in proposed reclamation areas 197; planning revisions 1992–2012 195; transforming governance 194–198
Stevenage 124–129; context 124–125; impediments 128–129; origin 124–125; proposed Stevenage West development 127; Stevenage West Narrative 125–128
Sydney 59–85; City of Cities 66; comparison of housing outcomes (Green Square, Rouse Hill, Sydney) 78–83; dual occupancy development 64–65; formal elements of Australian planning 59; house price inflation 65; increased housing density 65; mortgage and rent payments 81; urban renewal and growth centres 59–85; see also Green Square; Rouse Hill
system of housing production 15–16

Thames Gateway Development Corridor 139
Tung Chung New Town 204–208

urban planning and housing 2–3, 6–9, 13–15; see also Australia
urban settlement and housing demand 8–9

Taylor & Francis eBooks

Helping you to choose the right eBooks for your Library

Add Routledge titles to your library's digital collection today. Taylor and Francis ebooks contains over 50,000 titles in the Humanities, Social Sciences, Behavioural Sciences, Built Environment and Law.

Choose from a range of subject packages or create your own!

Benefits for you
- Free MARC records
- COUNTER-compliant usage statistics
- Flexible purchase and pricing options
- All titles DRM-free.

Benefits for your user
- Off-site, anytime access via Athens or referring URL
- Print or copy pages or chapters
- Full content search
- Bookmark, highlight and annotate text
- Access to thousands of pages of quality research at the click of a button.

REQUEST YOUR FREE INSTITUTIONAL TRIAL TODAY

Free Trials Available
We offer free trials to qualifying academic, corporate and government customers.

eCollections – Choose from over 30 subject eCollections, including:

Archaeology	Language Learning
Architecture	Law
Asian Studies	Literature
Business & Management	Media & Communication
Classical Studies	Middle East Studies
Construction	Music
Creative & Media Arts	Philosophy
Criminology & Criminal Justice	Planning
Economics	Politics
Education	Psychology & Mental Health
Energy	Religion
Engineering	Security
English Language & Linguistics	Social Work
Environment & Sustainability	Sociology
Geography	Sport
Health Studies	Theatre & Performance
History	Tourism, Hospitality & Events

For more information, pricing enquiries or to order a free trial, please contact your local sales team:
www.tandfebooks.com/page/sales

The home of Routledge books

www.tandfebooks.com